Everything Under the Sun

Everything Under the Sun

My Life in West Indies Cricket

JEFF STOLLMEYER

STANLEY PAUL

London Melbourne Sydney Auckland Johannesburg

To Sara and all cricketers' wives

Stanley Paul & Co. Ltd

An imprint of the Hutchinson Publishing Group

17–21 Conway Street, London W1P 6JD

Hutchinson Group (Australia) Pty Ltd
30–32 Cremorne Street, Richmond South, Victoria 3121
PO Box 151, Broadway, New South Wales 2007

Hutchinson Group (NZ) Ltd
32–34 View Road, PO Box 40–086, Glenfield, Auckland 10

Hutchinson Group (SA) Pty Ltd
PO Box 337, Bergvlei 2012, South Africa

First published 1983
© Jeff Stollmeyer 1983

Set in Linotron Sabon by Input Typesetting Ltd, London SW19 8DR

Printed in Great Britain by The Anchor Press Ltd
and bound by Wm Brendon & Son Ltd,
both of Tiptree, Essex

British Library Cataloguing in Publication Data
Stollmeyer, J. B.
    Everything under the sun.
    1. Stollmeyer, J. B.   2. Cricket players — West
    Indies — Biography
    I. Title
    796.35'8'0924   GV915.S/
    ISBN 0 09 152420 2

Contents

	Acknowledgements	7
	Foreword	9
	Introduction	13
1	The Beginnings	15
2	The College Years	25
3	Cricket Before the War	31
4	The War Years and Afterwards	42
5	Test Cricket Resumes	52
6	India	58
7	West Indian Summer	75
8	Ramadhin and Valentine and the Three Ws	107
9	Down Under 1951–52	117
10	The Aftermath of Australia	134
11	Hutton's England Team of 1954	142
12	Australia Visits Us for the First Time	151
13	Time to Retire	156
14	Back to the Land	161
15	Ten Years in the Senate	168
16	1966 and All That	175
17	Selection Duties	182
18	From Agriculture to Business	190
19	President of the West Indies Cricket Board of Control	193
20	The Packer Intrusion: The West Indian Viewpoint	203
21	The Aftermath	212
22	Reflections and the Future	222
	Index	225

Acknowledgements

A debt of gratitude is owed to my old friend E. W. 'Jim' Swanton, OBE, who kindly consented to write the foreword to this book. This is an honour bestowed on only a chosen few, for there is no greater lover of the game alive today, and no shrewder critic has graced the Test match grounds of the world.

Philip Thomson of Trinidad, popular and well-known host to touring cricketers and something of a cricket encyclopaedia, filled in some of the missing dates and scores.

Great credit is due to my daughter-in-law, Catherine Stollmeyer, who, appropriately, was discovered to be expert at reducing my wayward handwriting to neatly laid out typescript and painstakingly corrected drafts. My wife and family also contributed considerable encouragement and criticism.

Finally, my unstinted appreciation goes out to the successive editors of *Wisden*, without whom so many books based on the game of cricket, including this one, would not have been written.

PHOTOGRAPHIC ACKNOWLEDGEMENTS

For permission to use copyright photographs included in this book the author and publisher would like to thank: Associated Photo Service, Delhi; Central Press Photos Ltd; Patrick Eagar; Guardian Photonews Service, Trinidad; Sport & General Press Agency Ltd; and the *Sydney Morning Herald*.

Foreword

by E. W. Swanton

Despite the proliferation of cricket books, there is no up-to-date definitive history of West Indies cricket. For the beginnings of the story we have C. R. Nicole's well-researched *West Indian Cricket* and for a chronicle of the contemporary scene Tony Cozier's admirable *West Indies Cricket Annual*.

There should, therefore, be a warm welcome throughout the cricket world – especially, of course, in the Caribbean – for the memoirs of the man who, first as player, next as Test captain, and since as administrator and, finally, President of the West Indies Board of Control, has been at the heart of the matter for more than forty years.

The West Indies were admitted to the Test circle in 1928 when Jeffrey Stollmeyer was a youngster in short trousers at Queen's Royal College, Port of Spain. Eleven years later, at the age of eighteen, he was opening the innings against England at Lord's and scoring an elegant and auspicious 59. After the war, he and Allan Rae of Jamaica formed a successful partnership, paving the way for the brilliant young Barbadian discoveries, the three Ws, Clyde Walcott, Everton Weekes and Frank Worrell.

He and John Goddard captained the West Indies in the decade, beginning with the visit of G. O. Allen's MCC side in 1947–48. Goddard's contribution was the example of his own determination and a proper infusion of dignity and discipline in sides brought together from the four traditional centres of West Indian cricket: Barbados, British Guiana, Trinidad and Jamaica. The theorist and tactical thinker was Stollmeyer, who in this book acknowledges handsomely the debt he owes to the first of the great West Indian

Test batsmen, George Headley. 'He taught me most of what I know about the finer points of the game,' says the author, who, for all the genius of Sobers, of Viv Richards, of Kanhai, and of the immortal trinity of Walcott, Weekes and Worrell, rates Headley 'the greatest batsman West Indies have produced'.

When Jeff and George watched together and one of their fellows was the victim of some fatal indiscretion, George, who before the war carried the side's batting on his shoulders, would ask 'Why him don't like to bat?'

Looking back, it seems even more evident now than it did at the time that Stollmeyer should have been the bridge between the white leadership of the early days and that which was available from the middle fifties in the shape of the exceptionally gifted Frank Worrell. In extenuation of the regime, it should be mentioned that Sir Frank (as he became on his retirement in 1963) was twice offered the West Indian captaincy before he was able to accept it. But Everton and Clyde also proved to be intelligent and popular Shell Shield captains when the opportunity came to them late in their careers.

But for a certain physical fragility, Jeff would have made rather more than the 2000-odd runs he scored for the West Indies, with an average of 42, and notched more than his tally of fourteen 100s in first-class cricket. At his best he was a beautiful player, as he showed especially, in my own recollection, with the 43 and 78 he made on a terrible wicket against England at Old Trafford in 1950. His 100 against the speed of Lindwall and Miller at Sydney in 1951–52 is quoted as a classic by those present. But if he had lasted longer as a player there would have been less time in which to establish his second reputation as a negotiator (and, incidentally, a tour manager) in the often difficult political field of West Indian cricket and beyond. In his efforts in his own Trinidad he has worked often in close collaboration with his contemporary and great friend, Gerry Gomez.

Finally came the honour of the Presidency of the West Indies Board. That office has never been a bed of roses, but none of Jeff's predecessors had to deal with a situation so demanding as that of the Packer affair and the wholesale absorption of almost all the finest West Indian players. All this, and much more, Jeff deals with, diplomatically and conscientiously, in these memoirs. The book is a full, fair and at times outspoken commentary on West Indian cricket from 1939 to the present day.

Yet it is more than that. The present Stollmeyer generation is the third since great-grandfather crossed the seas in 1846. Jeff's roots are deeply embedded in the soil of his native island. He has been a planter, and represented agriculture in the Trinidad Senate in the first decade of its existence. Lastly he has moved into the world of business, as banker, newspaper chairman and director of divers companies. In short, this book, in addition to cricket as its main thread, has its value as a social document. It could have been called *Jeff Stollmeyer: His Life and Times.*

Introduction

I decided to write this story, a cricketing autobiography, for two reasons. First, because I thought I had lived a life interesting and varied enough to warrant the attention of an adequate readership and, second, because little has been written *at first hand* about West Indies cricket, its players and its development since the Second World War.

In this latter respect, my position is unique for I have been a player, captain, selector, manager and adminstrator, so perhaps I have been privileged to see and appreciate all sides of our cricketing problems, and to have played a not insignificant part in trying to shape our cricket destiny with a view to having the game in the West Indies and, not least, the West Indies team (at the time of writing, world champions) continue to be *sans peur et sans reproche*.

In private life, I have been fortunate. Born of German and English stock, although several generations West Indian, I was brought up on a cocoa plantation seven miles outside of Port of Spain, the capital of Trinidad. Having gained admission to one of the two finest secondary schools in the island, Queen's Royal College, I received a secondary education second to none, and learned there, through an assiduous and highly capable staff, that 'the way of the transgressor was exceedingly hard' (to quote our celebrated maths master, Grant Elcock Pilgrim) and along the way something about the game of cricket.

It was a totally happy existence spiced by several trips abroad both near and far, commencing in my mid-teens – and all, with minor exceptions, due to the game of cricket to which I confess to owe a tremendous debt of gratitude. The game has taken me to

England (twice as a player and once as a manager), Australia, India, Pakistan and New Zealand. Wonderful experiences all – though admittedly it is not uncommon for cricketers these days to visit all these countries in the span of a single year!

At all times, humour has been a close companion, and if some of the stories I tell appear to be at the expense of my colleagues, I ask them to believe that it is because of the high esteem in which they are held and my wholesome regard for them as people. Apart from this there will be passages which are critical of my friends. It is impossible for it to be otherwise when writing of cricket at the highest level, its tactics and its strategies. They are obviously, however, one man's opinion and should be treated as such.

In all these experiences one makes friends, not only with those with whom one travels but also with one's hosts. Cricket creates its own bond of friendship, and one's greatest 'enemies' on the field of play often become one's closest friends at the end of the line.

Cricket is a wonderful game. It was always so and though changes in the laws are necessary from time to time, especially in view of the so-called more 'scientific' approach of modern times, its essential elements must not be altered. While I accept change and indeed have seen many in the game since I first knew it, I would hate to see it become, at the highest level, a professional circus. As I write these lines, there is a Test match being played in some part of the world almost each week and a triangular tournament, between Pakistan, Australia and the West Indies, is being planned for this winter in Australia to include at least eleven one-day internationals complete with '30-yard circles'. Will all this last? And will 'instant cricket' eventually supersede Test matches simply because the present generation seems to want instant action? I hope not.

I subscribe fully to the dictum of Lord Harris who in his essay, 'A Few Short Runs' wrote as follows: 'You do well to love it, for it is more free from anything sordid, anything dishonourable, anything savouring of servitude, than any game in the world. To play it keenly, honourably, generously self-sacrificingly, is a moral lesson in itself, and the classroom is God's air and sunshine. Foster it, my brothers, so that it may attract all who can find the time to play it, protect it from anything that would sully it, so that it may grow in favour with all men.'

1

The Beginnings

Mon Valmont was as beautiful as its name. And it was our home. Set in the delightful Santa Cruz valley, a mere seven miles from Port of Spain, my father, a cocoa planter to the core, used to call it 'an oasis in the desert' and under his loving care it was just that.

A. V. Stollmeyer loved his cocoa trees and, after a largely unsuccessful foray into the business world, he returned to his estates which he developed with unbelievable faith and tenacity into veritable gardens. 'I am returning to my trees,' he used to tell me. 'People are too devious.' It is interesting to note that about ten years ago I did exactly the opposite. With the full approval of my brothers and sister, we decided to sell our agricultural estates and I entered the 'jungle' of business. But this commonsense decision is another story.

The present Stollmeyers are third generation West Indians, my great-grandfather having arrived in Trinidad on a brig in 1846 with, it is said, 'five dollars in his pocket'. Their emigration was due to involvement with the anti-slave-trade movement and my great-grandfather left the USA because of his anti-slavery beliefs. This, in essence, precipitated their flight to the West Indies.

Many tales are told about the settlement and development of the family in the island. It is not my purpose to recount too many of these, but suffice it to say that

the man who wedded technology and utopianism and who comes for a short space of time into the history of Trinidad was J. A. Etzler, one of those intriguing figures of the Victorian age who was partly a visionary and partly a charlatan. He was German by birth who went to England in 1840 from the United States. There he had tried unsuccessfully to muster adherents to form a community in which the drudgery would be performed by machines, many of his own invention, in which the people, relieved of their daily chores of life, could devote their time to leisure and the pursuit of useful knowledge and the arts. His companion from America was Conrad Frederick Stollmeyer,* a bookseller from Philadelphia who had published Etzler's tracts. He had also been a committee member of the Anti-Slavery Society in Pennsylvania and it was said that he was forced to flee because he had rashly founded an abolitionist newspaper in the slave states.

. . . In October 1844 the Tropical Emigration Society was formed with Etzler as President and Stollmeyer as Treasurer. Although its offices were in the Strand in London, much of the campaigning, carried out by the new didactic device of the public lecture given by its two leading members, took place in the industrial towns in the North, where there was much proletarian discontent. An appeal was made to all Socialists, Chartists and other reformers to join them. The chosen land was Venezuela. Etzler had been awarded about 200 acres by its Government at Guinamita on the Gulf of Paria, some four hours sailing from Port of Spain.

Etzler had variously described Trinidad (only 11 miles off the Venezuelan coast) as an earthly paradise and it appears that he formed a company known as the Trinidad Great Eastern and South Western Railway Company and it was under the auspices of this picturesque Company that Etzler and Stollmeyer arrived in Trinidad in 1846.

. . . Etzler vanished from the story and the Tropical Emigration Society quietly went out of existence. Conrad Stollmeyer, however, settled in Trinidad and he lived on until the early years of the twentieth century. He remained a reformer to the end and for a time was the editor of *The Trinidadian*. His main business interest became the exploitation of the Pitch Lake; he was an active member of a company exporting pitch to the United States and Europe and an ardent experimenter in the distillation of petroleum from pitch. Stollmeyer lived to see something of the fulfilment of Etzler's vision of technology transforming the tropics; in his later years he was a director of electricity, telephone and ice-manufacturing companies in Trinidad.†

My mother, Ada Kate, was born in England and actually lived at a house on the border of Hertfordshire and Bedfordshire. Her maiden name was Baxter, which is the reason for my second name and for the fact that I have saddled our four children with it as a third

---

*My great-grandfather. He wrote a book in 1845 entitled *The Sugar Question Made Easy*.

†Donald Wood, *Trinidad in Transition*, Institute of Race Relations, pp. 85–86, 89.

name. She married my father in 1906 after a whirlwind courtship. 'I am going to marry that girl,' he is said to have stated after seeing a mere photograph of her. Through her brother Alex 'A. J.' Baxter, a noted explorer, mountain climber and 'man of the world', he manipulated himself into a position to propose marriage to this much-sought-after lady and was successful. My mother came out to Trinidad in the same year that she got married when, she often told me, there was only one house between Port of Spain and our home in Santa Cruz. Today they are cheek by jowl and there is no room for any more buildings along the major artery leading to the area.

What it was like for a young English girl arriving in the humid tropics to a somewhat primitive island in those days takes some imagining. Trips to Port of Spain were more like excursions. A horse and buggy were used, and streams, which to this day become raging torrents in the wet season, had to be forded, among other hazards.

Life on the estate, although not luxurious, was comfortable. Servants abounded but there was complete mutual respect between master and servant, and whatever may be said of the system which obtained at that time, there is no gainsaying the fact that the happiest of relationships existed between my family and the labourers and servants who were in our employ.

All this made for a happy home, and seven children were born of the marriage, six boys and a girl. The eldest, Rex, who died at the age of sixty in 1967, spent much of his life in Canada where he was Trade Commissioner for, at varying times in accordance with their political status, Trinidad and Tobago, the Eastern Caribbean, the West Indies Federation and finally, once more, Trinidad and Tobago after independence and the dissolution of the Federation. Rex became quite a legend in the city of his adoption, Montreal. He knew and genuinely loved all the islands dearly and the people of the islands loved him. He was largely instrumental in the early development of trade and tourism between Canada and the West Indies. The inauguration of the Canadian National Steamship Line's 'lady boats' to the West Indies was largely due to his promotional work. Flour and salt fish were major cargoes outwards in exchange for sugar on the return journey. Unhappily all these fine ships were sunk in the Second World War and thereafter the accent was placed on air travel, and here in the promotion of the tourist trade Rex was once more a pioneer.

I recall one of our great QCs and cricket benefactors, Sir

Courtenay Hannays, saying to me one day while watching the cricket at the Queen's Park Oval, 'Boy, your brother Rex is a giant.' Sir Courtenay had recently been *Chef de mission* of the Trinidad Olympic team to the Commonwealth games in Vancouver. 'We arrived in Montreal on a Sunday without any money,' he recalled, 'so I called Rex. "Just a minute, I'll see what I can do," said Rex.' The amazed Sir Courtenay could hardly believe his eyes when Rex arrived with the Chief Executive of the Royal Bank of Canada who had come down to open the bank himself to get some money for the beleaguered team. 'I would do anything for Rex,' the grateful Sir Courtenay told me. Rex was a man apart.

Rex died in 1967 of cancer. Shortly before he died, I visited him and his wife Marjorie. He was but a shadow of himself, a disillusioned, dispirited man. He had just finished organizing and engineering Trinidad and Tobago's highly successful booth at Expo '67. The twin islands, his homeland, had one of the prime sites at Expo and the shows put on by Trinidadian artistes were the talk of the exhibition, but Rex received no thanks and minimal cooperation from the Trinidad and Tobago Government, and much of what was achieved was *despite* the uncooperative attitude of his superiors in Port of Spain. This shattered him after all the years of hard work he had put in and, in my view, hastened his demise. There has never been nor is there likely to be another Trade Commissioner in Canada of Rex's ilk – just ask the many West Indian students whose friend and counsellor he was over the years!

Alex, the second son, now the head of the family, made his life in the 'good old' USA, no West Indian life for him. All of my three eldest brothers went to American universities – Rex and André to Dartmouth and Alex to Harvard – after their secondary education was finished at Queen's Royal College. This was more or less unheard of in those days, but my father thought an American education more appropriate to the times, the days before the stock market crash in the USA. It was traditional that post-secondary education would be in the UK if you were of British stock or in France if you were of French-West Indian origin.

So Alex went to Harvard, became a chartered accountant with Coopers & Lybrand and settled with his American wife Elizabeth (*née* Faraday) in Forest Hills from where he commuted to New York daily for more than thirty-five years. He became more attached to the land of his adoption than most Americans and has now retired and lives at Southold on Long Island.

André also returned from Dartmouth with an American-born girlfriend whom he subsequently married. From Pennsylvania of Lithuanian parents, her name was Teckla (*née* Plasky) and they now live quietly in Trinidad. André was my boyhood hero. He was a marvellous athlete, one of the best soccer forwards ever produced by Trinidad, and he represented the island in some wonderful contests, particularly against neighbouring Venezuela. The Trinidad goal-keeper in these series was none other than his friend, Rolph S. Grant, debatably the finest amateur goalkeeper ever to keep for England and, undoubtedly, for Trinidad. Rolph was, of course, destined to play for and captain the West Indies cricket team to the UK in 1939, and it was under him that I had my baptism of fire in the world of Test cricket. After a successful business career with Geo. F. Huggins & Co., André has now retired. He has become, over the years, a fisherman *par excellence* and it is said that even the pro-fessional fishermen would follow him if he didn't go so far and so deep to find his precious red snapper.

Hugh, the fourth brother in the family, was an artist – a painter. A confirmed bachelor, he had more or less lived the life of a recluse, particularly in his later years. He had literary qualities as well and was one of the first contributors to a magazine called *The Beacon*, considered avant-garde at the time, to which several local notables contributed articles. Albert 'Bertie' Gomes, its editor, was to become Trinidad and Tobago's Premier up to the time of Independence in 1956, and among other contributors was C. L. R. James, the noted man of letters and author of *Beyond the Boundary*, one of the masterpieces of cricket literature. Hugh lived latterly in New York, where he died in 1982. His paintings, full of intense tropical colours, are scattered around our family's households and several are in the keeping of his close confidante, my sister Daphne. He has often made the statement: 'I shall be the only member of this family who will not be forgotten in the course of time.' He may just be right about this.

And so to brother Victor, number five on the list, the brother closest to me in age and habit. V.H., if you refer to *Wisden*, toured England with the West Indies cricket team in 1939; he played in only one Test match, the third and last, and scored 94. Thereby hangs a tale or two. Victor was selected as the No. 1 opening batsman but was plagued by ill health on the tour, suffering repeated attacks of tonsillitis. When Ivan Barrow, the other accredited opener, failed to find his form and Victor was ill, I assumed the mantle of one of the opening batsmen and our skipper, Rolph Grant, decided to open the innings with me. This policy was followed for all the Test matches, and when brother Victor came into the side for the third Test he was sent in at No. 4. After the war, when Test cricket was resumed, Victor had retired from the game and so we never actually opened together in a Test match; this would, I believe, have been some sort of a record. We did, however, have several successful opening partnerships together for our club, Queen's Park, and for Trinidad. Among his Trinidad crowd he was known as 'the Rock of Gibraltar', a regular and patient scorer of runs with considerable powers of concentration.

At an early age Victor qualified as a solicitor and is now a senior partner with one of the island's major law firms specializing in conveyancing and company law, bringing the same painstaking care that he showed on the cricket field to his practice.

Daphne, my only sister, was understandably something of a tomboy having to contend with six brothers. She was also blessed with creative talent and has held her own by organizing and maintaining a cottage industry in Caledon East, a suburb of Toronto. She specializes in leather work, and designs brooches, earrings and ornaments of all sorts which she then produces in leather. She markets under the name of 'Daphne of Canada' and her products have become well known and recognized in many parts of that vast country. Daphne told me once of a visit to her craft shop by a party of Japanese who, apparently impressed by her work, wished to place orders for five gross of this and six gross of that. Since each product was produced by hand, this was something of a tall order!

Daph was fortunate to be of independent nature and spirit, for after her husband Don Lingwood died, she has carried on her shop with the help of her neighbours, many of whom sold their 'productions' at her shop. Some developed the art of producing ceramics, others sculpture, batik, etc. The shop, open all the summer, is quite often attended by celebrities, and a stay at Caledon East with Daphne of Canada can be a wonderfully rewarding experience.

While I hesitate to inflict family history on readers, my father, Albert Victor Stollmeyer, was also something special. He was elected to the first legislature in 1925, and although the franchise was limited on the basis of income, he faced the hustings and defeated his friend but political enemy, Albert Cory Davies.

A.V.S. was the major pioneer of the citrus industry in Trinidad and Tobago, and as children we spent many hours wrapping and packing by hand 'Humming Bird' brand grapefruit for export to Bermuda and Canada. In 1929, however, he submerged his private interests in the formation of the Cooperative Citrus Growers' Association of which he became the first Secretary-Manager. The Association moved from strength to strength until, in 1965, it handled 1.3 million crates of grapefruit and oranges. It is somewhat sad to record that, from the most recent crop, the Association processed only 113,000 crates, but that is another story. It was of immense satisfaction to me to sit on the Board of the Association for eighteen years for twelve of which I was vice-president to Sir Harold Robinson, one of the great pioneers in the field of agriculture in Trinidad.

The citrus industry in Trinidad was started largely to offset the effect of witches broom disease which devastated the cocoa fields in the late twenties and early thirties. My father, however, was basically a cocoa planter. He knew the trees that grew in the fields around our home 'personally' and could be seen most afternoons trimming them with his cutlass (machete). In the late twenties, he was involved in the merchandising of cocoa, and when the market crashed in New York, he was caught with a great deal of cocoa for which he had already paid, in warehouses in New York unsold. He lost all his assets at this time and was forced to mortgage his home and properties – a virtual bankrupt.

Being a man of indomitable spirit, however, he did not take matters lying down. Helped by Barclays Bank in the person of its manager, Courtenay George, who had confidence in him and his ability to fight back, he began the slow climb back to solvency. This financial setback was the reason why the last three members of our family did not go abroad to university. Suffice it to say that the standard of education to which we were subjected in Trinidad was second to none at that time, and in my case what I missed by not seeing something else of the world was more than made up for by travelling as a cricketer.

Above all, Dad was a liberal father. As the one who followed in his footsteps as manager of the family's agricultural estates, I came to marvel at his courage in the face of adversity and his capacity for hard work. When it became necessary for us to fight bush fires in the hills, as it invariably did between March and May of each year, he used to scamper up the hillsides, all 120 lb of him, leaving me, much less than half his age, faltering behind. When the time came to hand over the reins to me, he couldn't have been more accommodating. He never once interfered with my efforts, much as he must have felt like putting the youngster on the right track.

My mother, a product of the Victorian era, was the focal point around which our well-knit family developed. A woman of rare beauty and poise – not only the members of her faithful domestic household would refer to her as 'Madam' – she was a fountain of knowledge, and it was said of her that there was no book in the central or public library which she hadn't read, although she did express in forcible terms her abhorrence of the 'trash' that was being written in those days.

Mother presided over our house like the matriarch she was. There were family gatherings at Christmastime and on other ceremonious occasions such as when the family assembled for her golden wedding anniversary in 1956, the last of our family reunions. Four members of the family were then living abroad and their presence was an added occasion for celebration. The event was recorded in the *Port of Spain Gazette*, an excerpt from which read:

'In the peaceful and picturesque Valley of Santa Cruz, a happy couple yesterday celebrated a big event in their lives – their golden wedding anniversary. In their beautiful home, surrounded by their seven children, some of whom had travelled thousands of miles to be with them on this occasion, and with many of their young grandchildren running around, Mr and Mrs A. V. Stollmeyer recalled the romantic meeting of fifty years ago which brought them together.'

Her death in 1974 at the age of ninety-four marked the end of an era. She lived in the 'great' house at Mon Valmont until the end, and not long after her death I had the unenviable task of having the house, built all of wood and literally held together by the termites, dismantled and taken away. The house was constructed, first as a bungalow, in 1880 and the upstairs was added as and when the family increased in size until it became too small to contain it. The house was unique and we had often hoped it would have been preserved to form part of a National Trust. As I write, no such thing exists in Trinidad and Tobago, which is regrettable.

When I married Sara (*née* Hutchinson) in 1947, my father gave me an acre of land next door to the Mon Valmont great house on which I built first a small bungalow and then, in the course of time, a much larger edifice which has been our home, 'Baxters', ever since.

In front of Mon Valmont was a lawn about 80 feet by 150 feet which was our cricket and football field. With so many brothers, not to mention neighbours and friends, I did not lack for companions to play these games, and many were the contests played on 'Melbourne' as we used to call it. My schoolfriends from Queen's Royal College would arrive early on Saturday mornings after I had been up at dawn cutting and rolling the 'wicket'. Neither the grass nor the soil was really suitable for cricket and it was a considerable advantage to win the toss and bat first because the wicket deteriorated considerably as the day wore on.

Apart from my brother Victor, who at that time represented an earlier generation, there were others who became names in Trinidad and West Indies cricket. Chief among these was my friend and later companion of innumerable tours, Gerry Gomez. Regular visitors and players were Arthur and Dick Trestrail, 'Chappie' and 'Boysie' Burke whose humour ensured never a dull moment, Edgar Marsden who subsequently captained Trinidad, and Phil Thomson, a great cricket enthusiast to whom visiting teams to Trinidad owe so much and a walking encyclopaedia of cricket statistics and records.

Games were played very seriously. England vs Australia was the order of the day, and woe betide the man who batted for Bradman or Hammond and failed! In those days I never dreamed for one minute that I would ever meet far less play against such great players. Players' averages were strictly kept, and as 'out' or 'not out' was by common consent there were many serious arguments and it was not seldom that matches were abandoned. It was most undignified to be caught at slip, where stood the roller invincible but safe as a house.

When we were tired of cricket we played football. Most of us were either in or near to the college first XI in both games and the standard was pretty good. 'With Shirts' vs 'Without Shirts' formed the identity of the two teams and naturally we all played barefooted.

The third great interest of most of us was horseracing, and by a complicated process of releasing water from a Roman bath into the open gutters of the back of the house, we raced 'jockeys' (small bits of wood carved in the shape of boats) named after prominent local racehorses of the day. It was described by a celebrated horse owner as 'good clean fun'. An ante of 6d per race was made and after Chappie Burke lost four races in a row, he was heard to say, 'I'll have to sign a cheque!'

Our love of sport was encouraged by the deeds of our seniors at Queen's Royal College. In 1933, QRC won both the island-wide cricket and football competitions, a feat never emulated before or since and never likely to be. The college captain in both games was none other than Harold J. Burnett, until recently Secretary of the West Indies Cricket Board of Control. In a celebrating speech at a dinner held in honour of our schoolboy heroes, 'H.J.B.' referred to the college's success as the *annus mirabilis* which indeed it was.

2
The College Years

Queen's Royal College in the Thirties was a wonderful educational institution. All the staff were graduates, the majority expatriate. Discipline was of a high order and there was a magnificent team spirit encouraged by enthusiastic masters who devoted much time to their pupils on the field of play after classes were over.

Several of the masters played for the college first team in club cricket at varying times and helped to instil a discipline which proved valuable to us students in later years. Arthur Wilkinson or 'Wilkie' to everyone, Achilles Daunt ('Doodles'), the Rev. C. Stokeley Doorly ('Stokes') and the one and only Grant Elcock Pilgrim ('Piggy') were four of the stalwarts. The rivalry with St Mary's (College of the Immaculate Conception to give it its full name) was intense and the Inter-Col. cricket or football match was the scene of immense patriotism and noise. 'Send your children to QRC' was one chorus and the QRC war cry 'Hicka boom-a-lack-a' was another.

Some of us in the lower forms found, however, that there was not enough organized cricket and football for our age group and, arising out of this and a large circle of friends, we formed a club named 'Triumph'. A highly organized club, fees, collected regularly, were 1d per week. We put out very good cricket and football teams and were regular applicants for the college concrete pitch on Saturday mornings. When this pitch was unavailable we were relegated to an area 'between the palm trees' on the Queen's Park Savannah where the bounce was far less reliable. One of our players claimed to have developed a 'shooter' bowled at will by holding the ball firmly in the palm of his hand, but I suspect that the pitch was the responsible factor.

We did not allow youths with only one initial to join the club. When David Merry, younger brother of C. A. Merry who toured England with the West Indies in 1933, and a fine left-hand batsman in the making, came to the college, we let it be known that we were prepared to consider him for membership of Triumph. However, on being told that he had no other initial than 'D', he was advised that this was totally unsatisfactory so he became D. A. Merry on our books, and it was as D. A. Merry that he played for Trinidad in a career tragically shortened by his death while engaged as flying instructor in Alberta, Canada, during the war.

Among my souvenirs, I still have the Triumph records and perhaps it would not be remiss to quote the pen-portrait of one of our better-known first XI members, written in 1935:

Gerald Ethridge Gomez – 16 – a player of exceptional merit, who is looked upon by many, including myself, as a future West Indian player. As a batsman he is a tower of strength, and is 'leaps and bounds' ahead of any of his 'Triumph' rivals. His strokes are on every side of the wicket, and best of all he mingles attack with defence very successfully so that he can bat in accordance with the position of the game. His batting is extremely orthodox and he is a master of the 'cover-drive', and when in an aggressive mood is a treat to watch. As much can be said for 'Gerry's' bowling. In this department of the game he has been no less effective, and time and again he has come out 'tops' in our bowling averages. As stock bowler of our first XI, his slow spinners are always a menace to the opposing batsmen. Again, when runs are to be kept down, Gerry supplies an indefatigable length with his medium-paced off-breaks. His fielding also is second to none on our team, for he possesses a very safe pair of hands and can be used both near to and far from the wicket. Lastly, as a cricketer on the whole, there is no sounder judge of the game than is Gerry, he is a fighter, and it would be a treat to have eleven men as keen, if not as talented, as Gerald Gomez.

There is no doubt that the training in organizing this club and the many cricket and football matches which it played helped me a great deal in later years when I was called upon to captain the West Indies, serve as President of the West Indies Cricket Board of Control and chair a number of companies including Barclays Bank of Trinidad and Tobago Ltd, now renamed Republic Bank Ltd.

Mention of Barclays reminds me of a fortuitous connection. One of my boyhood friends at QRC was the Triumph wicket-keeper,

Ken Ball, whose sister Sheila later married my brother Victor. Ken and I were close friends in the early thirties at which time he left to go to Worksop College where Ken Farnes taught arts, crafts and cricket. Ken Ball was a Triumph stalwart and we were up to all sorts of mischief together. Little did I suspect then that it would be Ken who, some forty years later, would be in a position as Director in charge of North America and the West Indies, to ask me to join the Board of Barclays Bank of Trinidad and Tobago and later to be its Chairman. Ken was the first of us young 'uns to buy a 'box' and he certainly needed it to keep wicket for Triumph.

When we purchased that 'box' at the age of thirteen from a Port of Spain store, three or four of us lads approached the store clerk with a whisper: 'I wish to buy a box.' When the store clerk called out loudly to his colleague, 'A box for this boy', great embarrassment followed and I remember feeling like beating a hasty retreat from the store.

The Triumph days were happy ones and our young club produced not only two West Indies cricketers but also six Trinidad first-class players.

Cricket at Queen's Royal College was serious business and to get selected for the first XI required more than average ability, for the competition was keen. As a youngster of fifteen, I was selected to go to Barbados with the college team to take part in a series of sporting events with its Barbadian counterpart – Harrison College. This was my first experience of a tour 'abroad' and it proved an eye-opener. The matches were well attended, and the standards high.

It was only afterwards that I learned that mine was the final place selected on the team and that it was because of our top sprinter declining the invitation to tour as his younger brother was not selected in my place. Still, I felt I made some sort of impression as a young lower-order batsman, judging by reports in the Barbadian press. The captain of the Harrison College team was Charlie Manning who later became a doctor and eventually set up practice on Mustique – an island in the Grenadines best known for the frequent visits of Princess Margaret who has a home there. Charlie was prone to get a thick outside edge to our fast bowlers, included among whom was Prior Jones later to play for the West Indies. The ball often proceeded through the slips along the ground to the boundary, and when this stroke was repeated two or three times, the home supporters described it vociferously as 'Charlie's own shot'.

It has often been said that international cricketers devise their own form of learning to play during their formative years and I was no exception. For hours on end, I threw a table tennis ball against the wooden wall of our drawing room. The ball would rebound on to the polished surface which was warped and therefore slightly uneven. It would then deviate and I would hit it hither and yon between the furniture – fielders. I had my own 'league' with names manufactured under the first six letters of the alphabet. The As played the Bs and so on, and all the mythical players had their different styles and patterns of play.

At QRC the promising cricketers and first XI were coached by A. J. Richardson, the Australian Test player. This was fortuitous for he was a wonderful coach. He never quarrelled with young players when they did the wrong thing, his method being to encourage the players in what they were doing well. Encouragement is the essence of coaching. 'Play the good ones quietly, hit the bad ones,' he used to say and his 'good ball, boy' used to be heard frequently during the afternoon's practice. A. J. coached in Trinidad from 1935 to 1938, and the 1939 and 1950 West Indies teams to England included between them no fewer than eight players who had come under his hand. Richardson could bowl and bat both right and left handed, a wonderful attribute for a coach, and his forearm was almost the size of my thigh. Above all, we held in awe and admiration that baggy green Australian cap.

Although we could not repeat the exploits of our 1933 *annus mirabilis* team, the QRC cricket and football teams were always a force to be reckoned with and we often proved to be giant killers. In those days, the two senior colleges took part in first-division club cricket and consequently played regularly against the Trinidad players, on pitches of clay covered by jute matting. Although these were true pitches, they gave the bowler a bit of bounce and true spin was rewarded. Their sameness, however, tended to produce big scores and some batting records in intercolonial cricket were established on them.

At this time, football took up as much of our sporting time as cricket, and both Gerry Gomez and I played consistently for the college, he at inside left and I at right wing. We both enjoyed football as much as we did cricket and subsequently the two of us played for the island in the forties. However, while football could take us only as far as another West Indian island, there was no horizon that was not open to us through cricket. So when the time came and the choice had to be made, cricket it was, and football had to go.

Apart from playing cricket for the college, I played every Sunday 'on the Savannah', that great open park, about four miles in diameter, just north of the city of Port of Spain wherein there were no fewer than fifty-seven cricket pitches.

At one time, on Sunday mornings I rode a bicycle from my home in Santa Cruz, seven miles away, to play for a team called 'New Zealand', ate briefly under a balata tree over the lunch hour and then joined my colleagues of 'St Clair Athletic' for an afternoon game in the Slazenger Competition. It was all serious competitive cricket and no quarter was either given or asked. Our team consisted of players drawn from both colleges, Queen's Royal and St Mary's, and their ex-pupils. St Mary's were our great rivals during school-days, but afterwards boys of similar backgrounds from both schools joined together to form cricket and football clubs. These matches were played over five hours and finished in one day. Although draws were not infrequent, most of the games were completed.

During that period, I played under the captaincy of R. E. ('Raffie') Knowles who, besides captaining Trinidad at football, in later life became a well-known sports commentator and broadcaster. His enthusiasm knew no bounds and his keenness and will to win was communicated to each member of his team. Raffie died in 1975 at the age of sixty, but his memory will live on in the sporting life of Trinidad and Tobago for many years to come.

Just about this time some of us were afforded the opportunity of embarking on a schoolboy tour of England, Scotland, France and Germany. It was during the August holidays of 1937 and what a wonderful experience it turned out to be!

About forty of us embarked on the Hamburg–Amerika line SS *Caribia* and, travelling second class – which was like heaven to us – we did a tour which took us to London, Paris, Baden Baden, Trier, Wiesbaden, down the Rhine to Koblenz, Frankfurt, Brussels, Dieppe, then back to England and up to Scotland. All this for the princely sum of £45 out of which we received pocket money!

In Germany we stayed at the Jugendherbergers – Youth hostels – and were entranced and amazed at the blind obedience of the Hitler Youth. We used to delight in copying the then fashionable greeting

'*Heil* Hitler' with the arm outstretched in the Nazi salute, too young then to realize the more sinister implications of it all. We did, however, take delight in convincingly defeating a football team from one of the hostels in Frankfurt. The German youth were no less surprised than we were that some unknown West Indians of their own age could play a useful standard of soccer.

I stayed on in England for a time with my cousins, the Taylors, at their home in Surrey, and was able to play a few cricket matches for East Molesey. It was my first and unfortunately very nearly my only taste of English club cricket, surely one of the most fundamental pillars of the sport. My performances at this level were mediocre at best and I often wondered what my colleagues of those days thought when my name appeared two years later among those chosen for the West Indies to play against Hammond, Bowes, Verity and Co.

Back to Trinidad then, for my final year at QRC. Senior Cambridge exams in the offing and more cricket and football ahead.

3

Cricket Before the War

In 1937 the regular triangular intercolonial cricket tournament was played in British Guiana ('BG', now Guyana) between the host country, Barbados and Trinidad. Trinidad possessed a strong team captained by an astute Barbadian, Lionel Birkett, who had toured Australia with the West Indies in 1930–31. My brother Victor, a member of the team, was considered to be the No. 1 opening batsman in the Eastern Caribbean at the time. In the previous year, he had scored a chanceless 136 against BG at the Oval in Trinidad, an innings in which he never looked like getting out. Gerry Gomez was the youngest member of the party.

At all events, a tremendous row broke out between BG and Trinidad over the umpiring, and at the celebration dinner at the end of the tournament, which was finally won by BG, harsh words were spoken. It seemed that the dark clouds caused by this friction would never blow away.

So it was that, in August 1938, Rolph Grant, the Cambridge double blue (cricket and soccer), egged on by his cricket-conscious family, decided to take a 'goodwill' team of Trinidad cricketers to BG. This proved to be the start of a cricket career for me. At seventeen, I found myself included in the party of goodwill cricketers and playing my first first-class game.

It proved a lucky break, for we won the toss and batted. Opening the innings, I had my first experience of batting on the billiard table which was Bourda. In the first over I recall playing a firm forward defensive shot to David Hill, a slow medium inswerve bowler. There followed a ripple of applause as the ball sped between mid-off and cover point to the boundary. Such was Bourda. I scored 118, but Bourda was never one of my lucky grounds in subsequent years.

In those days I did as much bowling (leg-spin googly of doubtful length and direction) as batting and I recall serving up a wrong-'un to Peter Bayley the star BG batsman at that time. As the ball approached Peter, always a comedian, I heard him say quite loudly, 'Don't bowl that here, boy,' as he despatched it summarily over my head out of the ground into the Lamaha.*

Following on this tour and having left Queen's Royal College, I started a long association with the Queen's Park Cricket Club which has continued up to the present time.

At Queen's Royal College, my studies had inclined to the classics – history and geography were my favourites – so when, at the conclusion of the summer term, it was time for me to move on, I was faced with a problem. None of my brothers had followed in my father's footsteps and involved themselves in the cocoa and citrus estates which he was in the course of developing with such loving care. It seemed only natural, therefore, that I should make agriculture a career, but with what training?

It was then decided that the authorities at the Imperial College of Tropical Agriculture should be approached and asked whether they would accept as a student a pupil who had received, at secondary level, no scientific training whatsoever. It was thus that I found myself in the holidays being tutored in the foreign subjects of botany, chemistry, zoology and biology, peering down a microscope examining minute objects such as cocoa thrips. 'Magnificent huge beast – look at him there around five o'clock': This unusual language spoken by my professor of biology became common parlance in the three years which followed.

If QRC was the college of the élite in Trinidad and Tobago at that time, ICTA was in no way less so. The staff of both institutions were of the highest calibre, and it was to ICTA that post-graduate students not only from the UK, but from all over the world, were sent to do their theses before proceeding to various parts of the British Empire to serve as agricultural officers in the Colonies. And who can say that they did not perform great deeds in this capacity? Professors of the calibre of E. E. Cheeseman, F. Hardy and C. Y.

---

*The Lamaha was a large ditch full of water which ran parallel to and outside of Bourda.

Sheppard, were men of international renown in their particular fields. I spent three very happy years as a student at ICTA, receiving my diploma in 1941 and playing a great deal of cricket and soccer along the way.

Trinidad (we did not play then as Trinidad and Tobago) visited Barbados in the January of 1939 to contest the triangular intercolonial tournament and I was included in the party. We had a strong team captained by Rolph Grant and including C. A. Merry, Tyrrel Johnson, Gerry Gomez, Ben Sealey, L. S. Birkett, and my brother Victor among others. It was not surprising that we won the series, although we were lucky to get British Guiana in on a sticky dog (wickets were not covered in those days). My personal contribution was minimal, and a finger injury put paid to my playing in the final games against BG.

We then returned to Trinidad to take part in the trials for the 1939 tour of England. The Jamaica team was visiting Trinidad for the first time. After all, they were 1000 miles away and there was no connection by air at that time, so they came by sea and had to adapt to the matting wicket – not really all that difficult once one got accustomed to the sight and feel of the thing!

It was my first sight of George Headley and soon this young aspiring leg-spinner was to feel his presence. I was actually bowling at the time the great man came in to bat – dragging his bat behind him and slowly putting on the wrap-on type of batting glove which he invariably wore. My first ball to him was hit very hard back to me along the ground. I fielded it with my right hand and thereafter bowled a very bad over. My first lesson was learned. It was George's way of ensuring that spin-bowlers did not give him much trouble.

When the team was announced for England after the trials and my name was included among those selected, I was as surprised as the public. A crescendo of objections came from every quarter of the Caribbean. 'What has Stollmeyer done to be pitchforked into the team?' said the *British Guiana Chronicle*. It was my first taste of public controversy; it was not to be my last!

Even then I was not at all sure that I would be allowed to go. What about my first-year exams at ICTA? The tour was due to take place from the end of April to the beginning of September and this clashed directly with the college examinations. But I suppose where there is a will there is a way, and the college arranged for me to sit a specially set examination before I left. So with the help of extra tutoring and a certain amount of cramming, I got through. It was a noble gesture by the college but I have often wondered what my fellow-students thought about this unusual procedure.

So off to England on the third official Test tour of the West Indies. The team selected was: R. S. Grant (capt.), I. Barrow, H. P. Bayley, C. B. Clarke, L. N. Constantine, J. H. Cameron, G. E. Gomez, G. A. Headley, L. G. Hylton, T. Johnson, E. A. Martindale, J. E. D. Sealy, J. B. Stollmeyer, V. H. Stollmeyer, K. H. Weekes, E. A. V. Williams, with J. M. Kidney, manager, and W. Ferguson, scorer and baggage master.

Looking back at the selection of the team, there no doubt was a certain amount of hit and miss but, as things turned out, it was not those who were criticized most who were to be the biggest failures. Of the Trinidadians who missed out, the most unfortunate were Cyril A. Merry and R. P. Tang Choon. The former, blooded in 1933 when he probably did not deserve selection, was now without doubt the best batsman in Trinidad. Experienced, mature and with a resounding cover drive, I can only conclude that if he had been selected I would have been omitted. Cyril never showed any animosity towards me, however, and continued, as always, to be my mentor. I used to look upon him as a bit of a lucky charm and, whenever I saw him enter the ground while batting, knew I was in for a big score. He married my cousin Clara and his early death at the age of fifty-three was sad indeed.

To get back to the selection, there was another omission which called for comment and that was the Chinese cricketer, Rupert Tang Choon. Before the tournament and trials in 1939, this dashing cricketer must have been considered a certainty, but poor form at the wrong time spoiled his chances. Several times while on tour I could not help thinking what an attraction this dynamic cricketer would have been to the cricketing public of England. Rupert was an explosive player batting, bowling or fielding and no better team man ever graced the cricket grounds.

The tour produced variable results. We lost the only Test of the three that was finished and it was the first played at Lord's. In our second innings when we needed to bat on for some time in order to save the game, Learie Constantine was in, together with K. H. Weekes. Weekes got out, but with Learie still in and well set the game looked safe. Suddenly Learie guided an arm ball from Hedley Verity into the safe hands of Wally Hammond at slip, a diabolical stroke undoubtedly conceived in advance and played at the wrong moment. When he came into the dressing room, his younger colleagues gathered round and asked the inevitable question, 'Learie, what happened?' 'Well, it was the inswinger,' he replied vaguely. Every time thereafter one of us got out playing a bad shot and was questioned, our standard answer was, 'Well, it was the inswinger.'

While Learie was not the cricketer of yore, his immense talent would explode from time to time. He made 79 in the Oval Test and, together with K. H. ('Bam Bam') Weekes who made 137, had the fielders scattered to all quarters of the ground. It was the first time that I had seen fast bowlers of the calibre of Reg Perks and Maurice Nichols bowling with no slip and all the men in the outfield. And then there was the time when Learie ran out Maurice Turnbull at Swansea. Turnbull played the ball sharply into the gully where Learie was fielding; in one movement he fielded the ball and had the stumps down with Turnbull following the stroke a yard out of his ground. In the same match he hit Cyril Smart for 6 barely over the head of square leg to win the match for us by 2 wickets. If he had got out, we would probably have been beaten.

Learie Constantine, great cricketer that he was, was coming to the end of his career and we never saw him at his best on this tour. He was, when batting, inclined to premeditate and decide what he would do before the bowler bowled, not always with the desired results. When he was bowled behind his back by Bill Bowes in the Old Trafford Test, Neville Cardus wrote the next day, 'Only a clever pedestrian could have got his legs out of the way!'

As young players we used, at first, to hang on to Learie's every word, but as time went on we found many of his theories foreign to our thinking. When in later years we were discussing Learie with Don Bradman, the latter made a rather caustic assessment: 'It was a different game when he talked about it.' Fair comment. It was. Of course, Learie played it differently and that was why he was such a great attraction despite his complicated theories of events.

His theories were not always to be discarded, however. One example was in our match against Gloucester at Cheltenham. It was the first over after the luncheon interval with Charlie Barnett just beginning to look dangerous. Going out on to the field, Learie said to Mannie Martindale who was about to bowl the first over, 'Bowl one short outside off-stump and I will catch him on the cover-point boundary.' The ground was a small one at the sides and he was prophetic. It happened exactly as he said. Barnett square-cut firmly in the middle of the bat, Learie swallowed the catch and, as he so often used to do, put the ball in his trouser pocket. Fantastic.

If I have appeared to be unfair to this great cricketer, let me say here and now that it is a fact, not disputed by any who saw him, that he was the greatest all-round fieldsman of all time. Didn't Neville Cardus write in *Good Days*, 'I swear I once saw him keep wicket to his own bowling'? He was, probably after Bradman, and possibly W. G. Grace, the greatest crowd attraction of all time. His eye and reflexes were incredible as was his ability to improvise.

In 1950 when our team comprised of such stars as the three Ws, Ramadhin and Valentine, it was the rule rather than the exception to find young autograph hunters on the railway station platforms asking, 'Is Mr Constantine with you?' Such was the measure of the man and the esteem in which he was held in the land of his adoption.

Another great bowler who was past his best was E. A. Martindale. Watching Martindale bowl to Bob Wyatt's team of 1935 struck fear into me as a youngster of thirteen. When we saw Mannie in the nets in 1939, his arm had 'dropped' after several seasons of bowling on slow wickets in the Lancashire League, and on this tour he was nothing more than the purveyor of rather gentle outswingers. A fine cricketer and great bowler in his day was Martindale. Perhaps he was too much of a gentleman, although those who faced him in his heyday would not agree with this.

My cricket benefited immensely from batting and listening to George Headley, to my mind the greatest of all West Indies batsmen. Here I admit to prejudice if only because I saw him in the formative years and he taught me so much about the finer points of the game. Above all, he never looked like getting out. His Christian names were George Alphonso, but C. B. Fry christened him George 'Atlas' in view of the fact that he so often had to carry our team on his shoulders.

When George turned seventy in 1979, I was asked by the Jamaica Cricket Association to write a tribute to him. This I did in the following terms:

I first met George when he came to the trials in January 1939 for the selection of the West Indies team to tour England that year. He was already a legend in West Indies cricket and as a 17-year-old at the time I viewed him from the bowling crease with some degree of awe and reverence.

During the tour of 1939 and after the war, both in 1948 at home and in India in 1948–49, I continued to pick his brains. For in addition to being the 'supremo' among West Indies batsmen, he had a greater tactical sense than any cricketer with whom I have played. He would never let a game get out of hand. There was always some strategy, some tactic, that he would suggest which could be tried and furthermore, if expertly carried out, could pull the irons out of the fire and make a match out of a game which, to all appearances, had been irretrievably lost. Witness the final Test in India in 1949, a game which was saved by the West Indies and with it the series won. George was the tactical architect on that occasion (using 'leg theory' as a defensive measure), despite the fact that he was not on the field himself.

He was the greatest batsman that the West Indies produced. Of this I have no doubt and my association with Test cricket in the West Indies spans a period from 1939 to the present day, during which I have seen and/ or played with the three 'Ws', Gary Sobers and Rohan Kanhai in their prime; also, Viv Richards of the current crop, great players all. Why should I be of this opinion? Simply because George never looked like getting out. He liked to bat; 'Why him don't like to bat?' he used to ejaculate when one of his team played a rash or unbecoming stroke! He reduced error to a minimum and he played as well on difficult wickets as he did on good ones. His 61 vs Yorkshire on a sticky dog at Harrogate in 1939 was the best innings, technically, that I have ever seen. The manner of his dismissal on that occasion was indicative of the character of the innings. He was out to a magnificent catch at forward short leg c. Leyland b. Verity, pulling a ball which 'popped' downwards!

Watching from the other end as I was privileged to do many times on that tour, I gained the impression that George knew exactly where the coat of varnish was on his off-stump!

Few, except those who played with and against him late in his career, knew how well he could bowl. He bowled flighted off-spin with great cunning and subtlety and could have been a considerable asset in this department were it not for the excellence of his batting and the necessity for him to play long innings regularly and consistently.

As a fielder he was quick and alert in the cover region and safe, even brilliant at times, in the slip area.

Long-sleeved, two-eyed stance, I see him now a scourge to all bowlers and a star batsman without peer in the firmament of West Indies cricket. Seventy not out is just another landmark. George being George the hundred beckons . . .

For me, I acknowledge personally a great debt to George. He taught me most of what I know of the finer points of the great game of cricket; a debt which, unfortunately, I shall never be able to repay.

Personal memories of the tour are more obscure but I do remember not being able to get my legs to obey me during the first overs of the first Test at Lord's. This was probably for the best because it meant that I couldn't get near enough to the ball to touch it. The England bowlers of the day were Bowes, Copson, Verity and Wright – not a bad combination. I went on to score 59 until bowled by a ball from Bill Bowes which 'came down the hill'. I had, in the game previous to the Test, scored 117 against Middlesex in my first appearance at Lord's.

The real difficulty was learning to cope with the ball that moved off the seam, something rarely seen on wickets in the West Indies. All the fast and fast-medium England bowlers could do this. One merely had to get accustomed to it, but it was no easy task. Perhaps the most difficult part of being an opening batsman is learning which ball *not* to play. George Headley was a past master at this, and so often was a virtual opener anyway. I could only stand and admire his technique at the other end. Unfortunately, being of a somewhat different temperament, I was never able to emulate his ability to leave the right one alone.

One proud moment was when, at Taunton against Somerset, I scored 45 out of 84 against Arthur Wellard and Bill Andrews on a day when the ball moved around in the air prodigiously. I stood at the other end and saw some of my colleagues bowled while playing anywhere from six inches to a foot away from the ball. At the Queen's Park Oval in Trinidad where much of my cricket was played, we learned to play the 'moving' ball by virtue of the fact that the Northern range, along the North coast of the island with its frequently humid atmosphere, encouraged swerve. The Trinidad players were often, in those days, better able than their counterparts from the other islands to cope with swerve through the air.

I remember playing at Leicester and having a stand with Gerry Gomez against Bob Sperry bowling huge inswingers. Several of our colleagues had failed. Peter Bayley, short of form and match play and suffering from a bad knee, opened the innings with me and was bowled first ball. Peter knocked on the door of the dressing room which he found closed on his return to the pavilion; the skipper was not particularly pleased when he opened the door to see Peter standing there saying, 'Good morning, skipper.'

In this game Les Hylton, the fast-medium bowler, was put in to bat at No. 3 and he too was out without scoring. Les had been complaining about not getting a knock in spite of his ability to bat, but it didn't quite work that way this time. While Hylton was not a big success on the tour, I remember him bowling Len Hutton comprehensively in the Lord's Test with a ball which came down the hill.

An unusual incident in which Hylton was involved took place at Cheltenham in our game against Gloucester. Hylton had been bowling none too successfully before lunch when, in the over before the interval, George Headley, apparently on his own initiative, moved from slip to leg slip. Hylton was seen to pause and show a certain amount of disapproval before continuing to bowl. After the interval we found ourselves out on the field two men short and, being the junior member of the team, I was ordered into the pavilion by the skipper to find out what was amiss, only to discover Hylton and Headley sitting on opposite sides of the dressing room both in high indignation, having had the most fearful row. After some pleading they both came on to the field. These two cricketers, both of them keen students of the game, often held contrary views and there was a bit of 'needle' between them. Nevertheless I learned more of tactics and strategy from them than anyone else with whom I played. I would place L. S. Birkett also in this category.

Les Hylton had not been originally selected for the tour but well-wishers in Jamaica had got together and subscribed his fare, board and lodging, etc. Here was another studious cricketer and one with whom I spent many hours in the late forties and early fifties watching and learning. He was a fine figure of a man. Six foot two or three with broad shoulders, he was a commanding personality, but he also possessed a fiery temper which had got him into trouble and was probably the cause of his missing the 1933 West Indies tour to England. While playing in the trials prior to that tour, an LBW appeal by him was turned down by the umpire who happened to be the elder brother of the captain-elect. When Hylton threw the ball down in disgust, his 'goose' was not unnaturally cooked.

Hylton's temper was to prove his undoing. In 1955 in Jamaica during the first Test match against Australia, I visited him in the Spanish Town gaol in the company of his lawyer, who was also a renowned cricket administrator, N. N. 'Crab' Nethersole. Leslie had been convicted for the murder of his wife, having shot her after an argument. His appeal had failed and he was living in Death Row;

dressed in a white gown, he looked like a high priest. It seemed a great shame that one so powerful and vital should have to pay the full penalty, but his temper had let him down for the last time.

The third and final Test of the 1939 tour was played at the Oval. The team had been selected and brother Victor omitted, and so, I was later told, he went out on the town the night before the game. On the morning of the match, he was awakened by 'Mr Jack' – our nickname for Manager Kidney – and told, 'You are in the team. Get ready to play.' Bleary-eyed, he made his way to the ground and luckily for him we fielded first. When he batted he was put in as No. 4 and, in his only Test, made 94. It was an innings of great character for, during the course of it, he was batting with George Headley when the latter was run-out, normally a disaster for our team. But Victor soldiered on and was finally out stumped Wood bowled Goddard only when a thunderstorm was threatening to end play for the day. There was much evidence to suggest that we should have opened the innings together in this match.

The 1939 tour of England came to an abrupt end. Although war with Germany was in the air, we cricketers used to read the back page of the newspapers rather than the front, and our captain nearly had a riot on his hands when he called the team together and informed us that we were going home. Of course he was a party to information which we did not have and his decision proved to be the correct one.

Almost overnight, we were shepherded on to a train for Greenock in Scotland and put on board SS *Montrose* in small cabins holding four passengers each. The cabins were so tiny that the feet of such as Les Hylton and Tyrrel Johnson extended into the corridors. It proved an eventful trip for more than one reason. During the course of it, we were up on deck one night for dubious purposes (there were forty Canadian schoolgirls returning home after touring England) when we noticed that the moon was on the opposite side of the ship. Persistent enquiries of 'Sparks' finally got out of him the fact that the ship had turned around – recalled by the Admiralty. Fortunately this lasted under twenty-four hours and we continued our voyage, arriving in Montreal on 3 September 1939 – the day war was declared by England on Germany.

It is a sobering thought that, in retrospect, had we missed the SS

Montrose, the next ship of the same line doing that crossing was SS *Athenia*, the first ship sunk in the war.

It was to be nine long years before the West Indies played their next Test match.

4

The War Years and Afterwards

En route home, after a short period in Montreal where my brother Rex and his wife Marjorie were resident, we then went on to New York to stay with another brother, Alex, and his wife Elizabeth at Forest Hills. Gerry Gomez and I spent many hours commuting in and out of the big city. Much of the time was spent in the environs of Times Square and most of that time at the Paramount Theater on Broadway, where the great Glenn Miller band was performing as part of a programme before a film in which Bing Crosby played the part of a priest. We saw the film at least five times, but we were really paying homage to Miller. Benny Goodman's orchestra was playing at the World's Fair and Artie Shaw was at the Strand. We enjoyed the big bands to the full.

In the early days of the war, I found myself immersed in studies for my diploma at ICTA but at the same time found adequate time to continue playing cricket for the college and for Queen's Park, and football for the Casuals Club.

The Casuals Club in those days was affectionately called the 'Red Army' by the crowd, and many and great were the battles fought against Shamrock, Maple, Notre Dame, Fleet Air Arm and the other top football clubs of the day. We possessed a great forward line by local standards and, at our best, in 1941 scored 83 goals in a season. In one FA trophy game, we beat a team called Vandals, from one of the outlying towns, 16–1.

The Casuals forward line comprised, from left to right, V. H. Stollmeyer, G. E. Gomez, H. De Silva, R. Littlepage and J. B. Stollmeyer. Three of us who had played international cricket had seen the great pre-war Arsenal forward line in action and it served us in good stead. I remember trying hard to introduce the 'third-back' game, which had recently become popular in England, into Trinidad football, but this required a coach who had seen it practised and was fully conversant with all the consequential charges. It was not put into practice in Trinidad until the Fleet Air Arm football squad played it on a continuous basis.

Football and horseracing were to take up much of my time during the years that followed. In the mid-Forties I captained the 'Maroons', as the Casuals were called because of our maroon jerseys, and thoroughly enjoyed playing with and against players who have since become firm friends. Both at club and island level, playing at right wing with such as Gerry Gomez inside of me brought forth many fond memories. We played together for Trinidad in intercolonial tournaments and toured Jamaica in 1946. The Casuals were usually near the top of the league and in contention for the FA Cup, but the standard of football achieved was far below that of cricket. This obtains even today and no West Indian football team has yet made its mark at international level.

In many of the islands today, the game is even more popular than cricket, but it would appear that the absence of professionalism is taking its toll and the time for the rigid training which is required for ninety minutes of 'total' football just does not exist. This does not mean that West Indian footballers are not talented and it should be merely a matter of time before they make their mark in the World Cup.

Our circle was always keen on horseracing and in 1943 ten of us purchased, for $120.00 TT currency ($1.00 US = $2.40 TT), a half-bred colt born in Tobago which we christened Bob. Rumour had it, however, that we paid only a 'bob' for him. The horse was put in the name of the member considered least likely to own a racehorse, Oliver 'Maffy' Burke, and great was the fun which we were to have through Bob's performance.

The stories of Bob are legendary in Trinidad racing. He was trained by another part-owner, Joe Crooks, who in the course of time became a civil engineer and town planner for the Trinidad and Tobago Government and later on acted in a similar capacity for the United Nations.

When we brought Bob over to Trinidad from Tobago to be trained, he looked rather like a diminutive mule and we were the objects of a great deal of chaff and what, in local parlance, was called 'fatigue'. We received much encouragement from Dr Cyril Gittens, one of the leading owners of the time, who possessed a successful but equally small horse called Lady Bird. 'Lift him up and let me see him,' was the wry comment of H. R. 'Dick' Murray, the foremost racing commentator of the period.

Bob, however, blossomed as a result of loving care and attention and went on to win many races. On one memorable occasion when he carried a top weight of 130 lb in a five-furlong event, there was a false start of which his jockey Padilla was not aware. He was ridden out along with more than half of the field of twenty-three runners and won the false start comfortably. There followed general confusion outside the parade ring. A majority decision was taken to send the horse back to the gates for a second run – a decision no doubt dictated in part by the jockey and those owners who had placed a substantial bet on the horse. Bob did not disappoint, winning the second start by a long neck. I was in hospital at the time recovering from an appendix operation, and listening in to the race on the radio, I almost burst the stitches. The horse had become such a favourite with Dick Murray that after mentioning his position once at the start of the race, he continued by saying, 'He's third now, moving up to second behind Bread Boy, he's challenging the leader. He's going to win. My goodness, he's done it.' It was only then that Dick remembered to say that Bob had won again – a feat unparalleled in the history of the local turf.

Bob had previously won the Anchor Cup, one of the more important races for the lowest class. The celebrations that took place that night were considerable if not entirely memorable. The cup was filled first with champagne, courtesy of the stewards, then any drink that was similar in colour, including rum, ginger ale and cider. Owners, trainers, stewards, jockeys, stable lads and sundry friends all joined in sipping out of the cup through their straws.

Bob won more than $26,000 in stakes – a tidy sum for those days. His deeds are still recalled by those who remember local racing in the Forties.

During the war years, Trinidad was a centre for the assembly of convoys going around the Cape to the East. It became more and more important strategically and not the least because of the oil which the country produced, albeit in small quantities, and because of the Trinidad Leaseholds Ltd refinery, which was then the largest in the British Empire. In succession, therefore, we had the establishment of a Fleet Air Arm training base at Piarco airport and subsequently, under lend-lease, the setting up of a US Navy base at Chaguaramas on the western peninsula of the island. A US Army base known as 'Fort Read' was also built in the north central area.

The presence of these bases was the direct cause of great changes in the domestic life of the population. The 'Yankee dollar' began to make its presence felt and the economy received a considerable boost from it. As food and other supplies to the local populace had been largely cut-off, the 'grow more food' campaign introduced by the government of the day caused a shift in the emphasis from export crops to domestic agriculture.

It proved a trying time for the owners of agricultural estates, especially the cocoa estates. The price of cocoa was pegged at 13¢ per lb which was completely uneconomical as labour was drawn away inexorably by the comparatively high prices being offered by the Americans to work on the building of the bases, and the dreaded witches broom disease was ravaging the trees at the same time. A combination of these two caused my father to dispose of those properties which had the least potential for the future. Sad to say, the food farms into which they were presumably to be converted never really got off the ground. History is repeating itself at the present time but for quite different reasons. Now it is full-scale industrialization, spin-offs from the oil industry, the black gold that has turned the world upside down. Having oil reserves, Trinidad has been fortunate; it is a 'rich' country but, by the same token, its agriculture has taken a back seat.

West Indies cricket did not suffer to any extent during the war. In fact it blossomed. This was due mainly to some far-sighted administrators – such as Allan Collymore and Fred Clairmonte of Barbados, and Sir Errol dos Santos, E. J. 'Dal' Marsden and Joe Kelshall of Trinidad. They started a series of 'goodwill' tournaments between Trinidad and Barbados on an annual basis. Later on, British Guiana was included with significant contributions on the administrative side from such as Alty O'Dowd and Lionel Drayton.

These games, played in the keenest and most competitive of spirits, served to develop the talent which existed in the area and, indeed, were responsible for the strong West Indies teams of 1948–54, teams which were to put West Indies cricket firmly on the international map. The tournaments were started in 1941 and continued uninterrupted until the end of the war. There developed terrific rivalry between the two islands. In general, Barbados would win the tournament when it was held at Kensington Oval, Barbados, and Trinidad would return the compliment the following year when the games were played at the Queen's Park Oval on the jute matting wicket.

In the first games of the series in 1941, Trinidad had a singularly powerful team which, in batting order, was V. H. Stollmeyer (capt.), J. B. Stollmeyer, D. 'A.' Merry, G. E. Gomez, Len Harbin, Ben Sealey, R. P. Tang Choon, A. G. Ganteaume, P. E. Jones, S. M. Ali and Lance Pierre – surely one of the most powerful ever to represent the country. All departments of the game were covered. Pierre and Jones were just about the best fast bowlers in the area, the former bowling huge and well-directed outswingers with a wonderful off-spin change ball, the latter capable of cutting the ball both ways off the unsympathetic matting wicket.

The Barbados openers, Stanton Gittens and C. L. C. Bourne, invariably had a torrid time against Pierre and Jones and on one memorable occasion, as recalled by Stanton Gittens, when 'Bourney' had played and missed for 2 successive overs from Lance Pierre, he walked down to his partner and said, 'Stanton, you take Prior, I have Lance covered!'

And then there was the controversial S. M. Ali. Batting against Ali, whom we met frequently in club cricket, was like playing against Tom Goddard or Jim Laker on a sticky dog. He bowled cart-wheel-type off-breaks which bit, broke and bounced. In those days several fielders could be placed behind square leg and Ali had most of his victims caught in the leg-trap or bowled. He was truly an extraordinary off-spinner, but (for more than one reason) he never played in a Test. First of all, his career had more or less ended by the end of the war and, secondly, this end was precipitated by him being no-balled by Umpire Ward in Barbados for throwing. He was no-balled thirty times in the innings and at one stage resorted to bowling under-arm. In retrospect, the umpire was probably correct and it was inevitable that his doubtful action would have caught up with him. For years I played against Ali in club cricket and it was always a battle for survival. 'Get him before he gets you' was the general attitude I adopted, but he did make one learn how to counter off-spin on a turner.

These were great days for Victor and myself as an opening pair, and we had many long and enjoyable partnerships together. Victor captained us and was universally popular with the players of both teams. He also seldom failed with the bat. Gerry Gomez was no less prolific and later on Ken Trestrail showed promise (never quite fulfilled) of the highest class.

On the Barbados side, these tournaments developed the skills and talents of the three Ws – Frank Worrell, Clyde Walcott and Everton Weekes – among others. The first two came on the scene initially, and at the tender ages of sixteen and seventeen respectively, they made their first-class debuts on the 'mat' in 1942. Frank Worrell, batting at No. 11, scored 29 of a last wicket partnership of 56 on his first appearance and bowling left-arm spin, took 3–70 and 3–58 in a match won by Trinidad by 2 wickets. A warning had been well and truly sounded.

Later in 1942 in Barbados, I became involved in a record of sorts by being a member of the Trinidad team which made an all-time low score of 16. Barbados had scored 329 for 7 on the Saturday. It had rained heavily on the Sunday night, and with the wicket uncovered and the sun shining, there was no doubt in our minds that we were 'for it'. The Barbados innings closed at 339 and in an effort to try and stave off the inevitable, our batting order was substantially altered, but to no avail. Of the 16 scored, Andy Ganteaume, opening the innings, scored 9. There were no fewer than eight 'ducks', mine being one of them. Derek Sealy, bowling well-directed half-volleys, took 8 for 8 and five catches were taken by the Barbados captain Tom Peirce at short-leg. Watching the other batsmen getting out to balls which lifted perpendicularly off the turf, I decided to leave alone any normal good-length ball even if it pitched on the stumps. This ploy proved successful for only two balls. The third skidded along the turf and hit the bottom of the middle stump!

Accompanied by our manager, Mr Joey Agard, we surprised the Bajans that night by playing 'carnival' and singing calypsos on the streets of Hastings. A remarkable celebration in the circumstances.

These tournaments were to become run feasts. When Worrell and Walcott became accustomed to the mat, they plundered the Trinidad bowling both in Trinidad and in Barbados, and John Goddard, too, was involved in some record partnerships. Two of the more famous ones were when, in 1944 in Barbados, Worrell (308) and Goddard (218) scored an unbroken partnership of 502 for the fourth wicket, then a world record. Previously, in the same match I had scored 210, the highest score made by a Trinidadian against Barbados at

Kensington. There followed the great partnership between Clyde Walcott and Frank Worrell in Trinidad in 1946 when they made 574 together (Walcott 314 and Worrell 255), breaking the record established between Worrell and Goddard. Fortunately for me, I was sidelined in this game through injury so was not one of those subjected to this rather traumatic experience.

The Trinidad batsmen were not to be outdone. Victor and I had several partnerships of over 100 for the first wicket and Gerry Gomez scored a magnificent 216 and, later in 1946, 213 not out to save Trinidad from certain defeat in the game of records played at the Queen's Park Oval.

Towards the end of the war, I was invited to take a team, largely consisting of Queen's Park Cricket Club members, to St Kitts and Antigua to play cricket and football against representative teams of those islands. We ended up playing them at tennis and table tennis as well and returned undefeated in any of the sports.

In retrospect, this was truly one of the most enjoyable tours I ever experienced. The camaraderie, the hospitality and the friendships gained have survived the passing years, and I am happy to feel that we left a lasting and favourable impression in those islands which has continued to this day and has helped me in my efforts to encourage the game in the Leewards and Windwards during my term of office as President of the West Indies Cricket Board of Control. Recently while speaking at a dinner in Antigua at which the Shell Shield was presented to the Combined Islands for the first time since the competition started in 1966, I asked whether there were any surviving players of that tour among the guests and, if so, whether they would kindly stand. There were three – Sydney Walling and Leo Gore (Antigua) and Calvin Wilkin (St Kitts). We had also played against Viv Richards' father, but he was not present at the gathering that night.

In 1946, in the absence of my brother Victor who had decided to retire from first-class cricket, I was asked to captain Trinidad in a goodwill series against Jamaica. Our team was the guest of the Kingston Cricket Club, and it was the first time that a Trinidad team had visited the 'Isle of Springs' for forty years – an indication of the distance by sea (over 1000 miles) which separates the two largest islands in the cricketing Caribbean.

While the tour provided a great deal of entertainment and some keen cricket and we tasted not only defeat but the wonderful hospitality of our hosts, I was disappointed in our team's performance and especially in my own contribution, which was not helped by a nagging leg muscle injury sustained while fielding. Both teams were strong, and Jamaica was captained by Cecil Marley who was to be my predecessor as Board President later on, a man of considerable vision and intellect who served West Indies cricket faithfully and well. Their team included the great George Headley, Ken Weekes, Ken Rickards, Hines Johnson, J. K. Holt, Jr, John Cameron and Dickie Fuller, all of whom either had played or were to play for the West Indies. Trinidad, on the other hand were served by the following Test cricketers: A. G. Ganteaume, P. E. Jones, G. E. Gomez, W. Ferguson, N. Asgarali, J. E. D. Sealy and myself. Captaincy I enjoyed and always have enjoyed. When one gets tired of playing the same shots and playing within one's limitations, there is no such side to captaincy. There is always a new situation to face, a new opponent to dismiss, another game to win or to prevent the opposition from winning. The tactics and strategy of cricket are, in my view, the game's greatest attraction.

Two records fell to me during this period. Playing against British Guiana in 1947 at the Queen's Park Oval, I scored 324, a record for the ground and in intercolonial cricket. An appeal for LBW by Berkeley Gaskin, the BG in-swerve bowler, was disallowed by the umpire when I was not yet off the mark. The bowler, I believe, felt disillusioned by the decision, as well he might because no chance was given until he bowled me between bat and pad a couple of days later. Ken Wishart, who for many years in later life successfully discharged the duties of Secretary of the West Indies Board, captained BG and one recalls his 'help' while fielding at mid-on. Ken was getting on at the time and was possibly over the hill. He was no greyhound in the field, and whenever the bowling was 'tight' and scoring difficult, there was always a run in the direction of mid-on, a run which became known as 'the Wishart single'. During this innings I enjoyed a long partnership of 434 with Gerry Gomez (191) who was much alive to this particular single.

The second record took place in the same year in a club match in Trinidad. This was considered to be first-class competitive cricket at local level, but was not a first-class match. Queen's Park were playing against one of the weakest teams, Stingo, when S. G. Guillen and I opened the innings for our club. The records show that we scored

290 for 0 wicket in 156 minutes and that our opponents were beaten by an innings. Has this happened before or since, I wonder. Perhaps the statisticians will know of many similar cases.

The most important event of 1947 for me, however, was my marriage to Sara. It had not by any means been a whirlwind courtship. We had met some ten years before and had been 'going together' for much of the period. Sara's father, Henley, was Barbadian of English extraction but was living in Trinidad and was a senior executive in the firm of Boyd and Hutchinson, manufacturer's representatives. Her mother Ruby, *née* Gordon, was Guyanese of Scottish heritage. They lived at Oxford Street in Port of Spain and were hosts to several boarders from the other islands, many of whom worked at Barclays Bank.

Their house became a second home for me, for I was a country boy who often found himself regularly in Port of Spain where most of the cricket and football was played.

Ruby Hutchinson was what her name implied, a ruby, and her tragic death at the young age of forty-five left an irreplaceable void in the lives of her family and those of her many friends and admirers.

By mutual consent Sara left Trinidad for the US in 1944 to study nursing, but after one year as a 'probie' she returned to Trinidad. I met her on the wharf and, while taking her home together with loads of baggage, we made up our minds to spend our lives together. It was a decision I have never regretted.

We were married at Christ Church, St Ann's, on 4 October 1947. Our honeymoon was spent at a rather remote seaside house at Blanchisseuse on the north coast of Trinidad. We left our rather uproarious wedding reception about 8.30 at night with me driving an old Dodge estate pick-up some fifty miles over a tortuous and lonely road through the northern range forests. We were lucky, for the next morning we found a flat tyre. I would certainly not have relished changing a wheel under the prevailing conditions. Sara was to become a cricket widow for the next six years, but this was not entirely unexpected.

Parents are notably and naturally prejudiced about their children, but our four offspring – three boys and a girl, Allan (1951), Donald (1953), Brian (1954) and Kathryn (1956), all normal, healthy and strong – have given us no cause for worry and are all making their way reasonably successfully in this troublesome world of today. Not many families in these times can boast of this record which is in no small measure due to the care and devotion provided by their mother over the years.

5

Test Cricket Resumes

The advance guard of Gubby Allen's 1948 team were three English journalists who we were to meet for the first time: Charles Bray, Jim Swanton and Crawford White. They arrived – all travel was by sea – some considerable time in advance of the team, and long and many were the yarns exchanged about cricket and cricketers since the cessation of hostilities.

Gubby Allen, aged forty-six, brought out an England team noticeably without Len Hutton, Denis Compton, Bill Edrich and Alec Bedser. The team was plagued by injury during the tour and eventually Hutton was flown out to join the team in British Guiana and made his mark instantly. Allen himself was the first casualty of the tour when he pulled a muscle while exercising on the deck of the ship which brought the team out to Barbados.

Because West Indies cricket had thrived during the war it was not surprising that many new stars had surfaced. Of the three 'Ws', Worrell and Walcott were already established players and Everton Weekes came in for the final Test at Kingston.

With the minimum of time to find their sea legs, the MCC (as they were then called), losing the toss, ran into a tremendously powerful Barbados batting side on a perfect Kensington wicket. Runs simply flowed and I wonder whether the team ever recovered from this setback. Harold Butler, one of the faster bowlers, was approaching the end of his career and appeared somewhat overweight, while Maurice Tremlett, a surprise selection, had some difficulty in pitching the ball on the wicket at all. Their injuries continued, and Dennis Brookes had to go home with a broken finger sustained while fielding in the Barbados Test. On hearing the diagnosis, 'Gubby', who was not unnaturally shattered by this time, exclaimed questioningly to the doctor, 'Are you sure?' A remark which was not appreciated by the medic.

In those happy days, although Test cricket was a serious matter, an overseas tour to the West Indies was a more leisurely business and there was more time for entertainment and relaxation. There was much fun and camaraderie off the field and the players of both teams mixed rather more freely than obtains in today's 'rat race'.

It was in Barbados on the Sunday of the Test match that I had my one and only experience of dowsing. Billy Griffith, the England deputy wicket-keeper (Godfrey Evans was the No. 1), and I were strolling along the beach at Sandy Lane on the Barbados west coast when we came upon an unusual scene. Several young men including Mike Foster, a Barbadian cricketer, were standing around a block and tackle from which buckets were being lowered into a large square hole in the sand, withdrawing a combination of sand and salt water. 'What's going on here?' I asked Mike. 'We are digging for treasure' was the reply. 'Why do you think there is treasure there?' was my rejoinder. 'Ask Mr Branch.' An older gentleman then came forward, a forked piece of metal in his hand. 'This,' he said, 'tells me that there is metal underground here and we know that there is treasure buried hereabouts from the buccaneer days.' With that, he proceeded to demonstrate that, when he held the metal over the hole, it pulled his hand downwards. 'Try it,' he said to me. I did, with no result. He then placed his hand on my wrist, and for the life of me I could not stop the wretched thing from pointing downwards. It was as if my hand would not obey my brain for, try as I might, I could not prevent it. Billy Griffith had the same experience. We have oft since recalled the incident. Mr Branch was a well-known water diviner and many are the wells which he has discovered for Barbadian plantation owners under the coral on which the island is based.

Barbados, a mere 166 square miles in area, has produced more great cricketers per square mile than any other country in the world, including two cricketing knights. Just consider Sir Garfield Sobers, Sir Frank Worrell, Everton Weekes, Clyde Walcott, Wes Hall, George Challenor, E. A. Martindale, to name merely a few.

Sir Pelham Warner accompanied the MCC on tour. 'Plum' was born in Trinidad and spent his boyhood days there. 'I lived at the Hall and played cricket in the marble gallery in my nightshirt,' he used to say. When there I took him to his old place of abode, now part of the Bishop Anstey High School, the flagstoned marble gallery still intact. During the course of his visit, he found that P. E. Jones, the Trinidad and West Indies fast bowler, had rented a house owned by him in the Belmont district of Port of Spain.

'Plum' became a friend of all. He loved the West Indies as much as he did England, the land of his adoption and his forbears. I composed a verse on him to the tune of the calypso, 'Brown Skin Gal':

> Who is this little man that I see
> Wearing the colours of the MCC?
> It's Plum, a real personality.
> Hats off to him who guides our cricket destiny

West Indies cricket, mainly due to the distance between the islands and the difficulty of communication, was still in its formative years, and often compromises, of a nature inexplicable in present times, had to be made by the administrators. There was one such on this tour when three different captains were appointed. G. A. Headley was to captain in the first Test in Barbados, J. B. Stollmeyer the second in Trinidad, J. D. Goddard the third in British Guiana, and finally Headley again in Jamaica. This certainly did not lend itself to stability within the team, but in the event, because of the superiority of our team in every department, we won the series convincingly by 2–0.

Test match wickets were not covered in those days and this could sway the fortunes of a game completely, especially on West Indian turf wickets which became virtually death traps after a period of rain and sun.

The first Test was interfered with by the weather which washed out the last day's play and ended in a draw with West Indies firmly in the driving seat. It rained every night after the first day on which we scored 244 for 3, Gomez and I sharing a partnership of 104. The wicket before lunch thereafter presented problems. On this type of surface, Jim Laker showed the first signs of the promise that would make him the great off-spinner that he became. Headley was off the field with a back injury in the latter part of the game and John Goddard took over the captaincy on his home ground. George was not to play again in the series.

One of the more unfortunate events in my cricket career took place on the final day of the match, MCC vs Trinidad. Godfrey Evans, who was not out overnight, hit the first ball of the day through extra cover. I turned to chase from mid-off and in the process pulled a hamstring muscle. This meant a three-week absence from the game and caused me to miss my chance of captaining the West Indies at the early age of twenty-six. It also meant that I missed both the Trinidad and British Guiana Test matches.

Gerry Gomez captained in the Trinidad Test played on the matting wicket, the 'infernal mat' as Gubby Allen described it. In the event the game was drawn, and if blame was to be placed anywhere for us not winning this match, it fell on slow batting in our first innings when the position of the game called for the batsmen to push on.

In later years in the West Indies, much has been made of the sole innings in Test matches of Andy Ganteaume who scored 112 and never played in a Test match thereafter. On that occasion, however, Andy's innings in its latter stages was not in keeping with the state of the game and his captain was forced to send a message out to him to 'get on with it'. In any event, who should the selectors have dropped in British Guiana for Ganteaume to play without unbalancing the team? The same applied to the fourth Test in Jamaica. The anomaly, if it indeed existed, might have been corrected when the team was selected later in the year to tour India. George Carew was preferred to Ganteaume and the former, a fine player indeed in his day, turned out to be past his best and unable to cope with the rigours, trials and tribulations of six months of travelling throughout the length and breadth of the subcontinent.

It was in this Test match that S. C. 'Billy' Griffith made his first first-class 100. In the absence of Brookes and Place, both injured, Billy was called upon to open the innings with Jack Robertson. It was a gamble of the first magnitude and appeared to be even more so when he was responsible for running out his more illustrious partner early in the match. Not to be daunted, he soldiered on to 140 before he was out LBW – in his own words, 'an atrocious decision by a Chinese umpire'. Be that as it may, this innings was one of great character and one of cricket's big talking points at the time. Quite naturally, he received numerous cables from his many friends in England. Perhaps the most amusing of these was from Austin Matthews, the Glamorgan and England bowler, whose message was the single word: 'Really!'

The third Test match at Bourda produced many thrills, especially towards the end when West Indies were chasing 78 on a rain-affected wicket and lost the first three batsmen for only 26. Gomez and Walcott saw us safely home but there were many alarums and excursions and our visitors were convinced that Gerry was born with the proverbial silver spoon. Len Hutton had arrived on the scene and made his presence felt immediately scoring runs in both innings of the match against British Guiana. His presence alone, however, was not enough to save the day and the final Test at Kingston went the same way, and we emerged comfortable victors by 10 wickets, Goddard and I getting the 74 needed in the final innings in thirty-seven minutes.

John Goddard was quite rightly and not unexpectedly elected to captain the team in Jamaica and he handled the game well. The most significant events were as much behind the scenes as on the field. Weekes – called in for Headley who dropped out at the eleventh hour, still not match fit – arrived in Jamaica while we were already on the field, the aircraft in which he was travelling flying over Sabina Park. In the event, he had a tremendously successful match, scoring 141, the first of five successive Test hundreds and he would certainly have got his sixth the following year in Madras were it not for a shocking run-out decision by the umpire when he was 90. This was the start of this player's illustrious career.

A second notable event was the excellent wicket-keeping of Clyde Walcott. Clyde is a big man and most wicket-keepers are short. For one as tall as he is, it is a long way to bend and repeated bending did take its toll in Australia in 1951, but for the next two years he was to be a tower of strength in this position. He was two players in one and, as such, a tremendous asset to the West Indies.

Success came my way in this game, but as a bowler rather than as a batsman. In the second innings my figures were 19–7–32–3 and were more than a little responsible for us clinching the match.

Hines Johnson bowled well and still looked, at thirty-eight, a very good prospect. He did not make the team to India, and whether he would have withstood the rigours of that hard tour is a matter for conjecture.

An incident took place in the dressing room shortly before the start of the match which may have had a significant bearing on the future of West Indies cricket. Frank Worrell arrived at the ground in a lounge suit a few minutes before the start of play, after we had lost the toss and were going out on to the field. We already were one player short (Weekes) and there was a frantic search on for a second substitute. Three West Indies Board members, who were also selectors, happened to cross his path at the time. They followed him into the dressing room and Frank was quite rightly at the receiving end of a severe 'lecture'. Previously on the tour he had asked permission to leave the ground while fielding in the Test match in Trinidad in order to meet his sister at the airport. This request had been quite naturally turned down. It appears that the Board decided that our most promising player was in need of some discipline, and he was not selected for the tour of India.

I have no doubt that this had a salutary and beneficial effect on Frank in the long term, for he kept in close touch with the team throughout that tour and subsequently became the great leader of men that he was.

6
India

'Now, boys, you're living in a strange country.' These were the opening remarks of our manager, Donald Lacy, at our first team meeting in Bombay. At thirty-nine, George Headley was hardly a boy, but still – errors and omissions excepted – Lacy's remarks were strictly accurate.

Donald Lacy, Secretary of the Board under current President Karl Nunes, gave his all to West Indies cricket, first as Secretary and then for many years as one of Jamaica's representatives on the Board. Little did he know the difficulties which lay ahead of him on this tour, and we proved to be the last-ever international team to travel internally through India by rail. The mildest and friendliest of men, Donald almost had a rebellion on his hands in the latter part of our six-month tour when the players (and I confess to being one of the spokesmen for them) insisted that they would not undertake any more long overnight train journeys. Thank goodness, wise counsel prevailed, and we did the final leg of the tour by air.

The subcontinent of India is 1,269,346 square miles in area and our journey from Delhi to Poona had taken over two days and nights by rail – this immediately after the conclusion of a four-day 'Test' match against Pakistan. The justification for our protest was obvious to all who were present to see the team disembark from the train on that occasion.

This first cricket tour to India by the West Indies came about largely because of a close friendship which had developed between the two Board Presidents, Karl Nunes and Anthony de Mello. The finances of the tour were loosely arranged: the Indian Board were to be responsible for all of our team's expenses, and it was agreed that, if there was a profit on the tour, our Board would get a share of it. In the event our Board received a token £10 as its share. The crowds at the Test matches were enormous, and throughout the whole tour we never lost a single hour of cricket because of rain. Friends at Chepauk, the Test ground in Madras, stated openly that the Madras Test gate receipts would pay for the whole tour. But this is water under the bridge. What was started in 1948–49 has proved ever since to be of inestimable value to the cricket and cricketers of both countries. Perhaps the irony of it all was emphasized when our Board was presented with a cheque for £500 as its share of the profits from the two weeks we spent playing in Ceylon!

I have earlier made some reference to the selection of our team. I thought that two players unlucky to be omitted were A. G. (Andy) Ganteaume, a safe and intelligent opening batsman, and N. E. Marshall, elder brother of Roy Marshall, the steadiest off-spinner in West Indies cricket at the time; these two were preferable to G. Carew and J. H. Cameron. We had a great batting team but failed on at least two occasions to bowl India out twice when they were facing huge first innings deficits. The non-selection of Hines Johnson, the fastest and most accurate bowler of his type available, is commented on in the previous chapter.

The route taken by our team was from Trinidad to England via Jamaica by the banana boat, SS *Cavina*, and on to India by air. The whole journey took us twenty-four days, including a break of three days in London to get us outfitted, and the journey out was not without adventure.

When we were leaving Kingston for the banana ports of Bowden and Port Antonio, the Board's President, Mr Nunes, was on board to see us off. I overheard him make a remark to John Goddard, our captain, in the presence of George Headley which proved somewhat ironic to say the least. 'John,' he said, 'George is picked for his batting – don't ask him to bowl too much.' It is a pity these words were ever spoken because George's batting was never really required on the tour, but his bowling certainly was. Personally I had the highest regard for his bowling after facing him in 1946, and few knew how good a bowler of flighted off-spin he was, once he put his mind to it. As it turned out, Headley did not play after the first Test match until we reached Ceylon, as he had developed rib trouble, and was never fit enough to play in another Test on the tour.

It is a great shame that, in these 'commercial' times, cricketers no

longer travel by sea. To me, this was one of the most enjoyable parts
of cricket tours in the early days. Watching bananas being loaded
by hand at the Jamaica ports was a fascinating experience. Over
120,000 bunches were put aboard by a steady stream of local labour,
mostly women, carrying them on their heads and disappearing into
and out of the cool store chambers. I discovered the rate of pay was
3s 6d per 100 bunches carried, the distance being about thirty-five
yards each way!

One of the hazards of allowing bananas to be loaded in this
fashion was the risk of stowaways hiding on board. Apparently this
was the rule, and our voyage was not to be an exception. In addition
to the bananas, we carried nine stowaways and they became quite
troublesome as the voyage progressed. Tension developed when they
were earmarked to be transferred to a sister ship of the same line
going in the opposite direction. The two ships stopped within hailing
distance in mid-Atlantic but the errant stowaways refused to enter
the lifeboats. Apparently on arrival in England, the steamship line
incurred a fine of £100 for each stowaway aboard but, according
to international law, they could not be forced to return against their
wishes. Also, if anyone chose to pay a fine of £10 each, they would
be allowed to stay in England. Unemployment and the pay for
loading bananas tell their own story of why the stowaways were
there in the first place.

At the ship's concert towards the end of our trip, I composed two
verses to two calypsos, one called 'Perspiration on the *Cavina*' and
the other 'Excursion to England'. They were sung to the tunes of
two popular Trinidadian calypsos of the period and members of the
team made up a remarkably good chorus. It more than broke the
ice on board, and it was a pity that they had not been sung earlier
in the voyage.

In London, the cricket fraternity rallied round and Gubby Allen
got together a number of our playing friends from the 1948 tour,
together with old England players and administrators, for a party at
his flat. Among those present were 'Plum' Warner, 'Shrimp' Leveson-
Gower, Jack Hobbs (not yet Sir Jack), Bob Wyatt, Martin Donnelly
and others who had only been names to us previously. I recall Sir
Pelham walking up to Donnelly and saying, 'Good evening, sir – a
great player.'

We were especially happy with our new blazers and flannels for
which we had been measured at home and which were shipped ahead

of us by sea, but when the time came for opening the crate at our headquarters, the Cricket Club of India (CCI) in Bombay, it was obvious that something was radically wrong. It was discovered that the crate had been severely broached, and the Bombay police sub-sequently arrested some fishermen from Goa who had boarded the boat and done their dirty work while the boat was anchored outside the harbour before coming into the Bombay docks. The fishermen could not resist wearing the new burgundy blazers with their green and white piping and crests depicting the constellation of Orion, and this proved to be their downfall. Although we never got back any of the loot, they were brought to book after expert evidence had been given by manager Lacy in the magistrates' court in Bombay.

It was not long before our vast journeys across the length and breadth of India got under way. After a game at the CCI against the Combined Universities, in which Clyde Walcott scored 100 in even time and then had to be carried off the field suffering from heat exhaustion, and Polly Umrigar showed off his spurs, we were off upcountry. Baroda, Indore, Patiala – names that conjured up visions of palaces and jewels and, above all, the mystery that is India.

While the journeys were exhausting, the countryside for the most part parched scrubland, it was difficult, as indeed it always is when in India, to stop looking. There is always something to see. Extremes of riches and a hundred yards away the most utter poverty. And always people and more people, 600 million of them. We saw it all, the good and the bad, but still a fascinating country which could easily get into one's blood.

We drew at Baroda and won at Indore, both games played on matting wickets, coir mat and not the jute to which the Trinidadians were accustomed. However, we who had 'mat' experience knew that we would be called upon to put our best foot forward. We played against and met some of the top Indian cricketers for the first time: Hazare, Amarnath, Mankad, Shinde, Sarwate, Mushtaq Ali, Sohoni, Ghulam, C. S. and C. K. Nayudu – the latter in his fifty-fifth year, a fine figure of a man, still active, with an eye like a hawk and full of interesting stories of their 1936 tour of England.

Unfortunately I didn't get to play at Patiala where the wicket was a beaut and the outfield fast and true. It was a game full of character and good humour, played in a wonderful setting. The Maharajah himself, a commanding figure and no mean cricketer in his turban (frequently changed, first azure, then cream, then fuchsia), was there, and Patiala's private regiment colourfully dressed, marched across the field playing their bagpipes at the close of play. We were guests of the Maharajah at his palace, the kitchen of which consisted of thirty-seven rooms.

We batted second in this match, and when Allan Rae was out for 113 he found Everton Weekes padded to go in next. We were playing against Amarnath, India's captain-elect, for the first time and Allan had had a good look at him. 'What does he bowl?' asked Everton. 'Inswerve, back from leg, outswerve, back from off,' replied Allan quite seriously. 'I can't play that,' said Everton removing his pads. 'Skipper, ask someone else to go in next!' Weekes was 53 not out at the close of play and the next day, at his magnificent best, he added 117 in a hundred minutes before lunch. Lala Amarnath had none for plenty. He never troubled Weekes and Everton told us that he called his bed Lala. Amarnath got his own back, for he was undefeated with 223 in the second innings, an innings which saved his team from defeat.

More humour was in store, at the banquet staged by His Highness on our last night there. Muni Lal, who had opened the innings for Patiala, was sitting a few seats away from us. He had made 0 and 4 in his two innings, having been bowled comprehensively by Gomez on both occasions. 'Gerry, I'm sure you'd like to take this batsman around with you,' said Everton. Muni overheard the remark and a great deal of mirth followed. No one suspected that some twenty years later he would turn up in Trinidad as ambassador for his country and that one of the first people he met there was G. E. Gomez. It was as well that they had both retired from the game by then.

While we were wonderfully looked after as guests of the Maharajah of Patiala, an entry in my diary illustrates the other side of the story:

A visit to the Post Office was interesting from the point of view that to get there one wandered through a back street tripping over the odd goat, curry fire, and prostrate form, then up a dingy and absolutely pitch black staircase which opened up into a small room, covered inches in dust inhabited by two dirty men who had obviously never heard of the West Indies. It was a trying experience, and after 15 minutes during which time I achieved exactly nothing I had to leave, without posting my letters, as John [Goddard] was late for the game. Yes, there are two sides to Patiala. Thank goodness we saw only one – and that, the good one.

The first Test match was played at the Ferozeshah Kotla ground in Delhi. Our team was accommodated in the 'Central Vista' officers' mess of the Royal Indian Air Force, and my diary records that 'despite the stylish name, the rooms at our "hotel" are cold, dark, damp, and dirty.' Actually the accommodation at the ground was equally poor and the game suffered from a number of disabilities. Forty minutes were lost on the first day when the ball was changed no fewer than four times, which with the new ball taken at 200 meant that five different balls were used in the day's play. Old stock – pre-war, we were told. I suppose this must be some sort of record.

The Test started badly for me as I developed an abscess in a gold-capped molar two days before the game. The pain was excruciating and I found myself ringing Mr de Mello at seven o'clock in the morning, imploring him to recommend a well-qualified dentist. I was somewhat happier when the dentist reassured me by mentioning that numbered among his recent patients were Lord and Lady Mountbatten. He put me out with 'gas' and extracted old 'goldie'. The aftermath was not so good in that I was subjected to a number of penicillin injections the next day and on the morning of the Test match, so that when we won the toss and batted I felt distinctly shaky and batted likewise. There was an early collapse: 27–3, Rae, Stollmeyer and Headley all out; however, thanks to Walcott (152) and Gomez (99), we ended the day at 294 having suffered no further loss. It was a great partnership with Walcott continuing his great form. The scores he had already made on the tour in the four innings which he played were 103 retired, 71, 73 not out and 75, a truly wonderful sequence.

Humour or, better, 'picong' – an expressive Trinidadian word for leg-pulling – was never far from the surface and Weekes, one of its greatest exponents, was a master of the art. When Headley, who had been having a lean time with the bat, was out for 2, his 'castle' shattered by an outswinger from Rangachari, he came into the dressing room while I was still unbuckling my pads and Everton was putting on his. 'Wha' happen, old man?' said the young high-scoring Everton promptly to the great man. 'You not goin' make a run at all, at all, at all?' George understandably was not amused at the time, but sometime later, a twinkle in his eye, he said to the young champion, 'What do you, you don't have respect for age?'

There were some terrible umpiring decisions next day, both Gomez 102 (stumped) and Walcott (run out at his overnight score) being at the receiving end. In no time we had lost 5 for 302, but there were two more centuries to come, a dazzling 128 from Weekes and 107 from Bob Christiani going in at No. 8. Our innings closed for 631 early on the third morning of the match.

As was to happen again and again on the tour, we were unable to bowl India out twice in the time remaining. We missed Ferguson's leg-spin badly, and I proved a poor substitute although Bob Christiani, also an occasional bowler of leg-spin googly, presented some problems in the second innings. A pity Headley did not bowl more; the ostensible reason was a stiff neck, but personally I did not consider this an adequate excuse! The game came to a close with the chorus of 'Well played, Adi-Khari, well played, Adi-Khari' echoing again and again around the ground. The little soldier was not out 114 in the first and 29 not out in the second innings. India had saved the day.

After the Delhi Test we were off over the border to Pakistan, our destination Karachi. Just prior to our departure, however, there was some more drama. Cliff McWatt had found that his trunk, which he normally required assistance to close, now did so with no trouble at all. Becoming suspicious he investigated its contents and found that three of his suits, three dress shirts and two unworn cricket shirts plus some money were missing. Upon notification, the Delhi police immediately went in search of the bearers and they spent a sleepless night being questioned and inevitably being subjected to third-degree tactics. Our faithful bearer David (his correct name, according to him, was Davche) did not escape the blows. His already sad face reflected the height of anguish when, early in the morning, he told us sadly, 'Saab McWatt – he lose-um three suits and money, it's ve-r-ry bad, it's not ve-r-r-ry good. Bearers get-um more blows later.' McWatt's bearer incriminated himself by having volunteered the suggestion the day before that he should be very careful in Pakistan because he would not be there to look after his belongings and therefore would not be responsible for any losses sustained. He was dismissed forthwith and not seen again.

On the subject of not being seen again, another of the team's bearers, by the name of Rattan, was heard to be coughing dreadfully in the night out in the passage of that awful Central Vista mess where the bearers used to bed down for the night. Sometime late the next morning, one of the team said, 'Where is Rattan?' 'Oh Sahib,' said one of the other bearers, 'it's ve-r-r-y bad. Rattan not there. He died last night.' Apparently, it was no big thing. Human beings in India are expendable. Thereafter, West Indians, with their own peculiar sense of fun, were quick to call any colleague who coughed, 'Rattan'.

Customs in Pakistan were different, and in the absence of John Goddard I was asked to represent the team at the laying of a wreath on Jinnah's grave. It proved to be an unusual ceremony for the inexperienced. I described it in my diary as follows: 'We all removed our shoes and as we approached the tombstone there were strewn about several old copies of the Koran, a few brass lotas, some candlesticks and heaps of incense being constantly lit and burned. The grave was situated on a rise, absolutely clear of vegetation, about five acres in extent, resembling an area recently cleared by a bulldozer. There was a tent under which was the grave. A few dozen worshippers were present and during the ceremony a Mohammedan priest conducted an open-air service. Barefooted and facing the west where the sun was setting in a ball of fire, they spread their prayer mats and prayed to Allah. Their prayers were energetically said and the devotees looked rather like a class performing calisthenics. In a high-pitched voice, the priest, bearded and with his fez on, emitted loud beseechings, while together they performed vigorous body-bending exercises.'

The cricket ground at Karachi in those days bears description. There was a 30-yard square of grass in the middle of which was the pitch of sandy textured earth. It was covered by a coconut fibre matting no less than sixty yards long, for it served as the bowler's run up as well. The outfield had not one blade of grass and consisted of a reddish sand watered and rolled. The pavilion accommodation left much to be desired. There were virtually no toilet facilities and no running water. It was not conducive to good cricket and little good cricket was played.

At Rawalpindi, our next stop, the atmosphere was quite different. The war in Kashmir was not far away and casualties were being ferried in to the hospital. Above all it was cooler. We won a two-day match outright on an indifferent wicket. Acting as captain, I persuaded Headley to bowl in the second innings and he responded magnificently with figures of 6–49 off 23 overs. I was convinced that he could prove to be our match winner in the Tests, but unfortunately he didn't play again in a Test match on the tour. In this match we met and played against Jehangir Khan, father of Majid and uncle of Imran, and himself a Test player. An amusing incident which took place after play in 'Pindi is worthy of record. Gerry Gomez, who fancied himself as a tennis player, and indeed was more than passable at the sport, had arranged a game with a 'local' whom he had not met. Allan Rae and I lined up as spectators. A nondescript-looking man, barefooted and in a 'dhoti', arrived at the courts with some tennis balls. He had the appearance of a ball-boy, and Gerry asked him anxiously about the whereabouts of the opposition. 'Oh,' he said, 'I have been asked to play against you.' To our great amusement and to the considerable discomfiture of Gerry, the worthy gentleman proceeded to run him off his feet and delivered a sound thrashing. He proved to be the club's professional.

We found ourselves playing a four-day 'Test' against Pakistan at Lahore, although our itinerary only called for a three-day match. This caused the first instance of open rebellion by the team, for we knew that if we played the extra day we would be travelling next day to Delhi and immediately thereafter a long and horrendous train journey lay in store for us to Poona. A glance at a map of India is enough to indicate what this meant.

The 'Test' was played at the lovely Lawrence Gardens ground which had been recently re-named 'Bagh-i-Jinnah'. It was a Test only in name because Pakistan had not been accorded Test status as yet. The game ended in a tame draw and was highlighted by Gerry Gomez's bowling. His figures in the game were 79.2 overs, 34 maidens, 121 runs, 8 wickets in Pakistan's innings of 241, and 285–6. Imitiaz Ahamad, opening for our opponents, had scores of 76 and 131, but he was guilty along with some of his colleagues for not capitalizing on his team's formidable position by not attempting to press on in the second innings. It seemed that the making of a century was the prior consideration.

There followed that memorable trip to Poona. Six were fortunate to be chosen for the only air tickets available, myself among them. It seemed as though the choosing of 'the fortunate six' was done in an arbitrary manner, not the best thing for team spirit.

We played badly in a drawn game at Poona and no wonder, after that horrible train journey. From my point of view, I learned a tactic from George Headley which I used in subsequent games to some effect. On a pluperfect wicket such as it was at Poona, even a mediocre batsman took some shifting, and after one of the intervals

I suggested to John Goddard that he put Weekes on to bowl his slow 'would-be' leg-spinners, pitching on and outside leg-stump with an inner and outer ring of seven fielders on the leg-side. In the event, this broke a long 6-wicket partnership between Nimbalkar and Uday Merchant and proved to be a useful ploy under similar circumstances.

Brabourne stadium was packed for the second Test and once again the atmosphere of a true Test match was in evidence. Winning the toss on a very good wicket, Allan Rae and I scored 134 for the first wicket. This was a prelude to our huge first innings total of 629–6, including 104 by Rae and 194 by Weekes in only 301 minutes, a dazzling exhibition of stroke play, and 60s and 70s by all who batted except Gomez who missed out on this occasion.

India were all out in the first innings for 273, and at 95 for 2 with one day to go, it looked as though we would win, but it was not to be. India played out time with defensive centuries by Modi and Hazare ending at 333–3. Again our bowling limitations were sadly exposed but we dropped catches as well and at times our tactics in the field were inexplicable.

One lasting regret was that Vijay Merchant, the great Indian batsman, never played against us. He was seen in the nets attempting to get himself fit, obviously a player of the highest class, but he never got on to the field. This signalled the end of his illustrious career. Maybe it was just as well for us because India already had several fine batsmen in their team.

Vinoo Mankad was an immensely clever slow left-arm bowler. Although he did not spin the ball greatly, he varied flight and used the crease admirably. He was up to all the tricks of his trade, and after bowling his arm ball, he often ran away towards extra cover as though anticipating turn. His direction and length were well nigh perfect, but he was up against the magnificent stroke play of Weekes, Walcott and Co. and his bowling figures on the plumb wickets suffered accordingly. A few years later when in Australia, I asked Sir Donald Bradman what he thought of him. 'He wasn't a bad player,' was Don's rejoinder. 'I don't mean his batting but his bowling,' said I. 'Oh,' he said, 'he put all the jokers over here' (signalling the off-side) 'so I hit him over there' (signalling the leg-side).

Any cricketer aspiring to be a Test player, and even more so a captain, who does not make a study of the finer points of the game, is destined to be found wanting. Bowling at good players on helpless pitches needs something more than a stereotyped approach, merely trusting to luck that something will happen and the batsman will eventually make a mistake. In fact, sometimes this does happen, but in my experience there is no substitute for studying the strengths and weaknesses of the opposition and directing affairs accordingly, while paying due regard to the state of the wicket, the clock, and the overall situation of the match. In the Test matches in India as well as in England in 1950 and in Australia in 1951, far too little time and attention was paid to analysing the game by our captain who, on his own admission, had 'never read a cricket book'.

Soon we were back up country, Nagpur in the Central Provinces being our destination, but this time we did the trip by air. Our strong representations to the President of the Board of Control for Cricket in India had, at last, borne some fruit. In John Goddard's absence I captained the team there. It was another coir matting wicket and my opposite number was C. K. Nayudu, the grand old man of India's cricket. At fifty-three, he was fit and active and on a difficult pitch made 72 against us against some hostile bowling from Prior Jones.

We won a game of fluctuating fortunes by 6 wickets – all four dismissals in our second innings being LBW. Allan Rae had some anxious moments in the early part of his innings of 15. This precipitated a headline next day in the *Nagpur Times*: 'Rae plays bad.' The matting wicket presented difficulties for many, none more so than a usually silent member of our tour party, Ken Rickards, who commented that he would prefer hunting tigers than playing on the mat. It was Ken who, while travelling in the team's bus one day from Glenelg to the Adelaide Oval in Australia, was heard, on reading in the local press that a resident had been 'taken' by a shark, to exclaim in his Jamaican dialect, 'Not me, to bathe in the sea here, him don't know I am a cricketer, him going have to come through the shower to catch me.'

Calcutta was the scene of the third Test match and again we were exposed to a twenty-four-hour journey by rail from Nagpur. We arrived there on Christmas Eve, and played a match against the Governor's XI in preparation for the Test, which was due to start on New Year's Eve.

In the meantime, John Trim had gone down with chicken pox and, as luck would have it, on the morning of the Test match I suffered a similar fate. I can think of little worse than suffering from chicken pox – a distressing malady at any time – in a dingy hotel room in Calcutta. It was small comfort to know that I was housed within a stone's thrown of the notorious 'black hole'. Sara had cabled me a couple of days before: 'All best for Christmas and New Year. Thinking of you. Get pox and come home,' to which I could not resist replying: 'Got pox OK but regret cannot oblige come home.'

So I had to sit out this Test. An immediate problem presented itself. George Carew, who was to take my place in the team, could not be found. He had gone shopping. In the event Denis Atkinson was commissioned to open the innings when Goddard won the toss for the third successive time. This game was closer and more of a contest than the first two Tests. A huge crowd watched while we made 366 of which Weekes made his usual hundred, 162 out of 366, an innings described by his colleagues as his best of the tour. India replied with 272. Weekes scored 101 in the second innings – his fifth consecutive century in Test cricket and a world record – and Walcott 108, our innings being declared closed at 336–9. India, set 430 to make in about seven hours, once more saved the game, being 325–3 at the close. Mushtaq Ali, the most adventurous of India's batsmen, had a good match with scores of 54 and 106. Mushtaq was a dasher, often going over outside of the off-stump to hook even as the bowler ran up to bowl.

'Mas' Jeff, Fergie got pox.' This was John Trim poking his head through my bedroom door. Wilfred Ferguson, our leg-spinner and probably our most attacking bowler, had joined the afflicted. At the best of times 'Fergie' was no Valentino, but with pox he was a sight indeed. At the same time Ken Rickards was taken to hospital with suspected typhoid. So with Headley out, we were down to twelve players. Worse was to come.

When the team arrived at our next stop, Jamshedpur, Denis Atkinson became the fourth 'pox' victim. This state of affairs precipitated one of the most frustrating series of misunderstandings of all time. Our manager had cabled Mr de Mello suggesting that our next scheduled fixture at Allahabad be cancelled, following upon which de Mello in Bombay cabled Nunes in Jamaica asking for reinforcements for our team. This was done without reference either to our manager or our captain, and some of us persuaded our manager to cable the West Indies informing the Board's President of this state of affairs. However, Karl Nunes had acted promptly on receipt of his friend's cable and had dispatched George Mudie, a left-handed spin-bowler, to India via London. This action was greeted with unanimous displeasure by the entire team who had 'suffered' together the harsh and oppressive conditions which had existed on the tour. Immediately we drafted and sent a cable to the President which opened with the following words: 'Your cable. Do not send Mudie, etc., etc.' The appearance of Mudie would not have helped matters. It would merely have served to aggravate the situation and would have been equally embarrassing to the new arrival.

In the event, the unfortunate Mudie was stopped in London from whence he returned home.

With all this going on, and down to a bare eleven, at Allahabad we lost the only match on tour by 10 wickets, played on matting over grass, the one and only time I have ever encountered such a pitch in a first-class match. This event caused the Maharaj Kumar of Vizianagram, dressed resplendently in full evening suit with an MCC red-and-yellow striped blazer, to announce in his speech at a dinner in our honour that 'the West Indies had met their Waterloo at Allahabad'. After the dinner, there followed another interminably long train ride overnight to Bombay, a brief bath and change, and off to the airport to catch a plane for Madras. The fourth Test was due to be played at the Chepauk ground a week later.

With the exception of George Headley who did not pass a fitness test after practising, we were once again a full team. We had squandered South Zone by an innings and 200 runs, and Gerry Gomez and I had played the principal roles in this win. In their first innings of only 46 on a good wicket, Gerry took 9–24 in 18 overs, moving the ball around considerably and mesmerizing the opposition. Gomez had bowled only about 150 overs in first-class cricket before the start of this tour, in the course of which he was to bowl no fewer than 750. We were 136–1 the same afternoon, the only wicket to fall being Rae's by the run-out route. We went on to 514–6 declared of which I scored 244 not out, a record score for the ground.

Having seen a great deal of the wicket which was the first really fast one we had met on the tour, I was convinced that we should include both Jones and Trim in our Test team. Not all the other selectors agreed with my contention but I was insistent and eventually my view prevailed. It was to prove to be our trump card in the only Test match we were able to win – by the handsome margin of an innings and 193 runs. India unwisely had taken the field without any fast bowler, for Phadkar was no more than fast-medium; a cardinal error this turned out to be. In the event Jones, took 6–58 off 26 overs and Trim 7–76 off 43. Winning the toss for the fourth successive time, we batted, and Allan Rae and I put on a West Indies record 239 for the first wicket – one which still stands today. The wicket was a fast one as anticipated, and Phadkar made the mistake of bowling a number of bouncers, often with six men on the leg-side. He was soundly hooked, particularly by Allan, who hit him for two huge 6s. At the end of the first day we were 315–1 (Rae 109, Stollmeyer 157 not out).

The following morning I did not add many, being out for 160, but all the other batsmen pitched in, Weekes in search of his sixth consecutive 100 in Tests, being given run-out at 90, palpably an umpiring error. We scored 582.

This time India was not let off the hook and, despite a perfect batting pitch, were dismissed for 245 and 144, the match ending on the fourth afternoon. It was a splendid win. We had achieved a firm grip early in the game and never relinquished it, and our fast bowlers were certainly not relished by the Indian batsmen. It was our turn to bowl bumpers and we, too, used six men on the leg-side to Jones during a certain period of play; but to better effect than the opposition.

John Trim was a delightful character. He was close to nature and sired no fewer than thirteen children. When we were riding in the train together and had a separate compartment to ourselves, he told me proudly, 'All my children are well taken care of and I have no worries.' He was immensely strong and it was said that when he caught the CCI opener at Bombay fielding at short leg, the ball was found to be out of shape on its return to the bowler! John and Fergie were good friends, both powerfully built and deep-chested. Surprisingly, they both died in their forties, within a short time of each other.

The wicket at Bombay for the fifth Test had been so grossly underprepared that it could hardly be discerned from the outfield. It seemed to us that the ground authority had decreed a finish at all costs, which way no one could tell. The ground and wicket at the Brabourne Stadium is so flat, however, that the mere rolling at the commencement of play and between innings served to settle the wicket. In fact, the wicket improved for batting each day as the Test proceeded.

This was, therefore, not a good toss to win, and when Goddard won it for the fifth time in succession and we batted, it was not on the normal shirt-front pitch. We were 88–2 at lunch, and surviving this difficult period I went on to top score with 85 in an innings of 286. Meantime I found difficulty in running between the wickets due to a leg muscle strain contracted at Madras which seemed to get progressively worse as the day wore on.

This match turned out to be the most dramatic Test match in which I have ever taken part, although my strained muscle did not allow me to take an active part in the highly exciting final day's play. We seemed comfortably placed at the end of the third day when India had scored only 193 in their first innings and we were 152–3, a lead of 245 with 7 second wickets still standing. The situation had not changed much at the end of the fourth day for, although we had been dismissed for 267 in our second innings, India were not well placed at 90–3 going at 361 for victory, but Hazare and Modi were batting and the wicket had improved perceptibly.

Then came the absorbing and thrilling final day's play, one in which, for possibly the first time, negative leg-slide bowling was used in a Test match. This mode of attack is now outlawed and rightly so. The present rule, whereby not more than two fielders are allowed behind square, was not in existence at the time. The game was delicately poised. India needed 271 to win in 300 minutes' batting, but had only 7 wickets in hand, one of whom was P. Sen, the wicket-keeper, who had not fielded because of a damaged shoulder. We were certainly on the right side of the match at the start of play. By lunchtime, however, the situation had altered somewhat; the overnight pair were still together, having added 85 in the 120' minutes play. Gomez had bowled unchanged from one end and Jones, too, was accurate and difficult to score from. The new ball was due at 200, but at the interval I advised Goddard not to take it unless he had broken the partnership and even then to proceed with caution.

Runs came rapidly after lunch when we bowled to a packed off-side field and it was clear that more drastic tactical measures were necessary in order to staunch the flow of runs. On the advice of Gerry Gomez who acted as vice-captain, the attack was then shifted to the leg-stump with the majority of fielders placed on the on-side and this move proved to be as necessary as it was successful.

At tea, the score was 289–6 with both Hazare (122) and Modi

(86) out, the former playing a masterful innings – only 72 were needed in ninety minutes with 4 wickets to fall. Fifteen minutes before the end, the target was 21 with 2 wickets left intact. Excitement ran high and the tension became almost unbearable as Jones prepared to bowl the final over, with 11 runs needed, to Phadkar with Ghulam Ahmed at the other end. My diary records that over: 'Ball 1 – wide of leg-stump, no stroke possible. Ball 2 – short of length on leg-stump, Phadkar steps back and hits it past cover for 4. 7 runs needed in 4 balls. Ball 3 – on the pads again. A push to square leg, single taken. Ball 4 – another push to the on, single possible, not taken. Ball 5 – a bumper over the batsman's head. And as we waited for ball 6, the umpire signalled over and removed the bails. In the excitement he had miscounted. The match was therefore drawn in the most unusual circumstances. There was the usual scramble for souvenirs and the crowd, in a feverish state of excitement, invaded the field and the hallowed precincts of the CCI.' From the West Indies' point of view, it was Jones's match, his figures in the second innings being 48–8–85–5. It was as well that Prior Jones was one of the team's strongest and healthiest men. He needed all of his great reserve of strength for that effort.

I had watched the day's proceedings critically from the gallery of my room at the CCI in the company of George Headley. Our conversations that day taught me more about the tactics of the game than I was able to learn anywhere else at any one time during my future as a player. It was then that I was more resolved than ever to make a study of cricket tactics.

There is nowhere in the world like home and there is nowhere else in the world that I have seen which is as similar as Ceylon (now Sri Lanka) is to Trinidad: the flora, coconut palms, breadfruit trees, bamboos and the cosmopolitan population. The big difference was in the height of the mountains: in Ceylon, you could get up high enough to be in a temperate climate, and nestled in the hills were the beautiful tea plantations. Our visit there was as relaxing as it was welcome. Although the cricket was of secondary importance, Ceylon was keen to do well and the local press was not very complimentary to our team's standard of play when we arrived. Whether we then resolved to teach them a lesson or not, we certainly carried all before us. Besides winning the two 'Tests' convincingly, in one game against the Combined Universities we scored no fewer than 481–7 in 300 minutes.

When in Colombo, we played against and were warmly entertained by Derek de Saram, who had scored a century against the 1934 Australians while up at Oxford. He became a firm friend and when, some years later, acquaintances of ours from Trinidad in the telephone business were transferred to Ceylon, I suggested that they look him up. They did – only to find that he was in gaol! He was supposed to have taken an active part in a political coup against the Government. The trial went on for an interminable period during which time he languished in gaol before being eventually acquitted and set free.

7

West Indian Summer

The West Indies tour of England in 1950 was truly a West Indian summer. In 1950 – our Jubilee Year (the West Indies team first toured England in 1900) – we won our first Test in England and it was at Lord's, the headquarters of cricket. It was the coming of age of West Indian cricket, a mere twenty-two years after we were accorded Test status in 1928. It was also the year of Ram and Val and the three Ws.

We started as a team of one on 26 March, when R. J. Christiani, the lone British Guiana representative, left his homeland for Trinidad from where, three days later, SS *Golfito* sailed for England with the Trinidad contingent G. E. Gomez, L. R. Pierre, P. E. Jones, K. B. Trestrail, S. Ramadhin and myself.

I remember turning to 'Sonny' Ramadhin, only two first-class-matches' worth of experience, and a surprise selection, and asking him how he felt about things. 'I've never been on a ship before,' he said. 'Is this still Trinidad?' and so I explained to him that we were passing through the second of the Serpent's Mouths and soon we should be out in the open Atlantic with England a mere ten days away.

During a four-hour stay at Barbados, we picked up our captain, J. D. Goddard, and E. D. Weekes and C. L. Walcott (two of the three Ws), R. E. Marshall and C. B. Williams, the team's manager, Mr J. M. Kidney, and his clerical assistant, the Rev. R. C. Palmer-Barnes. At about the same time A. L. Valentine and H. H. Johnson were setting out from Jamaica on the *Cavina*, while we were to meet A. F. Rae, reading law in London, and F. M. Worrell, who had recently returned from a highly successful winter in India with the

Commonwealth team, at our destination. We were a party of nine-teen, including manager, clerical assistant and W. Ferguson, world-famous scorer and baggage man.

The selection of the team had, as usual, provided followers of the game in the islands with ample opportunity to let the public know their feelings through the medium of the press. While such enthusiasm is understandable, one could not condone the attitude of a section of the British Guiana public and press who seemed to look upon the selection of only one representative from that colony as an insult and as sufficient grounds for withdrawal from the West Indies Cricket Board of Control. This attitude was particularly unfortunate at such a time when West Indies cricket seemed to be on the verge of overcoming insular prejudice. Luckily no such drastic measures as were contemplated were in fact taken.

As regards the composition of the team, no one could deny that a balanced side had been selected, and if the gambles came off it was felt that all would be well.

The great gamble was in the selection of the spin-bowlers. All three were young and inexperienced. How would they react to conditions of climate, atmosphere and wicket all vastly different from those to which they were accustomed? Would they acclimatize or would numbed hands on a cold day render them understandably useless? Now, when it is all over, we may pause to appreciate our good fortune in finding that, in the youngsters Ramadhin and Valentine, we possessed two of the finest of their type in contemporary cricket. Their excellent work was all the more praiseworthy when it is considered that they bowled equally well under any conditions, and their feats of skill and endurance will live forever in the annals of West Indies cricket.

When Johnnie Lucas, the Barbadian off-spinner and a candidate for selection on the team, heard over the radio that Ramadhin had been selected, he is reported to have exclaimed in disbelief, '*Rama*-who?'

I was struck by the lack of publicity which accompanied our arrival in England. Whether it was because it was Easter Monday, or too far in advance of the cricket season, I do not know. Maybe we were still being counted as 'small fry', and I detected a tendency towards using the West Indies series as practice matches for the visit to Australia in the winter. There was little enough in the press and what there was concerned the amount of rum we had brought with

us, rather than information regarding our ability as cricketers. Very
few seemed to remember the crushing defeat suffered by the MCC
at our hands in the West Indies in 1948–9. I thought to myself even
then that the English cricketing public had a bit of a surprise coming
to them.

All recognized touring teams to England are invited to a series of
official parties, luncheons and dinners during the first fortnight of
the tour before the strenuous times begin. The pick of these functions
are the luncheon at the Savoy Hotel at the invitation of the British
Sportsmen's Club, and the Cricket Writers' Dinner held, on this
occasion, at the Press Club. At the former we were privileged to
meet the majority of the famous Old Brigade of the 'Golden Era' of
English cricket, professionals who, by their service to English cricket,
were, in 1949, elected honorary members of the MCC.

And so it was that we were able to rub shoulders with the giants
of the past. So rich were their stories, so engaging their company,
that it was small wonder that we missed our train to Eastbourne,
most of the team getting the wrong end of a photofinish decision.
It must have been embarrassing for the three members of the team
who did catch that train to find that the civic authorities of
Eastbourne had turned out in full force to welcome the team.
However, the situation was easily and satisfactorily explained away,
for when again would one meet at the same gathering Jardine,
Yardley, Chapman, Gilligan, Wyatt, Allen, Brown, Hobbs, Barnes,
Tate, Rhodes, Woolley, Hendren, Gunn, Mead, Strudwick, Duckworth, Gover, Paynter, Russell, Tyldesley and Voce, to name just a
few of the many cricket celebrities present? Harold Larwood was a
notable absentee, as he was off to Australia within the week, where,
strangely enough, he had decided to make his home.

It was natural, I expect, that I should have wandered off in the
direction of Douglas Jardine, most famous of all English Test
captains. I jested that he should follow 'Lol' to Aussie. 'I'm lunching
with him on Tuesday and will discuss the matter with him then,' he
replied jovially. 1932–33 seemed a long way away, but any Australian
who had at that time reached the age of understanding remembered
'Bodyline' or 'Leg Theory' – call it what you will – and Jardine
knew this. 'Lol will be all right,' he said, 'but I think there's only
room for one of us in Australia.'

An interesting interlude. I recall George Gunn, to whom fast
bowling was jam, being emphatic on two points. The first, that the

best cricket is played on the best wickets, and the second that county
cricket in England had been considerably affected by the law, then
in effect, which provided for the covering of wickets for twenty-four
hours before the start of a match. 'You'll find that most wickets in
this country have a bit of life before lunch on the first day and then
go easy,' said George. This we found to be very true. The Trent
Bridge Test match was a perfect example and who, if not George
Gunn, is qualified to express an opinion about the Trent Bridge
wicket?

George Duckworth was quickly surrounded by West Indians
plying him with questions about the Commonwealth tour in India
which had just ended. 'We did all our travelling by air,' said
Manager-ex-England-Wicket-keeper 'Ducky'. 'Couldn't have made
it without. You chaps gave me the tip-off after your tour there.'
Yes, one profits by experience. What a difference air travel would
have made to the performance of the West Indies team in India and
to our enjoyment of that tour!

Then there was Sydney F. Barnes who, in his own words, 'had a
game or two last season' at the age of eighty-two. Face full of
character and the devil, fingers long and strong – exceptionally so
– to help him be the master of the art of bowling. 'You've had your
fill of cricket, Mr Barnes?' I ventured. 'No, son, I've had my share,
but never my fill.' He asked me what position I occupied in the team
and when I explained that I was an opening batsman, he rejoined,
'It's the easiest thing in the world, batting. Just get your head over
the ball, like this, and the runs come to you. There's no one in this
country to bowl you out these days.' Of course, I held my own
views about this, but was nevertheless thankful that there was no
S. F. Barnes playing for England in 1950.

In addition to cricketing talent, we had for company many distinguished men of letters, some of them far more than mere cricket
writers, whose business it was to describe the world's most fascinating game. It was here that we met for the first time John Arlott,
whose broad Hampshire accent was familiar to all who followed
Test cricket by radio. John was a good friend to us and, more than
anyone else, seemed to be our fairest critic. A highlight of the
evening's entertainment was a speech by Neville Cardus, whose
remarks had the section of the audience nearest to him in stitches
of laughter. Unfortunately, I was on the other side of the room from

which point Mr Cardus was quite inaudible. This was particularly irritating because he spoke for well over forty-five minutes.

The sugar manufacturers of Jamaica paid us the compliment of an invitation to cocktails, a function also held at the Savoy. On this occasion we were welcomed most cordially by Sir Pelham Warner. I do not know of anyone anywhere who was as fond of cricket and cricketers as this famous personage. Often, when speaking of the game, one found Sir Pelham's eyes growing misty from memories, cherished and dear to him, of his cricketing life. His heart and soul were in cricket. Sir Pelham, in his address of welcome, pledged neutrality. Here was a man who was born in Trinidad, achieved the distinction of scoring the first hundred made at the Queen's Park Oval there, and then had the greatest honour of all – that of captaining England. 'Plum' Warner – '76 not out', as he said during the course of his remarks – seemed deeply moved by the affection and hospitality which had been accorded him during his visit to the West Indies in 1948 when he accompanied the MCC team.

I have been privileged to listen to Sir Pelham speak on a number of occasions and have never failed to delight in his reminiscences. In Trinidad he referred to the tremendous enthusiasm and the crowd which 'hummed and surged on to the ground like a swarm of bees when the spirit moved them'. He made reference to Gubby Allen's squabble over some turkeys which were caged under his bedroom window one night at the Queen's Park Hotel in Trinidad. They were ordered to the pot next day by an irate Allen. 'And how inconsistent and unreasonable the cocks are in your country,' he added, 'crow at all hours!'

'Plum' had sustained a nasty fall in British Guiana which caused him great discomfort during the weeks that followed. While in Jamaica he stayed with Karl Nunes, President of the West Indies Cricket Board of Control, and there 'due to my infirmity – couldn't sleep – I heard the most wonderful cat fight imaginable. I got out of bed and went to my window. I confess I laughed so loudly that I awoke the household.' Sir Pelham was indeed rich in memory and humour. You couldn't help but feel his sentiment for cricketers and the game as you talked to him.

We spent ten days loosening up at Eastbourne. The town advertised itself as 'The Sun Trap of the South'. It did not quite live up to its name, for on 26 April it snowed heavily, chasing would-be cricketers from the field of play. On this day, with a chilling wind crossing the ground from the sea, even the five sweaters which some of us sported were inadequate.

It so happened that it was at Eastbourne in the dim distant past that my father had met my mother for the first time, and I innocently mentioned this to the Lord Mayor when the team was accorded a civic reception. Little did I know that he would make this the focal point of his speech of welcome.

At this juncture we acquired two very important members of the touring party. Frank Worrell, fresh from tremendous successes in India with the Commonwealth team, looked the picture of good health and after his first net one suspected – nay, accused – him of practising surreptitiously over the weekend. Then emerged W. Ferguson, our eminent baggage man, veteran scorer of over 160 Test matches, seventy-three between England and Australia. This delightful character was to accompany us on our travels up and down England, and no member of the team had anything but the highest regard for Fergie's qualities both in his profession and as a man. He never got angry or irritable and with typical efficiency never lost a piece of baggage. As we sat watching the rain at Eastbourne he told us tales of cricket and cricketers down the ages. Soon a dozen of us were held in rapt attention. Fergie would not hear anything said against Don Bradman; for him there was, and always would be, only one Don. He accused Yardley & Co. of 'fuzzling the Don out with all them frills and things' when Hollies bowled him for 0 in his last Test innings at the Oval in 1948, and when asked about Borwick's famous decision at Brisbane in 1947 when Ikin appealed for a catch in the slips off Voce's bowling, Fergie offered, 'I couldn't see from where I was, but Don said he wasn't out.' And that was enough for Mr Ferguson.

Another famous personality in cricket journalism turned up to have a look at us at Eastbourne: R. C. Robertson Glasgow, 'Crusoe' to his friends, and a more charming and delightful person it would be difficult to find anywhere. An amazing wit, he, above all other cricket writers, records the game in its proper perspective – as a game – to be played and enjoyed in good humour and in the richness of its setting.

And so from fun and games to serious cricket. The sixth of May came around and we were off to Worcester. Another English summer loomed ahead. 'If we have a dry summer, they will be formidable opponents,' the newspapers blared. We did *not* have a dry summer.

If those in charge of the arrangements of cricket tours in England have consciences and want to keep them, then they will see to it that the first county game is played at Worcester. Apart from the traditional aspect, the Worcester County Ground is among the loveliest, the outfield among the smoothest in the country. The first two games against Worcester and Yorkshire were both rain affected and were a prelude to the wet summer that we would experience. Worcester served to give notice of the magic touch of Worrell, and at Bradford on a 'sticky' we scrambled home by 3 wickets.

Bob Wyatt, still playing at forty-nine, captained Worcester. When entering a discussion with him on the subject of cricket, one immediately sensed that one was in the presence of a cricketer whose knowledge of the game was deep and far-reaching. Wyatt was not content just to play and teach the game; he went into the theory of it with the same thoroughness that a mathematician would devote to a novel and interesting problem. Bob went into details of how he once proved that Mayer, the Warwickshire bowler, would have improved his average by 2.5 if he had used a third slip instead of a third man.

In the second innings at Bradford, Jones took 7–29 and Gomez, bowling off-spinners, had 5–34 in the first. Ramadhin meantime fooled a few of the Yorkshire batsmen in the first innings, but had not yet acquired the mastery over length and direction so necessary for bowling effectively on a bad wicket.

My scores in three first-class innings so far had been 8, 9 and 6 and I was not a little desperate about such poor form. I remember going to the great Len Hutton and asking with complete naïveté: 'What am I doing wrong?' Poor Len could only mumble a nondescript reply. Obviously he hadn't even noticed.

In our next game against Surrey at the Oval, some of our more obvious weaknesses were exposed. On the final day, Surrey needed 242 with 7 wickets standing to avoid an innings defeat. They achieved their target, although a simple return catch to Worrell was dropped when the last pair were in, 6 runs before the match was saved. Of our fielding on this day, the less said the better. One hoped that we should not suffer the like again. Our tactics in the field left much to be desired, for we often bowled to defensive fields when an all-out offensive was called for.

The Cambridge team of 1950 included in its batting line-up P. B. H. May, D. S. Sheppard, J. G. Dewes and G. H. G. Doggart, a formidable quartet to say the least, so it was not all that surprising that the University, electing to bat on the first day, compiled a total of 507–3 on the beautiful Fenners surface and fast outfield. It was the first time that Ramadhin had bowled on a wicket on which he was unable to turn either way and he was in an absolute quandary.

Our reply to their eventual total of 594–4 (Dewes 183, Sheppard 227, Doggart 71) was 730–3 (Weekes 304, Worrell 160, Christiani 111, Stollmeyer 83, Trestrail 56 not out). We left Fenners a little puzzled about how easily our full bowling strength, with the exception of Gomez, was knocked about, and even more worried about our limitations in the field.

The MCC game at Lord's which came next was our first real test of strength, and losing this game by 118 runs was largely the result of batting which was not only sub-standard but unintelligent. C. B. 'Boogles' Williams, our leg-spinner, took 7–55 in the MCC second innings which was the basis for a wonderful comment by Sir Pelham Warner (then President of the MCC). 'Boogles,' he said reflectively. 'Lovely name for a spinner!'

We were set to get 266 to win in the last innings on a wicket which gave the spin-bowler a little assistance and was inclined to keep low. When Allan Rae was out and the first wicket fell with the score at 61 trying to hit Jim Sims out of the ground, a rash stroke under the circumstances, he was asked by Everton Weekes on his return to the dressing room why he had done such an outrageous thing. 'I saw a gap,' said Allan. 'You must have seen Hart's Gap,' was Everton's rejoinder. (Hart's Gap is a small side street on the Hastings coast of Barbados.) In later years Allan could never pass Hart's Gap without his friends reminding him of his indiscretion.

Ken Trestrail, who was being tried in the No. 3 position (Worrell, Weekes and Walcott were scheduled to be four, five and six in the batting order), had scored 19 in only a couple of overs before lunch, but he had used the pull and square cut, thus hitting across the ball, and I warned him of the possibility of the ball keeping low as we went into lunch. In the event he was bowled immediately after the interval, middle-stump by Sims hitting across the line of a top spinner which hurried on and kept low.

In Ken Trestrail, there were many, including myself, who felt we had another batsman in the class of the three Ws. He certainly had the talent and the potential to be world class, but he never adapted to English conditions as he should have done on this tour and turned out to be a great disappointment to his many admirers and supporters.

After this match I felt rather better about my personal form, for I had top scored in both our innings, 53 out of 170 in the first, and 39 out of 147 in the second.

In the meantime, the trumpets blared the result. Back in the West Indies, newspapermen waxed warm at the expense of their favourite batsmen. Pictures of George Headley were rescued from the files. 'If George was there he would have been the answer,' they said.

All this while Jim Sims, happy character, walked off the sunny turf of Lord's with a bag of 11 West Indies wickets, all of them good ones, plums picked easily, skilfully and without bruising, and one visualized Bob Wyatt, Les Ames and Brian Sellers, the England selectors, reading their evening papers with knowing smiles.

There were four more first-class games before we were due to play the first Test at Old Trafford and, as expected, they gave us pointers as to whom we should finally select for that match.

The game against Oxford was hopelessly affected by rain but not before one incident occurred, laughable in retrospect. Towards the close of our innings Gerry Gomez was joined by C. B. Williams, a good player who, batting at No. 8, had had very little opportunity to bat on the tour. Players who had toured with Gerry knew of his desire to get off the mark quickly and his habit of playing the ball smartly to cover point and taking off head down for his first run. Apparently Boogles had not experienced this and was left stranded high and dry, run out for no score. Understandably not in the best of moods, he was unbuckling his pads in the dressing room when the innings closed abruptly and Gerry entered. 'Boogles, you weren't backing up,' launched Gerry into the attack. The mildest and most controlled of men, this was almost too much for the disconsolate Williams who, trembling with an accumulation of rage and righteous indignation, could only stammer, 'I'd rather not discuss it.'

C. B. Williams eventually became the High Commissioner for Barbados in London. A gifted and lovable character, I am sure that he did a splendid job in this capacity.

Our game against Glamorgan, the first in which I acted as captain, we won handsomely by an innings and 26 runs. It could have been described as Johnson's match, for Hines produced match figures of 8–67 and hit three 6s and four 4s in scoring 39 at the end of our first innings.

On the Sunday of this game, our scorer Fergie accompanied us on our visit to Wenvoe Castle, and *en route* one of us remarked on the fact that there happened to be a large sign – 'Welcome to Cardiff' – in a cemetery which we had just passed. 'That's nothing,' said the incomparable 'Fergie'. 'In Sydney, Australia, during the last war they posted a sign in a cemetery there: "Awake, your country needs you." ' This was a typical Ferguson comment. No wonder we all loved him!

We won the Somerset game, but not convincingly, and it was about this time that we read notices in the press regarding the inability of batsmen to detect Ramadhin's break. I remember well, after our first practice at Lord's, when Charles Bray, cricket writer for the *Daily Herald*, who had a quick eye for spotting talent, calling me aside and asking, 'Where did you find this Ramadhin? He is going to trouble our batsmen.' Charles had been through the mill himself, and his curiosity and interest in the youngster were, as subsequent events proved, fully justified.

Ramadhin did not, however, seem to hold any fears for Harold Gimblett, one of those unfortunate players who had failed to find favour with the selectors, despite scoring heavily and in an attractive manner season after season. He was eventually selected for the third test at Nottingham but was unable to play because of a carbuncle on his neck. The last Test which he had played in was against us at Lord's in 1939. At the end of the Trent Bridge Test he was heard to say facetiously to one of the selectors, 'Cheerio, see you in '61!' Not surprisingly, he was not selected again for a Test match.

Our match against Lancashire, immediately preceding the first Test, was interesting from two points of view: the fact that the wicket disintegrated early in the match and the bowling of Alf Valentine which was virtually unplayable on the crumbling turf. Batting first, Allan Rae and I had an opening partnership of 204 and he scored his first century of the tour.

There was no doubt about it that Valentine's performance meant that he could on no account be left out of the Test team. During a brief period when a wicket had fallen, Wharton, the Lancashire all-rounder who was batting at the time, turned to Val and said laughingly, 'I expect you'd like to take this wicket around with you?' There was a pause, then a shy smile, then, 'No, sir, the Lancashire batsmen!' from Val.

Two thoughts struck me. What if we had lost the toss? Would

the position have been reversed? And what of the future? How would the Test wicket play? With the game a mere two days away, there was no sign of any wicket receiving intensive preparation.

Strangely, there had been no rain in Manchester for some weeks and the morning of the first Test match broke warm and sunny and the weather continued thus throughout the match.

Anticipating a hard, fast, and true wicket, Goddard, Worrell and I went out to have a look at the wicket before the match and frankly we·were not prepared for what we saw. Worrell turned to Goddard and asked him what he would do if he won the toss and when the latter replied, 'Bat of course,' Frank didn't seem so sure. The most disturbing feature was the fact that there were cracks wide enough to allow entry of a finger, and generally the wicket gave the impression of unpreparedness. Withal, it was impossible to imagine the dramatic cricket which was to follow.

We had selected twelve men the evening before the game. The selection was straightforward. The main doubt centred around Johnson and Jones. Should we play both or only one fast bowler? Valentine had played himself into the team in the Lancashire game and Ramadhin had shown himself to be potentially our best spin-bowler. The team finally selected was Goddard, Stollmeyer, Rae, Worrell, Weekes, Walcott, Christiani, Gomez, Johnson, Ramadhin and Valentine, with Marshall as twelfth man.

England had selected Yardley, Hutton, Simpson, Doggart, Dollery, Evans, Bailey, Edrich, Berry, Laker, Hollies and Bedser, and it was no secret that, when the selectors looked at the wicket before play started, they decided to retain the services of all three spin-bowlers and Bedser was left out.

The game started sedately enough, Simpson and Hutton playing carefully to the bowling of Johnson and Gomez, and spectators were just preparing themselves for the ordeal of Test match first-day batting, when the drama began. A good-length ball from Johnson lifted abruptly, rapped Hutton on the forefinger of the right hand and Len had to retire to the X-ray room. Edrich came in and, shortly after, Johnson had to be taken off complaining of soreness in the abdominal muscles. He did not bowl again in the match.

Fortunes often change rapidly in cricket and England 74–2 at 12.30 were 88–5 just after one o'clock. Valentine had done the damage. Such was England's predicament when Evans joined Bailey twenty minutes before lunch.

With the England total 94 for 5 at lunch, West Indies were still well on top and there were very few on the ground who thought that England would get more than 150, especially with Hutton still on the doubtful list. One is forced to wonder whether Hutton would have batted again had Johnson been able to bowl.

There is very little doubt, now that the game had been won and lost, that the magnificent partnership of Evans and Bailey, which added 161 and was still unbroken at tea, won the game for England. Evans played in his natural forcing style and he richly deserved his first Test hundred. Bailey showed admirable patience and defence and swept anything pitched outside the leg-stump firmly to the leg-boundary. Together they first saved the day for England, then gradually consolidated and finally placed her in a winning position.

How was it, it might be asked, that Evans and Bailey could do what the more reputable batsmen had failed to achieve? Was it that the wicket had improved? Apart from a slight easing in pace, I do not consider that the wicket improved at all. Valentine still got the ball to turn sharply and lift as well, but Evans was a fine cutter and anything a bit short outside the off-stump was cut to ribbons. Well though Valentine bowled, he was guilty of sending down too many balls outside the off-stump on a wicket where the ball pitched well-up on the leg-stump and turning away was the answer. Later in the tour, in August, say, when Val was more experienced and accurate, he would not have made this mistake. In fairness to him it must be said that he was asked to bowl for very long spells and it may have been expecting too much of a twenty-year-old, playing in his first Test, to shoulder such a heavy burden. The same applied to Ramadhin who bowled well, but was luckless. His length and direction deteriorated as he became tired. Although it is easiest to be wise after the event, the earlier relief of these two bowlers in the post-lunch period might have been tried to advantage.

Eventually we found ourselves facing a total of 312, a very good score under the circumstances and a capital recovery.

Allan Rae and I survived a precarious half hour in light that was none too good and were there the next day to resume our uphill fight. The whole of the second day developed into a struggle for survival on the part of the West Indies batsmen. Against the accurate spin bowling of Berry and Hollies on a wicket which assisted them, their fields cleverly placed by Yardley, we had our work cut out to keep our wickets intact. Most of our batsmen fought gamely, although a few of the wickets which fell were due to a lack of appreciation of the situation.

Our innings closed for 215, a deficit of 97 and we were still in with a chance when England lost 3 second innings wickets for 43, but Yardley and Edrich stemmed the tide and England went on to score 288.

Honestly though our spin bowlers toiled, one could not but feel that they were not making the use they might have made of this remarkable wicket, and the earlier relief of one or other of the pair might again have brought about results.

The absence of a fast bowler in our ranks was noticed once again when Hutton batted with his hand bandaged. His gallant innings only served to emphasize how essential it was under existing conditions to play with the minimum of use of the right hand. It was significant that as soon as Worrell was brought on bowling fast with the new ball, Hutton, showing little further inclination to stay, was out caught and bowled.

Set 385 to win, we batted on a wicket that defied description and our score of 183 was a creditable one under the circumstances. We had to face the accurate spin attack of Hollies, Laker and Berry and what two of the three lacked normally in capacity to spin was more than compensated for by the receptive pock-marked turf which, in the words of the cricket authority, H. S. Altham, resembled 'a stretch of the dusty Sahara'.

Defeat, then, in the first Test by 202 runs. And yet we felt that it had not been a true test of strength. The conditions had been abnormal and the surviving impression was that we had been beaten, not so much by the superiority of the opposing players as individuals, but by the team possessed of greater experience and tactical knowledge.

Personally, I felt pleased with my own performances in the game. Second top score of 43 out of 215 in the first innings and top score of 78 out of 183 in the second. The latter was probably the most important innings I ever played.

My readers may be interested in what the well-known cricket journalist, E. M. Wellings, had to say about the West Indies team at this juncture. I quote the following extracts from his columns in the London *Evening News*:

This West Indies team has often been described as their strongest ever, but there is little backing for this claim. I very much doubt if they are as strong as the New Zealand team which toured this country last summer. They certainly have no batsmen of the class of Donnelly and Sutcliffe, no opening bowler as good as Cowie, nor a slow left-hander the equal of Tom Burtt . . . There has been a suggestion that the pitch helped England to win. England had the worst of the batting conditions – at the start the pitch was hard, rough, brittle and fiery. As the top powdered the ball did more remarkable things, but it came off slowly. Consequently the batting really became less difficult as the match proceeded . . . The truth of the matter is that an English team which could not by any stretch of imagination be described as our best – our key bowler (Bedser) was even omitted on the morning of the game – beat a much over-rated West Indies team fairly and squarely.

Shameful criticisms, no doubt hastily made. In the light of later events, these pills must have been bitter ones for this journalist to swallow.

Our next first-class game after the Test was against Notts at Trent Bridge where, on a perfect batting strip, Weekes scored 279 in 235 minutes.

In the pavilion I heard several of the old-timers compare Weekes's innings with that famous knock of 345 scored in a day on the same ground by Macartney in 1921. Certainly it was a treat to watch, and in spite of the admittedly mediocre attack against which this great score was made, it was an exhibition of stroke play the like of which will not often be seen, and it justified the tremendous ovation given him by the crowd and by the members in the pavilion who stood up for him as he made his way up the steps to the dressing room.

It did not seem possible that we could win this game under the conditions but win it we did when, having detected rough on and outside the leg-stump in the Notts second innings, I asked Frank Worrell, in the absence of Ram and Val who were not playing, to bowl slow left arm over the wicket at the leg-stump and into the rough. This he did accurately and to great effect, enabling us to record our fifth success of the tour.

Allan Rae (179) and I (198) shared an opening partnership of 355 against Sussex at Hove, a record for West Indies in first-class cricket. During this long partnership, George Cox exchanged a steady flow of conversation and witticisms with Billy Griffith who was keeping wicket. I heard him confide in Griffith that although his son, whom he hoped one day would be a great cricketer, didn't 'have a clue', he was supremely confident that he would play for Sussex as an amateur! Another crack from him referred to his 'poor skipper', James Langridge, whose wife, he said, took a keen interest in her husband's activities on the cricket field and followed his scores closely. 'It's tough, isn't it, Jim, to get home in the evening and have the wife say: So you got a duck today, did you! and that blighter Cox scored another hundred.' George Cox, they told me in Sussex, is a chip off the old block. He, too, is one of those unlucky batsmen who have, through no fault of their own, failed to get a summons from the Test match selectors.

We had bowled Sussex out in their first innings with the help of the 'tide' which was 'in' when the new ball became due. It was again Frank Worrell who, this time bowling quick, converted a score of 170–2 to 220 all out. Worrell, the ubiquitous! He had just finished winning the Notts game for us with a fine bit of good-length spin-bowling on a wicket which called for spin. Now, here at Hove, he paved the way for victory by an equally fine spell of fast bowling on a wicket which cried out for swing.

This convincing win was just the tonic we needed before taking the field for the crucial Lord's Test. Our confidence had been fully restored by two consecutive innings victories.

A prelude to the Lord's Test was the presentation of both teams to His Majesty King George VI. I overheard Sir Pelham Warner say to Mr Kidney later in the day, referring to the presentation, 'Well played, sir! You are a fine body of men.' And, if I may say so myself, we did look smart 'on parade' in our very attractive burgundy blazers, the colours of the West Indies cricket teams on tour overseas.

Our team had one change in it. Jones came in for Johnson, the latter not having yet been pronounced fit. He had not taken part in any game since the Test at Manchester. England, on the other hand, made five changes, bringing in Washbrook, Bedser, Wardle, Park-house and Jenkins for Hollies, Bailey, Simpson (all on the injured list), Laker and Dollery. While the majority of these changes were obvious, the England selectors were guilty of selecting two left-hand slow bowlers of similar type, both of whom, under the conditions which prevailed at Lord's, proved of little use to Yardley.

The first day's play was not a totally satisfactory one from our point of view. A score of 320 for 7 on a wicket which would reward a spin-bowler for honest effort but which had no real life in it, did not reflect much credit on our batting. One had a sneaking feeling that England had been 'let off'. But there were bright moments. Allan Rae, on whom we had begun to depend to add that touch of solidity to our batting, came out with flying colours, scoring a century in his first Test innings at Lord's. Our position was not enhanced when, within fifteen minutes of the start of the second day's play, we were all out for 326.

This was not a large enough total under the conditions and we knew it; that was the hard fact that had to be faced. Hutton and Washbrook collected 50 without much difficulty and it was not until the combination of Ramadhin and Valentine took over that the batsmen were forced to retire into their shells. Hutton was out in a strange fashion before lunch. He appeared to make up his mind to 'move' Valentine who was bowling an immaculate length. He seemed to go down the wicket even before the bowler had delivered the ball and, beaten by the flight, was stumped by yards.

But it was not until after lunch that real disaster overtook England. Hutton's error of judgment cost his side dearly; his responsibility then to the batting of an England team was immense. In the post-lunch period, we saw some bowling by Valentine and Ramadhin that was nothing short of sensational. Try as they would and did, both Washbrook and Edrich could not detect which way Ramadhin was spinning and, after a protracted period of prodding, both men fell victims to his subtlety.

England's innings closed for the inconceivably low total of 151, and with our score at 45–0, I left the ground in a far easier frame of mind than when I had walked on to it that morning.

In our second innings, when Weekes was run out with the score 199–4, Gomez and Walcott, as they had at Delhi in the first Test in India in 1948, came to our rescue. Both played extremely well in their different ways. Walcott drove with tremendous power and some mighty hits of his off the toiling left-handers left the fieldsmen in the covers immobile. Gomez, on the other hand, with admirable restraint, was content to play, as it were, 'second fiddle'. Rapidly we recovered, consolidated, and eventually established beyond doubt that the initiative was ours. The partnership added 211 runs, at the time a record for the West Indies in Tests in England. The West Indies had, during the last three international contests, a lot for which to thank these two players. They had been the hardest worked members of our team, had faced many crises and they had seldom failed us. Walcott's score of 168 not out was only one short of the previous highest score made by a West Indian in Tests in England.

At 12.10 on the fourth day, our second innings was declared closed. We left England 601 to win in eleven and a quarter hours. I mention the time merely because the wicket was still in excellent shape and showed no signs of wear. The fate of England was probably sealed when Hutton was out bowled by a ball from Valentine which came with the bowler's arm 'up the hill'. To my mind, Hutton was the only English batsman playing in the match who had the ability to concentrate for anything like ten hours and who could actually play for that length of time without making a serious mistake.

But of cricket more than of any other game it can be said that the game is never won or lost until the last ball has been bowled. England came out fighting. Washbrook and Yardley dug themselves in, but Ramadhin bowled as if fresh from a week's rest; he had never bowled better. For sixty-six mortifying minutes he bowled at Washbrook without him scoring a run. Of course, defence was the first consideration, but surely a batsman with Washbrook's experience must have realized that the bowler would get on top unless countermeasures were taken. But Ramadhin did not bowl even one bad ball during that hour and, at the end of it, he completely deceived Washbrook and bowled him. It was, I think, as fine a spell of spin-bowling on a batsman's wicket as I have seen.

Such is the spirit of England when faced with certain defeat, that even the last pair, Berry and Wardle, together after lunch, played for some time as though they felt that a draw was not impossible. Suddenly Wardle could restrain himself no longer and banged Valentine for three fours, all clean hits from good strokes and Goddard had to draft Worrell into the attack in order to finish off the game. There were scenes of wild enthusiasm from the West Indians present when Umpire Dai Davies signalled Wardle LBW to Worrell and, complete with guitar, a small 'carnival' band could be seen shuffling slowly across the turf at Lord's to the familiar rhythm of the calypso. I made out 'Lord Kitchener' at the head. He had immortalized Ramadhin and Valentine in calypso, and quite rightly too, for lest we forget, here are their match figures:

RAMADHIN: 115—70—152—11
VALENTINE: 116—75—127—7

It was certainly a great feeling to be a member of the team which had just won the first Test match for the West Indies in England. That win had not been a fluke as was subsequently proved. It was convincing enough, a handsome margin of 326 runs.

A convivial impromptu party developed in our dressing room after the game and, aided by several magnums of champagne provided for the occasion by the MCC, it proved a delightful gathering, and everyone, the opposition included, seemed to live with us those memorable moments. Sir Pelham Warner, Norman Yardley and his team, the umpires, broadcasters, the secretarial staff at Lord's, members of the BWI Sugar Commission, and former England and West Indies players joined in the celebrations. It was good to see among those present the faces of Learie Constantine, John Cameron, Bertie Clarke and Victor Stollmeyer of the 1939 side; it was as much their day as ours. I regret that I cannot give in such detail the happenings which took place in room 326 at the Kingsley Hotel, where another team party developed. Suffice it to say that the occasion was suitably toasted.

Perhaps the highlight of a drawn game against Hampshire at Southampton, apart from another double century from Weekes, was a dinner held in our honour by the Hampshire County Cricket Club at which John Arlott spoke. John was at his eloquent best and suggested that England could select the following imaginary team to beat the West Indies:

1. As wicket-keeper: the local income-tax collector – 'Nothing ever gets past him and he has stumped me for four years.'
2. Mid-off: the petrol inspector, who, 'since the advent of rationing, has stopped more drives than anyone else.'
3. Backward short-leg: Marlene Dietrich, who has 'stopped more leg glances than any other living person.'
4. First bowler: the landlord of the local, who 'mixes them up well and gets out awkward customers before time.'
5. Spin-bowler: the barmaid, who 'keeps everyone guessing and never gives information of what she intends. She draws men a long way down and then beats them.'
6. Her sister: who is 'not half so deceptive, but is very fast!'
7. Dorothy Lamour: 'scores with a magnificent figure without, as far as I can observe, any visible means of support.'
8. John Goddard's barber: who 'cuts regularly and accurately . . .'

And so he went on as roars of laughter greeted his every selection. He confessed to not having been a great cricketer himself. He was one of those who, in his own words, 'basked in the smiles of female friends of men who play long innings.' He has the master's touch, has John Arlott.

I captained the team against Lancashire at Aigburth where the light seemed to be perennially murky. Lance Pierre came into his own for the first time on the tour with figures of 8–51, and Frank Worrell contributed 159 to our total of 397–8. On the last day it was merely a matter of time, for a dusty surface was Valentine's wicket. Our catching was again uncertain, but the Lancashire batsmen kindly kept serving us with catches at regular intervals. It was a pleasure to meet once again Captain Sapsworth of the *Golfito* who had come to see us play in his native Liverpool. He didn't see much cricket, however, for the game was over by lunchtime.

Our convincing win meant that we had twice defeated the 1950 joint county champions by an innings. An unusual feat and one worthy of special mention.

A drawn game at Northampton in which we played some very moderate cricket was followed by a run feast at Leicester. Batting first we scored 651 for 2 wickets on the opening day.

An analysis of the day's play in figures will demonstrate effectively what I mean. Marshall, 93 not out at lunch, scored 188 in 210 minutes; Worrell's 225 not out took 275 minutes; while the irrepressible Weekes was only 146 minutes over his 190 undefeated. It is not often that any batsman can accurately prophesy exactly what he is going to do, but in this instance, Weekes did just this. Before he went in, he let us know that he was about to score the season's fastest 100 and that he proceeded to do. He scored 100 in sixty-five minutes, thus beating the previous fastest scored by Len Hutton in seventy-three minutes. By this achievement he won the *Daily Mail* prize of £100 offered annually to the player scoring the quickest century. It must be mentioned that Worrell cooperated magnificently by giving his partner as much of the bowling as possible. Significant was the number of 4s hit by our batsmen: Weekes hit twenty-three, Worrell twenty one and Marshall no fewer than thirty-one.

Needless to say, we won this game on a wicket which became a spinner's paradise as the game entered the last day.

Although I might, with some justification, be accused of telling tales out of school, passing mention must be made of a golfing episode which took place on our Sunday in Northampton. The team was well represented and no fewer than four couples borrowed implements from members of a club to which Freddie Brown introduced us. We had by this time told all and sundry about Ramadhin's prowess with driver and iron and, with a representative gathering in attendance at the tee-off, he was given the honour of driving first. All was set and I had proceeded some forty yards along the fairway when a roar went up signifying that Ram had connected. Surely enough there was a golf ball disappearing into the beyond but I became disconcerted by the sound of something dropping, almost simultaneously, a few feet away from me. Something was up. Everyone was in stitches of laughter and then I saw why. Almost at my feet lay the club end of Ram's driver. I noticed, too, that one of our hosts, a man of vast proportions, was laughing so much that tears ran down his face. They nearly became real tears when he was informed that Ram had used his wife's favourite driver.

A short interlude at Chesterfield followed, where rain had the final say as far as the cricket was concerned. We stayed at Smedley's Hydro, a place where the elderly and arthritic took the waters. It seemed to us that the presence of our young team reduced the average age of the guests to about seventy!

Trent Bridge was the scene of the third Test match wherein the only change in our team was Johnson for Jones: we played the fitter man. There was a suggestion that we should go into the game without a fast bowler, but fortunately wise counsel prevailed for it was Johnson's bowling before lunch on the first day of the match, backed up by excellent slip catching and wicket-keeping, that set us on the road to victory.

But I am getting ahead of my story. England did not share our good fortune for, of the fourteen originally selected, both Hutton and Gimblett had to decline due to illness. In addition, England were without Edrich, Compton and Bailey so, in reality, it was not the full strength of English cricket that we defeated at Trent Bridge.

Before a huge crowd, Norman Yardley won the toss and took first knock. Although it was impossible for him to do other than bat first, the morning dew gave the wicket just that extra life that was necessary to the fast bowler, and with Worrell and Johnson developing fine speed and accuracy, we were able to secure the initiative with the result that England were always fighting a rear-guard action.

The England innings closed after tea for 223 and we were left with just over an hour's batting during which time Rae and I put on 77 runs. In the fifth ball of the last over of the day, I was out caught and bowled low down by Jenkins with my score 46. I have seldom regretted losing my wicket as much, for the wicket was a 'peach' and I felt that I had at last found my best form.

On the second day, following a partnership of 143 between Rae and Worrell in which Worrell did most of the scoring, Weekes came in when Rae was brilliantly stumped by Evans on the leg-side.

From this point until play ended for the day, we were entertained to a 'Good Friday' feast of batsmanship. Neither batsman gave the semblance of a chance and the bowling was literally murdered. Despite the rapidity of the scoring, they never put a foot wrong and both looked as though they would be there for ever. It was unforgettable cricket, and as a batting spectacle, it can seldom have been bettered. We had secretly been hoping that these two would be associated in a long Test partnership, and what we had hoped and England had feared had now come to pass.

Just before closing time at half past six, a crashing stroke through the covers from Weekes tallied the 402nd run of the day. It is not often that 400 runs are scored in a six-hour day in a Test match. We must not lose sight of the fact that this was achieved against tireless bowling of uniform length and a high standard of fielding which never weakened, even in the face of such a terrific onslaught.

Play on the Saturday was not a repeat of the day before, however, and there is a West Indian cliché which reminds us simply that 'every day is not Sunday'. The infallible of yesterday were now quite obviously fallible, and the day's proceedings started with a series of streaky strokes off both edges by both batsmen. Runs still came quickly, but Bedser and Shackleton, with the aid of a new ball and overcast skies, looked better than they had done so far during the match. Watching was Wilfred Rhodes, that great English bowler of former times whose eyes sadly allowed him to see little of the play, although he seemed to sense in an uncanny way what was going on. He was quoted by E. W. Swanton as having remarked when told that the burst of applause signified Worrell's dismissal, 'Aye, I'm not surprised – his bat hasn't sounded today like it did yesterday.'

Our score of 479 for 3 at the end of the second day was taken to 558 all out, and at one o'clock we found ourselves taking the field.

Bedser had revived for England a glimmer of hope and so started her fighting for a draw.

One could never begrudge Alec Bedser a wicket. He was at the time the hardest-worked bowler in England, sending down close on 1500 overs every summer. After having taken a severe pounding the day before, he came back fighting and threw everything he possessed into an inspired spell of bowling. He had 5–36 to show for his morning's work.

We had to wait a long time for a wicket for Washbrook and Simpson continued to play carefully and well on the Monday. When the wicket did fall with England's score at 212, it was not due to any particular merit of the ball which secured it. Washbrook, his 100 just completed, seemed to lose concentration and had a wild dip at a ball wide of the off-stump from Valentine. He was taken safely by Worrell at cover – a good catch. This was the major turning point of the game.

As so often happens when a long partnership is broken, the loss of more wickets followed quickly, and 350 for 5 at the end of the day was better from our point of view than at one time seemed likely.

But England were not finished yet, and on the final day Godfrey Evans and John Dewes, after both had been given chances, prolonged the innings setting us 102 to get to win.

Rae and I knocked these runs off without being separated in even time, but not before we had survived some uncomfortable overs from Hollies, and Allan had given a couple of sharp chances. One of these was a full-blooded drive back to Hollies which split his finger and caused him to retire when his analysis read 7–6–1–0. I have no doubt that this incident aided and abetted our 10-wicket victory, and at close on 3.15 p.m. I had the privilege of scoring the winning stroke.

I am not going to dwell for any length of time on our game against Durham played at Sunderland. This is understandable for it was here that I made my first 'pair', but our game against Yorkshire at Sheffield deserves more than passing mention.

Of Bramall Lane, the cricket ground at Sheffield, Neville Cardus once wrote: 'It is a blasted heath, but as Shakespeare knew, it is on blasted heaths that matters of grim moment come to pass.' Our game, played there during Wakes Week before huge crowds,

subscribed to Mr Cardus' statement. It was grim cricket. Tight
cricket. Nothing was wasted. The first shattering appeal from Alec
Coxon supported by 30,000 enemy voices indicated that Yorkshire
were out to beat us. Not only the XI opposed to us, but every
Yorkshireman who watched the play had come to see to it that these
upstarts from the West were put in their proper place – and who
was best suited to do this job if not Yorkshire, top dogs of English
cricket?

There is more atmosphere at Bramall Lane than at any other
cricket ground on which I have played, except Lord's. It was an
atmosphere vastly different to Lord's, tense and full of the spirit of
combat, accentuated as it was by the squat chimneys looming black
outside the ground, and the air, which despite the holiday, contained
more than a trace of smoke from furnaces and steel smelters. It is a
terrible shame that this ground is no longer available to Yorkshire
CCC.

The crowd, unashamedly partisan, lived with the game and kept
it alive – not that it needed that, for it is unlikely that I shall ever
take part in a more exciting game of cricket, or one in which the
fortunes changed so abruptly. When we had achieved the impossible,
as it were, and had gained victory even as defeat stared us in the
face, the crowd stood there for some moments as if transfixed,
refusing to believe the scoreboard, and then, as if to give vent to
their feelings, they hurled their seat cushions on to the playing area.
It was a remarkable sight, and as it happened at a moment of
personal triumph, I shall not easily forget it.

Let us trace this match from its beginnings. It is worth it. Perhaps
it is best described by asking you to put yourself in my shoes and
live with me, sharing my feelings and thoughts during the course of
the game.

When still a quarter of a mile from the ground in the coach which
takes us there, I see the ends of the queues and feel that cricket is
in the blood here in Yorkshire. The air is charged with electricity
when I walk out with Norman Yardley to toss. We exchange pleasantries. Don Brennan, the Yorkshire keeper, has just become the
father of a son – one up for Yorkshire. Up goes the coin. I know I
have lost so wait placidly for Norman to tell me to prepare for the
leather-hunt, but no – 'You bat first,' he says. 'We want to please
the crowd, and anyway there is usually some early life in the wicket

here.' The die is cast. I take Roy Marshall in with me and we collect 40 runs without much incident. There are, of course, intermittent, violent eruptions from Coxon when he strikes the pad, for Alec is of the old Yorkshire school. I am out LBW in answer to one of these menacing cries, and before I have my pads off, there is a terrific roar which can mean only one thing. Frank Worrell is out. For a while it is Weekes and Marshall together, but Roy becomes too ambitious too early and Yardley bowls him out. It must be near lunchtime. I hope it is. No more wickets before the interval please!

After lunch we look like recovering but not for long. Trestrail and Weekes are soon asking each other how and why they got out, but the ball which bowled Everton was a beauty – a 'seamer' back from the leg-side. Coxon is bowling tight and someone reminds me that he has bowled unchanged before lunch. A wiry one, this Alec Coxon.

The only real resistance comes from Williams who sensibly hits at everything and tries his best to keep the bowling as our tail-enders come in. 'Farming' the bowling is no easy matter when playing against these Yorkshiremen, but 'Boogles' comes out with flying colours. All out 198 on a good wicket and Yorkshire still with 180 minutes' batting time.

I realize that trouble is imminent and call a team conference: 'Everyone expects', etc. Yorkshire produce Hutton and Lowson, the latter frail and uncommunicative. He shows no emotion even when Pierre uproots his off-stick first ball. The rest of the play is all Hutton. His magnificence dwarfs all else. Hutton is in the mood and in form, playing before a crowd which adores him. I stand at mid-off and can scarce forbear to cheer some of his beautiful strokes, the strokes of a master. That classic on-drive off Valentine, that masterful straight drive off Pierre, and now I hasten to rectify my mistaken impression that Jones can bowl to him in this mood *sans* mid-off. Very impressive and illuminating it all is, but worrying too and not at all conducive to my peace of mind. Close of play score: 178–3, Hutton 98 not out.

All day Monday, it is a grim battle, a battle of wits. We spar like a pair of heavyweight boxers. Every possible advantage is followed up, but at the end of the day there is not much in it either way, although Yorkshire slightly have the upper hand. The cricket is of absorbing interest throughout. When Gerry Gomez and I get to the ground we do not go into the dressing room, but instead make straight for the middle in our 'civvies'. How much rain has there been? Can we feel the wicket give to a push of the fingers? To the latter, the answer is 'yes'. That means a 'sticky' sometime during the day. The sun has been out during the morning and we fear the worst but do not say it. We expect the wicket to be easy for an hour and then become a sticky dog. This would mean almost certain defeat, for Yorkshire would have us in on it and we would be sunk.

But things don't pan out that way. I start in with Valentine. Hutton gets his hundred but not many more. The wicket is playing tricks, turning quickly and popping. I set attacking fields. Valentine and Gomez, bowling off-spinners, both have five men literally under the bat. Yes, it is a spin-bowler's wicket. Weekes keeps swallowing catches at first slip. In less than an hour, Yorkshire lose 6 more wickets and my attention is drawn to Yardley standing on the pavilion balcony. He had declared with his score 217 for 9 wickets and wants an hour at us before lunch.

This hour is all-important so I implore Marshall to 'dig in'. He plays a fine innings and by skilful cricket we are still together 40 runs to the good at lunch. The wicket is improving every minute so we are happy in the knowledge that we are now on terms with every prospect of a good score to follow.

But we do not reckon with Yorkshire guts. They fight hammer and tongs to get our men out and how well they succeed! Give nothing away is Yorkshire's motto. It is the only way to win matches. Luck in cricket is fleeting, never permanent. Fifty-three for 0 becomes 132 for 5 and we are in the doldrums. Worrell has failed to score, out on both occasions caught at long-leg, careless strokes. Weekes too has been deceived again by Coxon and the situation calls for courage and initiative. It is the old school of Walcott and Gomez who come to our rescue, and I thank my stars that in the West Indies we possess two such crisis players. Walcott goes from strength to strength but misses his 100 when he doesn't quite get hold of a colossal sweep at Yardley. Long-leg had been a thorn in our flesh all the match. He has caught five of our batsmen. Wardle crashes through our tail and we have made only 229. A rapid calculation tells me it's 211 to win — or lose — whichever way you want it and we decide to fight to the last.

There are barely fifteen minutes left for play that afternoon which means fifteen minutes of pace. Pierre is feeling good. He gets one to touch the inside edge of Hutton's bat, and I confess to showing emotion as Williams hugs the ball at leg-slip. Now, I feel, we have a chance to win. Yardley sends in his No. 11 Brennan as night-watchman. Pierre's tail is up. The last ball of the day lifts from a good length, there is a snick and a deflection. The appeal is like a slap of thunder as Walcott holds the ball aloft but the verdict goes against us. The umpire explains afterwards that Pierre's follow through takes him in line with the flight of the ball and he is therefore unable to see. Bad luck, Pierre, bad luck, West Indies, but perhaps our luck will turn on the morrow. In any case Hutton, our biggest menace, is out and we still have a sporting chance. It may even rain in the night – who knows?

It bids fair to be a fine day. Yorkshire, with Hutton out, need 198 to win. This is the grim fact with which we are faced as we walk on to the field.

Did I say our luck may turn? Well, it doesn't – at least not before lunch. The wicket has rolled out well, and there is little encouragement for the bowler from that source. Our task is a difficult one and our difficulties increase immeasurably when we fail to hold *eight* possible catches in the morning period. There is an epidemic of dropped catches the like of which I have never seen. One of the umpires and an excellent one at that, W. H. Ashdown, the old Kent player, tells me that in all his years of cricket experience he has never seen one batsman (Lowson) dropped six times in a couple of hours. Why should this be my misfortune, I wonder. Even Weekes, usually incredibly safe at slip, shows that he is only human. We have bowled well, our ground fielding has been tight, but catching the easiest 'sitter' has been beyond us. Brennan has made 24, very nearly his highest ever.

As we come in to lunch I calculate that they need only 92 to win with 8 wickets still in hand and almost unlimited time (120 minutes) at their disposal. Not so good.

As I prepare to take leave of Yardley who I had sat next to at lunch, I say, 'How many do you need to win, Norman?' 'Ninety-two,' says he. 'You are going to have to fight for every one,' I tell him and he replies with a cheery grin: 'Good, I hoped you'd say that.' That is how cricket is played in Yorkshire – quarter is neither given nor is it expected.

The tactics I have in mind are those we used in India in 1949 by which means the West Indies saved the day in the fifth Test played in Bombay. The situation calls for extreme measures so I decide to adopt the 'India Plan'.*

This plan, briefly, is a form of fast-medium leg theory and consists of bowling at the batsman's legs to a strategically placed inner and outer ring of leg-side fieldsmen. The essential difference to 'body line', as we understand it, is that the batsman is at no time being intimidated nor is there any attempt at direct attack. There is, therefore, little or no risk of bodily injury. The occasional bumper is mixed in certainly, but it is strictly occasional.

My key bowlers are Jones and Worrell. Jones has done it before and can do it again, but the whole idea is novel to Worrell. However, I feel that his natural swing of the arm will help him to put the ball just where he wants and his amazing accuracy of length and direction will help to pull us through. All is set, the rest is in the laps of the gods.

In half an hour, Lowson and Halliday have added only 3 runs and the capless Halliday's brow is furrowed. He glances at the clock over the pavilion for the first time. Then Lowson is out – at long last – gleefully caught at the wicket on the leg-side by Walcott as he swishes at a ball from Jones. Lester comes in. Before he has scored, he offers a chance to backward short-leg off Jones. This one too goes on the floor. It is difficult for us to believe our ill fortune, but the game goes on. Lester celebrates by sweeping Jones into the football stand for 6 and then he too is snapped up by Walcott, 139 for 4.

A problem has been posed: a left-hander, Wilson, has come in to join Halliday. We shift the field around. Worrell's task is now much more difficult. His natural action tends to make the ball move towards the left-hander's off-stump, but Frank keeps his head and Wilson is caught off his bowling as he mistimes a hook. The York-shire captain now joins Halliday. He is a strong on-side player, but still we attack his strength. He hits a lofted drive over my head at mid-wicket to the far end of the ground and they run four. The crowd is visibly excited but Yardley attempts to repeat the stroke, mistimes it and Jones catches him at deep mid-on. Coxon and Halliday now and the first signs of the tail in evidence. Wardle is still to come – a hard left-handed hitter, and he is the man I fear

*Leg theory of this nature was not considered to be sharp practice at the time this game was played and was not outlawed until some five years later.

most under the circumstances. Worrell slips one in on the wicket to Coxon and he is LBW – grudgingly so – for Coxon had put all he knows into this game, and is not a believer in wasting effort.

Now comes John Wardle who promptly lashes out at everything. There is a short boundary on the leg-side for the left-hander at Worrell's end and Wardle hits two 6s just over the head of one of two long-legs on the fence. Shall we abandon our plan at this end when Wardle has the strike? But even while I ponder this problem, Worrell bowls Halliday who has suddenly had a wild swing at a good-length ball on the middle stump – one of the few 'bad' balls bowled by Frank. Still to be safe we must move Wardle, for not until then is the winning of the game a practical certainty.

Worrell tries bowling shorter to Wardle who has been swiping at everything. This does the trick. He has swung once too often and Christiani, substituting for Pierre, is under the ball at square leg, 166 for 9. Leadbeater and Whitehead only are left to get the 45 runs now needed to bring Yorkshire victory. They are both bowlers and are unequal to the task. When Whitehead hits up a skier to Williams at cover-point and the fieldsman catches it, the tension leaves me and I feel limp. The strain during this day's play has been terrific, but I am now supremely happy. It has been the match of a lifetime and, proudly, we board the train for London.

An innings win against the 1950 joint county champions, Surrey, a game in which Walcott (149) and Marshall (143) scored centuries, followed.

In technique, Roy Marshall might not have pleased the discriminating coach but his effectiveness was unquestioned. Here was a stroke-maker of undoubted promise, and yet he was unable to get into our Test team. This certainly reflected our immense batting strength. A prominent English sportswriter whispered to me during Marshall's innings, 'If we had this lad in England we'd be cracking him up to be a world-beater.' In later years Marshall played several seasons with Hampshire and had a distinguished career with them.

A well-attended drawn game with Glamorgan at Swansea was next, where 'Wee' Willie Jones made a century for the county. This was the second successive long innings played against Ramadhin by left-handers who were prepared to carry the attack to the bowler, Fishlock of Surrey having done this in the previous game, and I wondered whether England would capitalize on this by including such a left-hander in the final Test at the Oval. In the event they did not, but first let me go into some detail about a match against Warwickshire, one of the most exciting in which I have taken part.

The Warwickshire groundsman's laconic comment to me before I tossed for innings with Tom Dollery was 'We don't go in for featherbeds here!' It was one of those tosses it would have been just as well to lose but perversely I won it. There was nothing for it but to bat.

Over the first two days, the game seesawed back and forth. On a seamer's pitch, we were dismissed for 156 with Charlie Grove who bowled magnificently in the circumstances having 8–38. At the end of the first afternoon we were back in the game having broken the back of their batting. Their score was 90–5. But on the second day we lost our grip on the game. A bad fielding lapse and a couple of loose overs which we could ill afford in such a low-scoring match gave Warwickshire a lead of 128 on the first innings. Although we fought hard in our second innings, we could not score more than 222 with Hollies (6–57) our bogey-man on this occasion. This meant they needed 95 to win. Was it impossible to stop them?

I went to Mr Kidney, our manager, before the final innings started and said to him, 'Mr Jack, I think we have a chance of winning, but it will mean that Prior Jones will have to bowl through the innings and he will be needed for the Test match tomorrow.' 'Go ahead and try to win,' was his reply. No county had yet beaten us on the tour. How well the team fought may be gathered from the following description of the last day of what I choose to call the finest game I ever lost.

There were forty minutes before lunch. Our tactics were clear. Close up one end with negative bowling if we could, and attack at the other end via the same rough spot which Hollies had used so well. We had the bowlers to carry out these tactics – Jones to supply the length stuff and Valentine to use the 'spot'. I fervently hoped all would go well in the field.

And so I started in with these two bowlers – the shine being rubbed from the ball in order that Valentine could spin the second over. So effective were the tactics that only 8 runs were scored before lunch – two snicks for 4 each through the slips off Valentine. Jones bowled 5 consecutive maidens.

The big difference between this and the Yorkshire game at Sheffield was that it was our job not only to save runs but, more important still, to get wickets quickly, an infinitely more difficult task. The time factor never entered into the scheme of things at Edgbaston. Warwick could score 1 run every two minutes and still win comfortably.

At one stage they were 72 for 6 and it was truly anybody's game. Our ground fielding was keen and tight and the greatest credit must go to the two bowlers who hardly bowled any loose balls all day. The magnificence of Jones' catch which dismissed Dollery for 0 at backward square leg off Valentine still stands out in my memory. It did one good to see our team fight so hard when faced with adversity, and if the day's play did take something out of us physically, it certainly did our morale no harm.

It was Don Taylor, a New Zealander, as yet unqualified to play for Warwickshire in county games, who saw the county through the final stages of the game. It was a pity that an important catch hit by him into the outfield was not held, for at that time we were still very much in the game. There were nought but rabbits left and the hutch would have been open.

They won by 3 wickets amid scenes of enthusiasm of a type not often seen on the playing fields of England. We had lost but we were happy in the thought that we had gone down fighting. Indeed, in the field we came out of the game most creditably. Only three bowlers were used in the county's second innings and it is with a keen sense of appreciation of their efforts that I record their analyses:

JONES:	21.4–12–33–1	
VALENTINE:	26–13–36–4	(bowled unchanged)
PIERRE:	5–1–17–2	

Yes, it was cricket at its best. A great tribute was paid the team by a crowd numbering about 800 who waited at the ground for two hours in order to cheer our coach as it drove away. The echo of that cheer and what it implied is still a cherished memory.

It was with a determined spirit that we entered into the fourth and final Test at the Oval. The only change in our team from that which played at Trent Bridge was the inclusion of Jones in place of Johnson. A balanced side was therefore maintained, and while Roy Marshall, owing to his recent outstanding batting performances, may have been considered unlucky not to gain selection, it was probably a wise move not to interfere too much with a winning combination. England were almost at full strength. Evans was a notable absentee, having suffered a fracture in a county game the week before, but

McIntyre, who kept wicket in his place, proved an able substitute. Another player on the sick list was Parkhouse, and D. S. Sheppard, the promising young Cambridge and Sussex player, was given his chance. Washbrook too was unable to play but Compton's name figured in the opposition's camp for the first time. England's team was F. R. Brown (capt.), Simpson, Bailey, Sheppard, Dewes, Hutton, Compton, McIntyre, Bedser, Hilton and Wright. It was Wright's first game against us in this series, and only Gomez and I of the 1939 West Indies team had ever played against him before. The selection of F. R. Brown as captain automatically followed the announcement of his selection to captain the MCC in Australia in the coming winter.

This game was one in which the weather played a considerable part and, in the end, the West Indies won comfortably by an innings and 56 runs, but had England on the third day made a greater effort to force the pace and go for a win, then it was the West Indies who might have been batting on the rain-affected pitch on the fourth day.

Our first innings total of 503 was built around a sound and sensible innings of 109 by Rae, together with a century from Worrell, whose normal brilliance was interspersed with inexplicable lapses of concentration. It was an innings during the course of which he left the field for a period suffering from giddiness – only to return later on to finish with 138. There was also a peach of an innings of 74 from Gomez. He has rarely played better.

When England were 229–3 in reply with Hutton and Compton together, the result could have gone either way, although the batsmen's progress had been too slow if winning the match had been the prime objective of the home team.

It was at this stage that we had a stroke of good fortune which proved to be the turning point of the game. Off a ball from Gomez, Hutton played around the corner wide of me at backward square leg. Compton called and ran but Hutton did not move, and I was able to correct an intended throw to the wicket-keeper and send a slow return to the bowler's end to run out Compton.

After this, no one could stay long enough with Hutton who batted right through the innings for 202 not out. He was the only batsman to play our spin-twins, Ramadhin and Valentine, confidently.

The fourth day of the match proved to be its last. The wicket had been affected by overnight rain, and once we had ensured that

England did not save the follow-on, then we were more than likely
to be home and dry. A mere 12 runs were needed to save it when
the last wicket fell.

When Hutton was out for 2 in the second innings, caught at short
leg off Goddard bowling with the new ball, the die was cast.
Goddard is the ideal bowler for a 'sticky' wicket. His off-cut is of
speed and length that denies counter-attack. His accuracy was superb
on this occasion and his figures were 4–25 off 17 overs bowling at
the end of the first innings and 1–11 off 9 overs in the second, but
it was Alf Valentine wheeling his left-arm-spinners away for 90 overs
with match figures of 10 for 160 who was the main architect of our
victory. Val never bowled better. There was a wonderful feeling of
satisfaction as I pocketed the ball when catching F. R. Brown at
extra cover off him, the match and the series conclusively won.

I have dwelt at considerable length on the subject of this 1950 tour
to England because, without doubt, it was a major turning point in
West Indies cricket.

Never, since this tour, has the West Indies cricket team been other
than world class. True there have been brief lapses and cyclical
failures, but seldom have we been other than rated among the top
teams of the world. If we are now undisputed world champions, it
may truthfully be said that it all started in 1950.

8

Ramadhin and Valentine and the Three Ws

With Ramadhin and Valentine
And give me any nine
And we can beat England any time.

So voiced one of our leading calypso singers in a composition appraising the performance of these two young bowlers. No one, not even our selectors, could possibly have foreseen the success which these two twenty-year-olds would enjoy on the tour of England in 1950. The origin of each player and his meteoric rise to bowling fame was as remarkable as it was simple.

Let us take first the case of Ramadhin. I have seen various descriptions of how he was 'discovered' but none of them has been quite in keeping with the facts.

One day, Clarence Skinner, a Barbadian ex-intercolonial cricketer employed with Trinidad Leaseholds Ltd in Trinidad, was watching some youngsters playing cricket in a public park. He noticed a young slip of a lad spinning his companions out. Skinner realized that he, an onlooker, could not with certainty say which way the ball was going to turn when it pitched, so he made arrangements for the boy to come and bowl at him at the nets at Pointe-à-Pierre, the Company's headquarters. Skinner's original interest in the boy increased when he found that not only he but also several of the leading batsmen of the Leaseholds Cricket Club were at sea when batting against Ramadhin, for that, the boy had told Skinner, was his only name. (His initial 'S' stands for his nickname 'Sonny'. The initials 'K.T.' often ascribed to him are purely fictional.)

Ramadhin was an orphan who was brought up by his grandmother. He had one brother two years his senior, whose bowling action greatly resembled his own. The only opportunities to play cricket that came his way in his boyhood days were with his school-mates on the streets, in public parks or in some clearing among the sugar-cane fields which surrounded the area in which he lived. The wicket more often than not consisted of an uneven surface of ground clean-weeded, with a dustbin or some similar object representing the stumps. The other implements were equally as makeshift – for instance, a bat shaped out of the stem of the coconut leaf. Yet, under these primitive conditions and without any tuition, the lad had developed a style of bowling which was quite different from anything yet seen in cricket. He had the natural ability to bowl a leg-spinner with an action so similar to the one he used for bowling the off-spinner that the batsman could seldom be certain of which way the ball would turn.

I first saw Ramadhin at the Queen's Park Oval, the headquarters of cricket in Trinidad, in the North vs South match of 1949, when he represented the South. I happened to be batting at the time he was brought on to bowl, a slight figure in a bright red cap. My partner was A. G. Ganteaume. Ramadhin's first ball to me was of good length pitched on the middle stump. Not being accustomed to the rather peculiar delivery and not too sure what to expect, I played forward somewhat feelingly. The ball whipped back from the off, passed behind my back and, with the wicket-keeper equally badly beaten, the result was 4 byes. I remember walking up the wicket to my partner and saying, 'It looks as though this lad may give us some trouble. Let's try to set about him before he settles down.' This policy paid off for, not being blessed with an experienced captain and at the best of times a difficult bowler for whom to set a field, we found gaps which were exploited to the full. As a result he never really bowled with complete confidence. Still, he performed well and procured some wickets later in the innings.

In January 1950, before selecting the Trinidad team to play against Jamaica in Trinidad in a series of matches which represented, in part, the trials for the selection of the 1950 West Indies team, Rama-dhin played and bowled in each of these games. He had 4 or 5 wickets on every occasion, all the leading Trinidad batsmen being included in his bag. He even withstood the acid test of being asked to come out of the pavilion in mid-afternoon when two batsmen were well set and take up the attack immediately. During all this time, Mr Skinner was a silent watcher with unlimited confidence in his find. He encouraged him, saw that he was properly cared for and instilled into the youngster the necessity for cultivating length and direction. The rest, he knew, was there.

Ramadhin bowled his way into the Trinidad team which played in February 1950. I captained Trinidad and well do I remember awaiting the chance to introduce him into the attack so that he would be likely to get an early wicket and so secure some confidence. I very carefully did this but – I realize now – that it was quite unnecessary. Ramadhin would have got to the top anyway. Against Jamaica, he was the outstanding bowler, but in spite of this there were few, apart from the selectors, who seriously considered him as a candidate for the West Indies team, for he had little or no experience, was only twenty years of age and was so slight of build as to conjure up fear in the minds of the experienced as to whether he would possess the stamina for such a rigorous tour.

His record in England that year can be appreciated by a glance at the list of averages for that tour, but this does not tell us everything about the quiet, simple, unobstrusive but neat little figure who first made the headlines because he bowled at the nets with his shirt-sleeves down and in a white cloth hat.

Everything in those times was novel to Ramadhin. He had never been on a ship before, never been out of Trinidad, the menu card on the morning breakfast table presented a difficulty, the diet was different, even the double-decker buses in London were a novelty: 'Let's ride in one of those upstairs buses,' he suggested to me one day. It is true that, when Ramadhin bowled to Hutton at Bradford, he did not know the Yorkshireman even by reputation! Hutton was just another batsman to him. Worcester, looked upon by every member of a touring team as the first big game, was just another game of cricket to Ramadhin. On the train to Worcester, he enquired naïvely why we were travelling so far to play a one-day fixture!

Ram, as he was affectionately known to the other members of the team, was well liked by his team-mates. Well do I remember the occasion on which half a dozen of us set off for dinner at one of London's many Indian restaurants. Ram was in the party, and we left it to him to do the ordering – a wise move, for his selection was beyond reproach – and shortly before we were due to leave, he disappeared into the precincts of the premises and it was subsequently discovered that he had settled the bill. Despite vigorous protests from the other members of the party, he insisted that the dinner was at his expense for, he said glibly, 'Today's my birthday.'

It was Ramadhin's amazing control of length and direction, in addition to his naturally deceptive action, that made him a great bowler. I still find it hard to believe that this slight, timid, inexperienced youth never once faltered or complained of fatigue because, make no mistake, he was asked to do a tremendous amount of bowling. He was, without doubt, the most colourful personality seen in the summer of 1950 in English cricket.

In later life, Ram became a highly sophisticated, self-confident family man, and together with his charming wife he runs a pub in the north of England, still playing the odd game to keep his spinning fingers supple.

From quaint old Spanish Town some twenty miles out of Kingston, Jamaica, came Alfred Valentine. Like Ramadhin, he was only twenty years old when he found himself a member of the West Indies team to tour England in 1950.

At the time the team was selected, the following reference to him appeared in *The Cricketer*:

The youngest member of the party, Alfred L. Valentine, has bowled in only two innings in first-class cricket, with figures of 2–190, and one might wonder why he is going to England. This left-arm spinner, with his left thumb cocked like a pistol-hammer at the moment of delivery, showed on the unresponsive jute matting in Trinidad that, in addition to being able to bowl a length, he could really spin the ball and get it to turn more than the average left-hander. At the moment his bowling is somewhat mechanical, but a long tour will do a lot to remedy this. Should the wickets give him any help, Valentine may be expected to have a good summer.

This was an accurate summary of the situation as it appeared to most observers at that time.

Undoubtedly, our selectors had learned their lesson. The absence of a left-handed spinner in England in 1939 and again in India in 1948–49 had cost us many matches as well as several extra hours in the field, and the net result was the realization that one had to be chosen at all costs. In the days of uncovered wickets it was sheer folly for any touring team to set out for England without a bowler of this type, provided there was available material. There was no substitute for the quick spinning left-hander on certain English wickets.

Jack Mercer, the old Glamorgan and Northants player, who had wintered in Jamaica for the past few years coaching the youngsters there, was impressed by the promise shown by Valentine, and it was he who encouraged the youngster and helped him along, giving hints that would be useful to him in the future.

As an apprentice machinist in the Parish of St Catherine, Valentine found time after working hours to play plenty of cricket, and representing St Catherine Cricket Club, he soon recorded some excellent analyses in club cricket in Jamaica. While his entry into first-class cricket was not impressive judging by figures, he showed, nevertheless, that he had the three main attributes of a first-class spin-bowler: length, direction and spin. What is more, under the most trying conditions for a bowler of his type, he had shown admirable persistence.

Valentine's record in England in 1950 was a fine one. When it is realized that he had only just turned twenty and was playing in his first season of first-class cricket, his record may be described as almost miraculous. If his rise to bowling fame was in any way less glamorous than Ramadhin's, it was certainly no less meteoric.

And what of the boy himself? He, like Ramadhin, was modest and unassuming. He had a sense of humour – he wouldn't have been the left-arm spinner who bowled 92 overs (a record) in the England second innings at Trent Bridge, 26 of them consecutively on the last day, if he hadn't. It was Val who, during the course of our game with Leicester, appealed twice in successive balls for leg-before without obtaining the desired result. At the end of the following over bowled by Ramadhin from the other end, he observed that the unresponsive umpire had forgotten to take up his position over the stumps in order to preside. Hailing Gomez who was nearby, he said in his West Indian accent: 'Gerry, tell the lickle blind umpire to come here!'

There was one unforgettable incident in which Valentine was the central figure. At Southend, after our game with Essex, there was some delay while the team congregated in the coach which was to take us back to London. As was apt to happen on such occasions, the coach became quickly surrounded by autograph hunters. A number of us were kept signing for several minutes, but there were many disappointed customers still left when, at last, we moved off. At this juncture, Val, to ensure that his admirers were not disappointed, plunged his hand deep into his coat pocket and produced innumerable slips of paper on which his name was signed. These he scattered to the four winds and a terrific scramble ensued. This incident was typical of the serious manner in which our two spin-bowlers took their autograph commitments. On consecutive nights of the Test match at Trent Bridge, they stood outside the hotel in Nottingham and signed their names for well over an hour.

Valentine's hobbies were collecting shoes and 'bop' recordings. He had accumulated some twenty-five pairs of shoes during the tour; multiply this number by five and you will have a general idea of the number of 'bop' records he amassed. As Fergie rightly exclaimed: 'Cor lumme, I've never seen anything like it!'

One thing I have discovered, and that is that Val's spectacles, which were acquired at the expense of National Health, failed to improve his batting average!

Worrell, Weekes and Walcott, the three 'wicked Ws', all hail from the tiny island of Barbados. Barbados, only 166 square miles in area but with a population of well over 1400 per square mile, has, I am sure, produced more talented cricketers than any other area of equal size.

It was not generally realized at the time that these three young men had most of their cricket before them, as in 1950 they were only twenty-six, twenty-five and twenty-four years of age, respectively. Together with Ramadhin and Valentine they formed a nucleus around which a team of world championship class could be built. To witness a long partnership between Weekes and Worrell was always a most stimulating experience.

One of the openers is out and there is a hush of expectancy among the spectators. A lithe athletic figure emerges from the pavilion and a prolonged cheer greets his arrival on to the playing area. He walks with head down, rather quickly and somewhat apologetically to the crease, the bat held in his left hand. As he passes the not-out batsman, he smiles, rubs his eyes (he has been sleeping in the dressing room for the last hour) and stammers laughingly, 'Wha-wha-what's going on out here, old man?' In due course, he takes his guard, has a word or two with the wicket-keeper and nearest fieldsman and then prepares himself for the fun of the day. Frank Worrell has started another innings. If it has been your good fortune to see a hundred from Worrell you will have seen batsmanship of the highest class. Classic late cuts, drives off the back foot through mid-on, hooks and straight drives all enchantingly played and executed with precision and wrists of steel.

Later on, Frank Worrell was to prove beyond doubt his great capabilities as a captain. The fabulous West Indies tour to Australia in 1960–61, encompassing the famous tied Test at Brisbane and the ticker-tape farewell at Melbourne when the team was leaving, after having lost the series by 2–1, was as much a tribute to Worrell himself as to the team which he captained. Then there followed the incomparable tour by the West Indies to England in 1963, a great West Indies team, possibly and arguably the greatest ever, superbly captained by Worrell. His greatest assets were his coolness under pressure which conveyed itself to the team under him, and his leadership qualities which enabled him to get the full support of his players.

He was destined to delight cricket audiences for many years and his death in 1967 at the tragically early age of forty-three cut short what would surely have been an active career in West Indies cricket administration.

But what's this? The other opening batsman has been dismissed and No. 4 on our scoreboard is E. D. Weekes. Here he comes now, a 5 foot 6 inch bundle of muscle, neatly attired, and looking good for at least 200. A wry smile to his partner and best friend (Worrell), possibly a brief greeting to the wicket-keeper, his guard is taken and right away he gets down to the business of the day. There was no nonsense about Weekes, no tomfoolery. Once on the job, he was purposeful. His business was to score runs and, believe me, Weekes liked nothing better. I hope that you have had the pleasure of seeing him score 100; this joy was mine on numerous occasions and I never tired of repetition. Each fresh boundary called forth renewed exclamations of approval. Weekes, the batsman, was an entertainer. He was business-like, yes, but he would take a chance. He was primarily a stroke-player. Playing strokes was the game he knew and loved best, and unless circumstances warranted discretion, Weekes would produce his smashing square cut, slashing cover drive, resounding hook and forceful on-drive for all to see and enjoy.

In later life, Weekes has become a cricket commentator of renown in the Caribbean and particularly in his native Barbados. His terse and often sarcastic comments are excellent value, for he is unable to tolerate bad cricket and incompetent cricketers; no one knows the game better than he does. He was certainly the easiest of players to captain. As far as I was concerned, he anticipated my every move and I pay myself a great compliment when I venture to suggest that we read the game alike.

If it is your lot to fall into a conversation with a West Indian on the subject of Weekes and Worrell, it is not long before the inevitable question will arise: which one was the better batsman? Arguments on this subject have occurred whenever and wherever cricketers gather in the West Indies, and it is a difficult question to answer. I saw a great deal of both players and greatly admired their talents and contrasting styles, but in assessing their relative merits as batsmen, there are differences invisible to the casual observer but known only to their close friends and associates. Personally, I should never attempt to answer this question directly, for my answer would depend entirely on existing playing conditions.

As batsmen both players bore comparison, and it may be of interest to set out briefly my opinion of their comparative rating under various conditions.

I considered Worrell the sounder in defence, Weekes the greater attacking force; Worrell the more graceful, Weekes the more devastating; Worrell the more effective on soft wickets, Weekes the more so on hard wickets. Worrell gives the bowler less to work on, Weekes has the wider range of strokes. Both are good starters, but Weekes is the more businesslike; Worrell appeared to be enjoying an afternoon's sport, whereas Weekes was on the job six hours a day. Due possibly to his wider stroke range, Weekes took more chances than did Worrell and the latter was probably, all told, the sounder in principle, but this did not extend outside the realms of actual batsmanship, for Worrell was not as capable a runner as Weekes was, nor was he as meticulous over the little accessories that make the complete batsman.

Both men were delightful characters on and off the field, cheerful and humorous. They were both match-winning cricketers. Worrell, in addition to his batting, bowled left-handed either at a pace well above medium, or slow-length stuff. Indeed, he was quite equal to the task of opening our Test attack in 1950, and whenever he bowled his slows, he kept the runs down. In the gully or at short leg Worrell took many brilliant catches which, together with his quickness of eye and footwork, were indicative of amazingly quick reflexes. He was the complete cricketer. Weekes I classed as one of the world's finest slip fielders. He had the ability to stand relaxed and what would to most players be difficult catches were made up to appear simple by clever anticipation. He bowled little in first-class cricket, but I am sure that if he had put his mind to it, he could be more than useful in this department, for here was a natural cricketer with a shrewd cricketing brain.

Clyde Walcott while being the most junior of the three, was certainly not the smallest: he is over 6 foot and a tremendously powerful man. At first sight one would be sceptical about his ability to keep wicket; such a huge man must be clumsy, one would feel. But see him stump on the leg-side the misguided batsman who lifted his back foot and you would have had cause to alter your opinion. He improved immeasurably as time went by, continual practice assisting him in developing his art, and he became far more than just a competent wicket-keeper. Over a period of time, Walcott missed little and took a lot, and he graduated into the front rank of wicket-keepers. Strong and safe, his reach enabled him to get to catches that other keepers would not consider even attempting. As a wicket-keeper–batsman he must have ranked with the best of all time.

Figures over a period of time are the most accurate means of measuring ability, and the immense value of Walcott to the West Indies team on two tours, India in 1948–49 and England in 1950, is best illustrated by the following record of his performances as a batsman and wicket-keeper in first-class matches:

	INNINGS	TNO	RUNS SC.	HS	AVERAGE
INDIA 1948–49:	22	4	1366	152	75.88
	Caught 19	Stumped 4			
ENGLAND 1950:	36	6	1674	168	55.80
	Caught 30	Stumped 18			

And even then we are not told by these analyses that he was our No. 3 batsman in India who, apart from his responsibilites as wicket-keeper, carried the batting of the team on his shoulders during the early stages of the tour playing more than one crisis Test innings. We may, too, lose sight of the fact that in England he scored no fewer than seven centuries, most of them at a time when runs were most urgently needed. Walcott, in the first Test match at Old Trafford, in the absence through injury of H. H. Johnson, took time off from keeping wicket to open our bowling. Needless to say, the 4 overs he sent down were of excellent length and little was given away in the process of removing the shine from the ball.

My respect for this powerful cricketer was unlimited. He was one of the very few who could take fast bowling by the scruff of its neck and literally tear it to pieces. Several times I have seen Walcott throw his weight on to the right foot and crash some unsuspecting fast bowler straight overhead for 6. Power was his métier. He could drive equally powerfully in either the forward or back stroke. Such driving, straight and through the covers, as we saw during his innings of 168 not out in the Lord's Test of 1950 will long be remembered by those who were fortunate enough to witness it.

Against the Australians in the West Indies in 1955, he scored five centuries in the Test matches, including one in each innings both in Trinidad and Jamaica. He also had scores of 73 and 83 – a phenomenal run – and this was against bowlers of the calibre of Lindwall, Miller, Johnston and Ron Archer.

A great leg-puller, 'Wally' was a wonderful asset to a team on tour. Few escaped his scathing tongue and woe betide him who did not accept his teasing in the spirit in which it was given!

Clyde Walcott is currently a highly successful and respected manager of several West Indies touring teams, including our all-conquering Prudential Cup winners of 1975 and 1979. There is no doubt that he has a considerable part to play in the future of West Indies cricket as an administrator.

9
Down Under 1951–52

It was while we were toasting our victory over England in the pavilion at Kennington Oval that we heard that the Australian Cricket Board had issued an invitation to the West Indies to tour Australia the following winter. Naturally we were keen as mustard to go. Hadn't we just finished beating England decisively at home? We had nothing to fear from the Aussies. The great Don had retired anyway.

We were in for a rude awakening and a chastening experience. Not for one moment did we realize that without an answer to the powerful Australian fast bowling attack, we would be found wanting on wickets which were generally fast and full of bounce.

Australian cricket was in full bloom. The majority of Bradman's 1948 team were still at their best and a team captained by Lindsay Hassett, and including Morris, Harvey, Miller, Lindwall, Johnson, Johnston, Hole, Ring and Langley, would obviously be no pushover. In fact this Australian team was, under the conditions, too good for us, and further proved that we were still comparatively immature as Test cricketers when up against a team of this class.

But I am getting ahead of my story. The bulk of our team – comprising Goddard (capt.), Atkinson, Christiani, Ferguson, Gomez, Guillen, Jones, Marshall, Rae, Rickards, Ramadhin, Stollmeyer, Trim, Valentine, Walcott, Weekes and Worrell – did the long journey by sea. Gomez and I were not so fortunate and, because of business commitments, were permitted to fly out, a journey which we did via Montreal, Toronto, Vancouver, San Francisco (where we were joined by Rae), Honolulu and Fiji, a total, in those days, of sixty-seven flying hours.

To me, it seemed that, in a seventeen-man tour party, room should have been made for another fast bowler, having regard to the opposition. We would need something to provide an answer to any rough stuff served up by Lindwall and Miller. In the event we had no one through whom we could retaliate and this proved decisive in the series. Four players who, in the event, were not selected – Frank King (fast), L. Butler (medium inswerve of the Bedser type), N. Marshall and B. Pairaudeau – had claims but to include one another player had to be left out. It did seem, however, that we had one batsman too many and one fast bowler too few.

The first mistake in a hastily arranged tour soon became apparent. We were in Sydney for nearly two weeks before the tour proper started. Nets at the No. 2 ground were hopeless so we were given the use of facilities at Cranbrook School. The nets there were so good that we all thought we were Bradmans in the making, but our euphoria was to be short-lived.

Our first commitment on the field was a testimonial game for that unique personality, Bill Ferguson, our baggage master and scorer. It was highly successful and all Australia joined in paying homage to someone who was universally popular and had made a unique contribution to the game. Bill O'Reilly and Alan McGilvray played in the match. The former was still able to 'drop them' and passed the bat of both of our star batsmen, Worrell and Weekes, more than once.

An early fixture against the Prime Minister's XI at Canberra was a highlight. The Rt Hon. R. G. 'Bob' Menzies was a great cricket enthusiast and his team was captained by Jack Fingleton, a member of the surviving Australian greats. The game started dramatically with 'Fingo' being caught at first slip off the first ball for 0. The batsman was not amused!

The dinner hosted by the Prime Minister was a wonderful occasion. He spoke fluently and held us all enthralled for an hour. I make no apology for having recorded some of his observations on the back of my menu card. Sam Loxton, in Parliament at the time, was at the receiving end of several of his caustic comments. He drew a comparison between Sam and Bill O'Reilly. 'They are both international cricketers and part-time cads,' he quipped. 'Both are ferocious cricketers, they are both bowlers – one good, one not – but both have this in common: they would like to bowl, stump, catch and eviscerate a batsman all in one ball. There is on record a time when Sam bowled a fast one, didn't like it so caught it.' He then broke into verse:

> Look out for Sam, oh gentle stumper,
> For Sam will bowl a frightful bumper,
> And follow through with fearful pleasure
> And murder the batsman for good measure.

Of Lindsay Hassett who was to captain Australia against us but who, in this game, could afford to relax, he had this to say: 'Lindsay Hassett, immortal man, I saw him today fielding at mid-on, the last refuge of mankind.'

The conclusion of his speech was full of words of wisdom: 'The world is for the people who play cricket and those who laugh and perhaps the future of the world will depend on whether these people are in the majority.' He then added, 'I shall now ask my captain, Jack Fingleton, to give a short talk on the rearing of domestic ducks.'

It was not long before we were faced with the stark reality that the tour would be no picnic. Shocks from a country XI at Newcastle were followed by more shocks from Queensland, after which we were pitchforked into the first Test at Brisbane, short of match play and form.

It was to be a great match, one of the first in Australia in which the wicket was covered throughout the game. This may not have been necessary for fine hot weather prevailed throughout and there was no need for covers.

We went into the Test without a fast bowler. Neither Jones nor Trim had been impressive so far on the tour; neither had they had enough bowling. This meant that our bowling attack consisted of Gomez, Worrell, Ramadhin, Valentine and Goddard. A great deal would depend therefore on our young spinning combination.

Goddard won the toss and we batted first and it was not long before the day's drama unfolded. Rae took the first ball from Lindwall. As we came to expect later, it was an outswinger (inswinger to the left-hander) of perfect length and direction. Allan shuffled across his wicket and tried to keep it out. He was either late with his stroke or a fraction outside the line and *crash*, the ball went into his pads. A thunderous appeal for LBW followed from the bowler and the slips. 'Not out,' said the umpire and so started the series!

At the other end, I looked heavenwards and thought, like the bowler, that Allan had got away with it. But not for long; the third ball, another of similar calibre, got the inside edge of Rae's bat and cannoned into the stumps. We were 0–1.

Keith Miller took up the attack from the other end. The newspapers said next day that he had bowled badly and off target, but there is nothing more unsettling to an opening batsman than a fast bowler moving the ball both ways on a wicket which has early morning 'life' and this was what Miller was doing. I breathed a sigh of relief when he was taken off after only 2 overs and Bill Johnston brought on, but my relief was short-lived. Relaxing somewhat I got an inside edge to a ball which lifted and was comfortably taken by Langley behind the wicket 18–2.

Strangely and quite erroneously, we had thought before the tour started that Australia may have been weak in the wicket-keeping department on the retirement of Don Tallon, but this proved to be anything but the truth. Gil Langley took fifteen catches during the series and I don't remember him missing any. Later in the tour, at a party at his home, he confided in Gerry Gomez that 'the only trouble with you, Gerry, is that you keep nicking 'em!'

Our innings never really got going, Lindwall saw to that, and we were all out for 216. Six players had got into the 20s but none had gone on to a big score, the highest being a plucky 45 from our skipper. Australia were 16–0 at the close.

The game moved quietly along next day until first Valentine and then Ramadhin were introduced, at which point a game which had begun to get out of hand became a match. Both bowlers were able to spin the ball and Ramadhin looked more like a conjurer than a bowler to the Australians, until Lindwall, missed badly before he had scored, and, to a lesser extent, Miller, hit their way out of trouble. In the end Australia led only by 10 runs on the first innings and the game was still wide open.

Our second innings was somewhat of a repetition of the first only this time it was the spinners, Ring and Johnson, who were the wicket takers. Only Weekes (70) and Gomez (55) played adequately. A turning point was when, in the last over of the day, Worrell went down the wicket to drive a ball from Ring well tossed outside the off-stump. He was stumped by a yard and the Australians capitalized on this mistake by claiming the wicket of Goddard, who went in as night watchman, caught and bowled in the same over. So 88–2 had become 88–4 and we were only 78 on with 6 wickets in hand.

It was a seesaw battle all through the third day. There was another turning point when Marshall, who was batting well with Gomez, had 'a rush of blood' and skied a slower ball from Miller to mid-off, trying to go over the top. It seemed from the ring that he might have been intimidated by the bouncers served up by the bowler earlier in the over (Roy Marshall wore spectacles). Nevertheless it was an injudicious stroke which cost us dearly.

Our innings closed at 245 and Australia needed 236 to win. The wicket would give some help to the spin-bowlers, and if we could field and catch better than we did in the first innings, we were in with a chance.

Splendidly as our two 'spin twins' bowled, they were asked to do too much. They were each given 22 overs consecutively when a short spell from Gomez and/or Worrell, both inexpensive bowlers, might have given them the breathing spell they needed. At the end of the day's play Australia were 108 for 2.

When, on the final day, Australia were 149–5 with all the recognized batsmen (except Hole) back in the pavilion, West Indies were back in the game, but a partnership between Hole and Lindwall thwarted us. The time for the new ball had long come and gone, but Goddard put all his money on Ram and Val. Even when he finally decided to take it, he rubbed the shine off in the dirt and continued with his two spinners. He was roundly criticized for this and his action called unsportsmanlike in some quarters, but he was within the laws and personally I saw nothing wrong in what he did. Where I may have disagreed with him was in his tactics of not giving his spin-bowlers some relief and at the same time presenting the batsmen with something different. The batsmen were under terrific pressure; they may have relaxed and been lulled into error, but these are the 'ifs' and 'buts' of this great game.

Australia scrambled home by 3 wickets but there were lessons to be learned. Our batting, strong as it was on paper, lacked both form and discretion. We had made obvious errors in our field-placing and our catching had been below Test standard; finally, it did not take a genius to imagine our plight if we were to be pitted against Australia on a fast wicket which was not conducive to spin. This is what we found at Sydney where the next Test match was played.

There were two games against New South Wales and Victoria between the first and second Test. We lost the first of them by 24 runs and the second was drawn. In the match against Victoria, I captained the team in the absence of Goddard who was resting. It was a source of disquiet within the team that no vice-captain had been appointed by the Board, and it was not disclosed until shortly before the match who would be asked to do the job.

In our second innings against Victoria, Rae and I put on 161 for the first wicket. It was our first decent partnership of the tour and made us both feel better about things. During this partnership, one of the little niceties of the game took place when, obviously struggling to find form, I received a friendly pat on the back from Bill Johnston between overs. 'You'll be all right, you'll come good,' he said. This didn't prevent Bill from doing his utmost to get me out and, believe me, he was anything but a friendly bowler. 'A shagga in the moss'* is what Weekes called him.

My innings of 94 ended in attempting a run to Neil Harvey at mid-wicket. There is no easier way to commit suicide.

I was privileged on this tour to have many a long talk with the three Australian radio commentators – A. G. 'Johnnie' Moyes, Vic Richardson and Alan McGilvray – and being shrewd judges of cricket and cricketers, they were of considerable help to me. Johnnie Moyes travelled around the country with us and we became firm friends. They suspected that my back-lift was too high to cope with bowlers of the pace of Lindwall and Miller and that I should try to correct this, particularly in the early overs, by taking a lower grip on the bat handle. I was to see the wisdom of their advice at first hand during the second Test at Sydney.

Hassett put West Indies in when he won the toss and Rae and I found ourselves up against the Australian fast attack on a lively wicket, Ray Lindwall bowling with a thirty-five-mile-an-hour gale behind him from the Randwick end. It was distinctly unpleasant and I was lucky to be still there at lunch with the score 68–1. Johnnie Moyes, in his book *With the West Indies in Australia 1951–52*, had this to say: 'Stollmeyer batted very attractively except for the one blemish, that of reaching into the unknown outside his off-stump. It seems to have a fatal attraction for him, like a piece of cheese for a predatory mouse.'

By a mixture of good and bad, we put up a first innings score of 362 with Worrell (64), Christiani (76), Walcott (60) and Gomez (54) all playing their part.

---

*A *shagga* is the local word for a sharp-pointed crustacean which lives hidden in sea moss around the coast of Barbados.

Australia in reply lost both openers with only 27 scored and should have been 31–3 if Walcott had been able to hold on to a chance given by Hassett off Jones. As it was Hassett went on to score 132 and, with Keith Miller (129), put the game completely out of our reach. I never tired of watching Lindsay Hassett bat. By 1951, Hassett had become largely a defensive player, but his style in defence was so neat and correct that one could not help but admire his flawless technique. He was troubled by Ramadhin when the ball turned, but then, who wasn't?

Miller was at his batting best in this innings, but it is as a bowler that I remember him most. He was the most unsettling bowler against whom I played and, of them all over the years, I liked to face his bowling the least. This wonderful character is much loved in the West Indies where he has been a frequent visitor both as player and cricket journalist. One of the great personalities of cricket, he could be as brilliant one day as he was ineffective the next, that is, if the mood did not move him.

Stories of Miller are legendary. He was a cricketer of contrasts. For instance, he took part in the Adelaide Test of this tour over the Christmas period and made no impression whatsoever on the game. He often stood with his arms folded in the slips as if completely disinterested in the proceedings. On the other hand, I saw him win the first Test for Australia against the West Indies in Jamaica in 1955 with a magnificent piece of new ball bowling, and when the back of our batting was broken by him, he tossed the ball to someone else as if to say, 'Finish it off now – the important work has been done.' It was Keith, the journalist, who was the author of one unforgettable phrase: some statistician had discovered that, in the West Indies vs Australia Test match at Port of Spain in 1973, Lance Gibbs had bowled 25,000 balls in Test cricket, 'and that's a lot bf balls' was Miller's published comment.

I firmly believe that it was during this innings of 129 by Miller that the potential menace of Ramadhin to the Australian batsmen was overcome. It was Miller's obvious dominance over the bowler in the circumstances that had a psychological effect far beyond appearances at the time.

The match got completely out of hand when after 7 wickets were down for 372, Lindwall and Ring added 85 runs, aided and abetted by fielding lapses and faulty tactics. Lindwall had taken great toll of our bowlers in three consecutive Test innings, but he was very much an off-side player and a driver of the ball, especially through the cover area. He was far less strong on the leg side, but we had not learned the lessons of Brisbane. The Australian innings closed at 517, a lead of 155.

When we started our second innings, I had a runner for a leg injury sustained while fielding, and it was not long before I was struck on the head from a fast one from Lindwall and felled like an ox. In retrospect, what happened subsequently was amusing although not so at the time. As the ball hit my head with a resounding smack, the last thing I heard before losing consciousness was Ian Johnson, who was at first slip, shouting 'Catch it' to Morris at short leg. He thought the ball had struck the bat! Then, as I was recovering my senses some thirty seconds or so later, I heard Ray say, jokingly, words to the effect that, 'When I drop them, they usually fall on their wickets.' But that was not all; there was a sequel when, in the Sydney Morning Herald next day, I read that 'An X-ray of Stollmeyer's head revealed exactly nothing'! I went on to score 35 but it would probably have been better to have retired and resume my innings later for I cannot truthfully say that I remember much else about what happened that afternoon. The bump on the back of my head where the ball hit me is still there to this day.

We were out for 290 in our second innings and I was forced to watch from the ring while Australia made the 136 needed for victory. They lost only 3 wickets in making the runs but I could not help feeling that we had lost the match by not taking the chances offered us.

It was palpably clear by this time that our team was not playing as well as it should. Our fielding and catching had been lamentable and our batsmen were getting out frequently when well set before they compiled a big score. At the same time, we were also being outplayed by the Australians tactically.

Things deteriorated still further when we were annihilated by South Australia, the margin of defeat being 227 runs. Our morale had reached an all-time low. In this match, Worrell had the dubious distinction of making a 'king pair'. Out to Geoff Noblet in both innings, first ball. There was a strong feeling in our camp that Noblet's bowling action was unfair.

The rot continued at Perth where we were again beaten, this time by one wicket by a moderate Western Australia team. There was one small consolation: John Trim, who had not taken a first-class wicket thus far on the tour, had figures of 10 for 112. I smiled to myself when John exclaimed to the Governor of Western Australia, 'We didn't concentrate and we lost the match – these Australian fast bowlers, they concentrate all the time.' A delightful character was J. Trim.

Better things were in store for us, at a time when we least expected it.

Adelaide was the scene of the third Test which was played over the Christmas season. Adelaide is also the home of Sir Donald Bradman in whose company some of us spent many enjoyable hours. If there is anyone living who is more knowledgeable on the game of cricket than this cricketing knight, then I would like to know him. The Don brought his great knowledge and perception into cricket administration after he ceased to play the game actively and in this area his contribution was in no way less great.

He has helped many struggling visiting cricketers to Australia. He certainly tried to help us despite being one of Australia's selectors. I remember him asking John Goddard a pertinent question: 'How many batsmen have you had out caught on this tour, John?' This loaded question referred, of course, to our field placing which to many of us had seemed, on occasions, to be inexplicable. It also highlighted the fact that we seemed to be paying little attention to opposing batsmen's strengths and weaknesses.

Stories about the Don are many and legendary. Some are no doubt true, some have been embellished, and I apologize to him if the two that follow are inaccurate either in content or detail. One was told to us by Jack Fingleton who captained New South Wales when the Don was in his heyday. Apparently Bill Brown, the Queensland captain, was passing through Sydney and met up with Jack who offered the advice that he had been able to contain the great man after he was set by a certain form of attack supported by suitable field placing. Armed with this useful advice, when South Australia played Queensland shortly afterwards and the Don had got to thirty and appeared set, Brown took some time to set his field and to put his plan of containment into effect. Bradman is supposed to have walked up the wicket and remarked to Brown, 'Billy, I see your little plan. I was going to get a hundred and give it away, now I'm going to get two.' The inevitable double century followed.

While watching the beginning of the first Test at Brisbane, Sir Donald was sitting among the players in the small players' pavilion.

Jim Burke, Australia's twelfth man, was sitting in front of him. Some eager West Indians sitting behind claim to having overheard the following exchange between Bradman and Burke. Bradman: 'Jimmy, what do you think about when a bowler is coming up to bowl at you?' Burke: 'Well, I would have found out something about him first, and be looking out for what he might be doing with the ball.' Bradman: 'Jimmy, you know what I used to think about? Where am I going to hit the next one for four.' Good advice? Maybe you'd like to try it some time.

I have to my great satisfaction and benefit kept up a stimulating correspondence with Sir Donald, and on several issues of cricket administration and the laws of the game, his opinions and advice have been of considerable help and encouragement. On one of these subjects, the LBW law, I will elaborate in a later chapter.

It was a sad and disappointed lot of West Indians who went in to the third Test at Adelaide. A further setback had emerged: Clyde Walcott's back had acted up, he was out of the match and we were told that he would no longer be able to keep wicket.

Allan Rae's form had been such that the opening partnership we had developed between us had to be broken. This was naturally a source of great regret to me for, over the years, we had developed a wonderful rapport and understanding. Allan was having difficulty in negotiating the short fast ball (he wasn't the only one). In India he had played the hook but it frequently cost him his wicket. He had cut the stroke out by this time, but had not yet found an answer to the short rising ball.

Roy Marshall took Rae's place and Guillen came in for Walcott. Atkinson was preferred to Jones, his fielding and late order batting weighing in his favour. Our attack was the same as in the first Test – hardly likely to cause the Australian batsmen sleepless nights, unless the slowish Adelaide wicket took spin.

The fates were on our side this time, however. Hassett was, on the eve of the match, pronounced medically unfit and he was replaced by Geoff Noblet instead of by a batsman, so the Australians put an unbalanced side into the field.

It had rained quite heavily on the morning of the match which got under way more than half an hour late. Morris, deputizing for Hassett, won the toss and decided to bat on a wicket which had more than one soft patch on it. It was a decision which surprised me at the time and it proved to be the wrong one. Two wickets were down with only 5 runs on the board and Worrell had got them both. The ball was stopping and lifting from time to time at one end, but this surprisingly was not the end at which the wickets fell. At lunch Australia were 41–5, and shortly before three o'clock they were all out for 82. Worrell bowling into the 'good' end had a bag of 6–38. Fine bowling indeed, but who could have possibly conceived the day's events beforehand?

We had looked a different team in the field, businesslike and more confident of what we were doing. Was it because of an exhaustive team meeting and tactical discussion the evening before the game? Whatever it was, we looked like a team for the first time on the tour.

Our joy was short-lived, however, because the Australians are never beaten, and at tea we had lost 5 for 51. As the afternoon progressed and wickets continued to fall, thought was given to whether we should declare and get Australia back in while the wicket was still impaired. In those days, however, the laws under which we were playing did not allow declarations on the first day of a match. Our innings eventually closed at 105, a lead of 23.

Johnson and Langley started Australia's second innings and the enemy found themselves 20–2 at the close. It was a day when so much happened to so many. Freakish cricket, yes, but very much worth watching. Twenty-two wickets had fallen in the day's play.

On the Monday, the game began to slip out of our grasp. Ring and Langley added 61, the former by some lusty hitting and his 67 was by far the top score of the innings. Australia eventually managed 255 with Valentine securing 6–102.

Set 233 to win, we achieved victory by 6 wickets, but not before we had our share of scares, and it was not as easy as it appeared from the figures. Gomez and Christiani were there at the end, both not out in the 40s, but everyone played their part. The game finished on Christmas Day and we had won in three days. It was the finest Christmas present we could have chosen for ourselves. Also the tour had been revived from the dead, so to speak. We immediately went on to Melbourne for the fourth Test with our hopes high and a new spirit in the regiment.

Marshall was unfit, having pulled a muscle at Adelaide, and was replaced by Rickards, while it was decided that a fast bowler would be more than useful on the Melbourne wicket and Trim replaced Atkinson.

Whether winning the toss was an advantage or not, we soon found ourselves in trouble against the three-pronged fast Australian attack. Our first three were out with only 30 on the board but, thanks to Worrell (108, his only really good Test innings on the tour) and to a lesser extent Gomez and Christiani, coupled with some very substandard fielding by the Australians, we totalled 272.

Australia fared even worse than we did and were all out for 216, the last 4 wickets falling for the addition of 2 runs. The burly Trim had more than justified his selection with 5–34, but Ramadhin and Valentine had both bowled as well as they ever did.

In the twenty-five minutes' batting time before the close of play, we lost 2 wickets. In fact, we were 2 down with no runs on the board. Night watchmen Guillen and Goddard both got ducks before Rickards stayed with me to the close. Blame was attached to Goddard for his altering the batting order, but to me this was unjustified for in the first innings Rickards had not looked the part of an opener.

The seesaw battle continued throughout the next day with first the West Indies and then Australia gaining the advantage. The ever-reliable Gomez and I both got into the 50s, but there was not much support from the others this time and the innings closed at 203.

Australia needed 260 to win in the last innings and, with the wicket occasionally doing the unpredictable and inclined to keep low as well, we felt we were on the right side of the match. At the close of play on the third day, Australia were 68–1 with Morris out and Moroney, their new opener, retired hurt but expected to bat next day. The game was evenly poised.

What happened on the final day of this game is a part of West Indies cricket history. It was an unforgettable – and indeed unforgivable – day's cricket as far as we were concerned.

Australia needed 192 to win with 9 wickets in hand, Hassett and Harvey together. Valentine soon bowled Harvey between bat and pad with a beauty. Moroney re-entered and was first missed by Valentine, a c. and b. chance, and then became a victim of Ramadhin. Miller perished by the hit wicket route, but Hassett was impenetrable. The new ball, taken with the score at 144, disposed of Hole but Lindwall was untroubled by it and it was not until Valentine returned to the attack that he was out caught at the wicket off Ramadhin. Valentine, the real danger man, was being handled by Hassett.

Above: Stollmeyer's Castle, a landmark in Trinidad, built by my grandfather. It is now the property of the Government of Trinidad and Tobago

Right: The family gathers at on Valmont in 1956 for my parents' golden wedding anniversary. *From left to right (in order of age):* Rex, Alex, André, Hugh, Victor, Daphne and Jeffrey

Inset: Mon Valmont

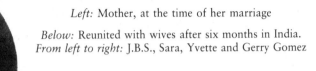

Left: Mother, at the time of her marriage

Below: Reunited with wives after six months in India. *From left to right:* J.B.S., Sara, Yvette and Gerry Gomez

Right: The J.B.S. clan in 1973. *From left to right:* Kathi (seventeen), Allan (twenty-two), Donald (twenty) and Brian (nineteen)

Signing autographs at the nets. Lord's Nursery, 1939

The West Indies Cricket team, England, 1939.
Standing, from left to right:
W. Ferguson (scorer), G. Gomez, J.B. Stollmeyer, L.G. Hylton,
T. Johnson, C.B. Clarke, H.P. Bayley, E.A.V. Williams; *sitting*: G. Headley, I. Barrow,
R.S. Grant (captain), J.M. Kidney (manager), J.H. Cameron, L.N. Constantine, E.A. Martindale;
front: K.H. Weekes, J.E.D. Sealy, V.H. Stollmeyer

Above: Opening the Trinidad innings with Victor, against Barbados in the Goodwill Intercolonial Series at Queen's Park, Trinidad, in 1941

Left: Learie Nicholas Constantine

Above: Donald George Bradman

Right: With 'Mas'' George (Headley), Calcutta, 1948

A controversial decision. Weekes run out for 90 at Madras. Had he made 100,
it would have been his sixth consecutive century in Test cricket – a world record.
Also in the picture are wicket-keeper P. Sen, V. Hazare, and G.E. Gomez (non-striker)

Clyde Walcott. 'Power was his métier.' Madras, 1949

Top left: His Highness the Maharajah of Patiala
in full cricket regalia

Top right: Elephant riding at Patiala.
Bob Christiani is draped across Jumbo's neck

Above: Queen's Royal College, Trinidad

Top: We arrive at Patiala
after thirty-one hours by rail

Above: The team is entertained by
Prime Minister Nehru at his residence nine months
after the partition of India

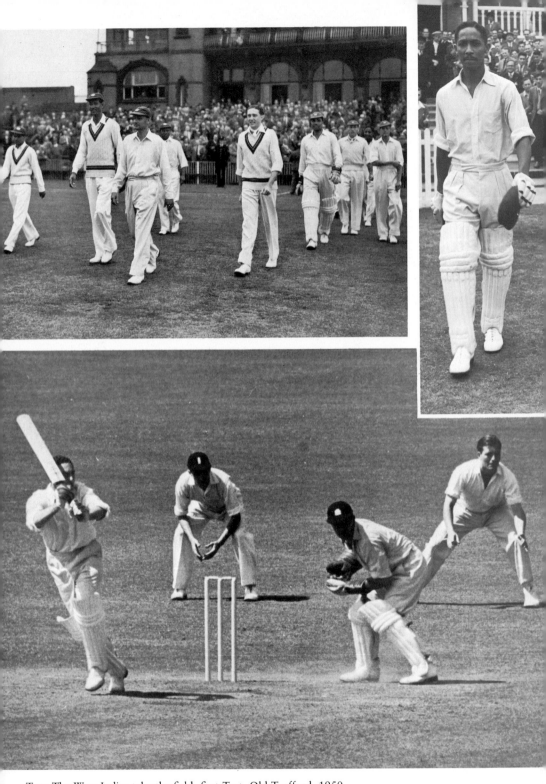

Top: The West Indies take the field, first Test, Old Trafford, 1950

Centre: Weekes and Worrell during their big stand together in the third Test, Trent Bridge, 1950

Above: Playing Bedser to leg, third Test, Trent Bridge, 1950

Top: Ram and Val lunch at Windsor Castle, 1950

Above: Being presented to His Majesty King George VI at Lord's, 1950.
Plum Warner is on the left

Goddard rubs the shine off the
ball under the watchful eye
of umpire H. Elphinstone.
The bowler is Ramadhin, the
batsmen are Harvey and Morris.
First Test, Brisbane, 1951

Hit on the head by Lindwall, second Test, Sydney, 1951.
'When I hit them, they usually fall on the wicket'

Ken Archer c. Weekes
b. Gomez, second Test,
Sydney, 1951

Miller appeals for LBW against me. He was not amused when the decision
went against him. Second Test, Sydney, 1951

Raymond Russell Lindwall

Frank Worrell demonstrates the back cut –
a model for the young player

The majesty and perfection of Len Hutton's cover drive.
England vs West Indies, The Oval, 1950

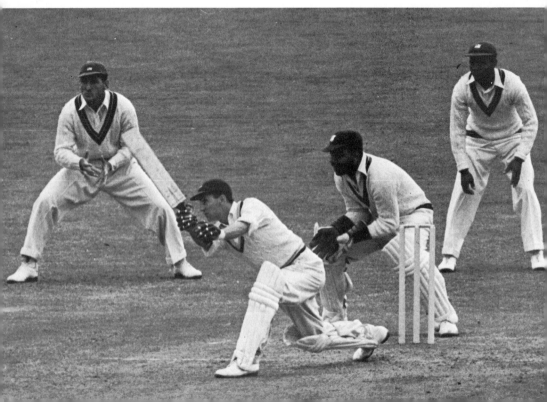

Above: Muhammad Ali watches the West Indies play Middlesex at Lord's in 1966. With him are M.C. Cowdrey and P.E. Richardson

Left: Fred Trueman prays before facing up to the bowling of Wes Hall

West Indies vs England, fourth Test, 1954. *Standing, from left to right:* K. Ramadhin, B. Pairaudeau, J.K. Holt, F. King, D. Atkinson, C. McWatt, W. Ferguson; *sitting:* C.L. Walcott, F.M. Worrell (vice-captain), J.B. Stollmeyer (captain), H. Burnett (manager), E. Weekes

Above: Lance R. Gibbs, master of flight and spin

Left: Garfield St Aubyn Sobers, a one-man team

Above: Clive Lloyd. He will be sorely missed when he retires

Left: Viv Richards. Don't bowl to him on his pads

Above: Sunil Gavaskar, 'the real master'
Right: Joel Garner – two bowlers in one

The West Indies in England, 1966. *Back row, from left to right*: J.S. Solomon,
B.F. Butcher, S.M. Nurse, J.L. Hendriks, P.D. Lashley, D.W. Allan and D. Pye (masseur);
middle row: W.F.B. Hoyos (assistant manager), R.C. Brancker, D.A.J. Holford,
R.A. Cohen, C.C. Griffith, M.C. Carew, E.D. McMorris, J.A. Griffith (baggage master);
front row: L.R. Gibbs, R.B. Kanhai, J.B. Stollmeyer (manager), G. St A. Sobers (captain),
C.C. Hunte (vice-captain), W.W. Hall

TWO MOMENTS OF CELEBRATION

Top: After our first Test victory in England,
jubilant West Indian supporters, including calypsonian 'Lord Kitchener',
invade the sacred turf at Lord's

Above: Presenting Viv Richards, captain of the Combined Islands, with the
Shell Shield at the Castle Harbour Hotel, Antigua, 1981

When tea was taken, Australia needed 56 with 4 wickets in hand. Left with Hassett to get these runs were Johnson, Ring, Langley and Johnston. Meanwhile John Trim had pulled a muscle and was not on the field. A second substitute, Rae, was fielding for Rickards whose leg muscle problem had recurred. Johnson was short-lived and immediately afterwards, prize of prizes, Hassett was LBW to a beauty from Valentine. His century was more than a captain's knock; it was the greatest contributory factor to winning the match for his side, but at his dismissal the match was again in our grasp. Langley was LBW to Valentine at 222 so 38 were still required with only Ring and the inept Bill Johnston to score them.

An epic partnership between the two followed, and the fact that they made the runs is a tribute both to their strength of character and their approach to the job. On the other hand, our team was exposed for what it was: unreliable in a crisis, with many of its members certainly lacking in the knowledge not only of what to do, but how to put it into practice.

Our tactics should have been clear. Put the fielders back and give the single to the hard-hitting Ring. Close them in on Johnston who was obviously going for the short single to give Ring the strike. Ring actually hit two 4s over a mid-wicket in no man's land, while Johnston appeared to get his short singles with ease. Our team morale worsened when, with 10 runs needed, Ramadhin left the field limping. There were now no fewer than three substitutes aboard. Valentine, our trump card, was brought back into the attack but it was too late: Australia won by 1 wicket and the series as a contest had been spoiled. It should have been two-all but Australia now led by 3–1, an unassailable position.

The feat performed by the two 'Richmond Tigers', Ring and Johnston, was suitably celebrated by their club a couple of nights later. The members of the West Indies team were invited, but only two attended, Allan Rae and myself. I did not consider this absence to be in good taste. We had lost a great contest fairly and we owed it to our hosts to be with them in their hour of victory.

As a result of the way in which our team reacted when under pressure, I made a vow that, when I returned to the West Indies, I would involve myself fully in the training of promising young cricketers in the finer points of the game so that, when confronted with a similar situation, they would react sensibly. This was to afford me many hours of satisfaction in the fifties and early sixties.

The tour continued in a more pleasurable vein. We enjoyed the beauty of Hobart and its environs, won a light-hearted second encounter with Victoria which heralded Allan Rae's return to form and his inclusion in the team for the fifth and final Test at Sydney.

At this stage of the tour, John Goddard was distinctly unwell. He had lost some 25 lb in weight and was seemingly in a state of depression. Things had not gone well for him on the field and he worried a great deal. Often an underrated cricketer, John had an abundance of guts and, as an all-rounder, could be counted to make a contribution in one or other department of the game. He was, however, only a shadow of himself and he unselfishly decided to stand down on the morning of the match and I was asked to captain the team in his place.

Although the series had already been sewn up in Australia's favour, the difference between the two teams in the Test matches had been so minimal that I felt that if we could marshal all of our resources we would give them a run for their money, even though our chances at Sydney, where the wicket suited their pace men, were less than elsewhere.

It was a hot steamy day when Hassett won the toss and elected to bat. It was to be another dramatic day's cricket in which no fewer than 19 wickets fell for 180 runs. The reason was the tremendous humidity, the lively wicket and some remarkable bowling and catching. Gomez, moving the ball both ways at medium pace, destroyed the Australian batting with career-best figures of 7 for 55, and Australia was tumbled out for 116. What a tower of strength Gerry was to West Indies cricket. Strong as an ox, he never gave in nor did he give anything away on the field or, for that matter, between the wickets. I was as pleased as punch. We had bowled and caught splendidly and we had looked like a Test team in the field.

However, my pride and pleasure was short-lived. The Australian team of that period thrived on the principle of 'anything you can do I can do better'. In retrospect, if our medium pacers Gomez and Worrell had been so successful with swerve and seam, we may have reasonably suspected the trio of Lindwall, Miller and Johnston to do even better. They certainly did bowl beautifully and, helped by the atmosphere and the slightly grassy wicket, we were hustled out for 78. Only four batsmen had got into double figures and the three Ws had only been able to muster a mere 7 runs between them!

Well as Lindwall and Miller bowled, there was a certain lack of resolution in our batting and one detected a tendency of some of the less qualified players to seek the company of the square-leg umpire when up against this great pair.

So we were 38 in arrears on the first innings when I thought we would be at least 100 ahead after Australia had collapsed for 116.

Conditions were not the same when Australia batted on the Saturday. The humidity had gone out of the atmosphere and it was much more of a batsman's wicket. They were 216-4 at the close, Colin McDonald, playing in his first Test, made 62 and there was another sound defensive innings of 64 from Hassett. It was palpably clear that the wicket was more suited to fast bowling, and well as Ramadhin and Valentine toiled, they could extract little or no turn.

A bad fielding mistake on the Monday morning saw Hole let off when he should have been run out by yards. He was only 5 then and went on to score 62. It was probably the turning point of the match.

Hole was inclined to overplay the sweep shot. He often took the ball off his stumps and did not always keep it down. I decided to attack him in this area, adjusting Ramadhin's field accordingly. It proved to be a mistake. The law of averages didn't work for me in this instance and too many 4s, which we could ill afford, were given away.

Meanwhile, Miller had been at his dashing best, scoring a swash-buckling 69, and although the new ball disposed of the Australians reasonably quickly, we found ourselves facing the daunting task of making 416 in the last innings. At close of play we had scored 112 of these for the loss of 2 wickets and I had not given up hope.

Continuing along with Weekes the next day, we were being subjected to a number of bumpers from Lindwall in particular. Weekes hooked at one of these and Neil Harvey, of all people, dropped him at long-leg. Knowing as I did that much would depend on a long partnership between us, I felt disposed to counsel Everton against repeating the stroke. It seemed to me that he was courting suicide. Almost immediately afterwards, Ray served him up another. It looked to me from the non-striker's end as if Weekes started to play the hook then decided against it; the ball hit the top of his horizontal bat and skied up for Langley to take the catch. While I must accept some of the blame for his dismissal, I felt sure I was right in asking him to refrain from repeating the stroke under the circumstances of the fast wicket and large outfield.

At lunch we were 189 for 3 and I had been joined by Worrell who dug himself in. But the fates played their part soon after. I was out immediately after the interval, LBW to Lindwall for 104, and shortly after this Worrell, in backing up, slipped and Richie Benaud, playing in his first Test, threw down the wicket. Our fate had been sealed. The rest of the batting folded up and we were all out for 213. It was a disappointing performance by a team which had promised much but fulfilled little on the tour.

What were the lessons to be learned from the Australian experience? There were many. Our batsmen would have to be more professional in their approach. We needed to find some young fast bowlers so that we would have bowling to suit all conditions and, thirdly, more attention would have to be paid to our catching, throwing and out cricket generally. But even if we could correct all these flaws in the team's make-up, we would not win Test matches against the best opposition unless our forces could be welded into a fighting unit which instinctively knew its purpose on the field of play.

Some of the lessons learned in Australia were put into effect in New Zealand to which beautiful country we flew for two Test matches.

The powerful New Zealand combination of 1949 had been depleted by the absence of such stalwarts as Wally Hadlee, Merv Wallace, Martin Donnelly and Jack Cowie, and some of their new blood had not yet come to hand.

We won the first of the Tests, a low-scoring game played at Lacaster Park, Christchurch, by 5 wickets. Christchurch is the garden city of New Zealand, but the weather for most of the game was overcast and gloomy and the wicket uncertain. Ramadhin was in his element and had the majority of the opposition guessing. It was not a convincing win, however, and apart from two fine innings from Frank Worrell, we still looked an indifferent batting team. The spectre of Australia was still with us.

By the time we moved on to Auckland for the second Test, form and confidence had been restored, and sent in to bat by Bert Sutcliffe on what looked to be a wicket full of coarse weeds but turned out to be a very good batting strip, we went on a run spree.

Our first innings totalled 546–6 (Stollmeyer 152, Walcott 115, Worrell 100, Rae 99, Weekes 51). There is no doubt that we were relishing the absence of Lindwall, Miller, Johnston and Co. and made hay while the sun shone.

I personally welcomed the return of Allan Rae to the team. Our close relationship based on mutual understanding and trust has been maintained in later life when we have continued to share as partners the burden of West Indies cricket administration and oft-times have represented our Board at the International Cricket Conference. To be associated with Allan over the years both on and off the field has been a rewarding experience, for he is entirely unselfish and utterly fearless with a keen legal mind but absolutely courteous in the presentation of his views. Above all he loves the game of cricket – and in particular West Indies cricket.

An incident took place early in our long opening partnership of 197 in this Test which is worthy of record in a day and age when niceties are no longer to be encountered in the arena of Test matches.

Allan was only 9 when, in backing up, he slipped and fell on to the turf some distance out of his ground. Alec Moir was the bowler and the ball was swiftly returned to him. Alec, quite deliberately, allowed the batsman to regain his crease. I have neither seen nor heard of the like in any class of cricket and this incident must rank with the greatest of sporting gestures ever to be recorded in the annals of Test cricket.

There was a rather unfortunate sequel to the incident. At the end of the over, Allan came down the wicket to me and said, 'Jeff, I don't feel happy about what Alec has done, I'm going to have a go at him and give him a chance to get me out.' In the event, Rae hit Moir out of sight and out of the attack as well!

Rain put paid to our chances of winning the match. New Zealand scored only 160 in their first innings and following on were 17–1 in the second, but the final day was washed out.

And so we wended our various ways back to the other side of the world, chastened by our cricketing experiences 'down under'.

10

The Aftermath of Australia

After our return from the Australia–New Zealand tour, the next encounter for us would be India's first visit to the West Indies.

Although we had been successful in defeating England at home, I was all too aware of the naïve approach to the serious business of Test cricket, not only by our captain John Goddard, but equally by some of the members of our team. Cricket at the top level requires study, and captaincy embraces knowledge of human nature. All men are different and individuals require separate attention and treatment. The ability to handle men, unfortunately, is seldom given to the young and inexperienced.

I felt that we were not making the most of our team's ability because many of our players were not sufficiently trained in the finer points of the game, nor were we paying sufficient attention to tactics and strategy. Surely anyone who aspires to play at Test level must try to learn not only cricket technique but also cricket tactics? A player may get tired of bowling the same ball or playing the same strokes, but can he ever tire of the new situations that occur in each day of each match, situations that must be met and dealt with promptly by the team's captain? And if the men under him are not alive to what is going on and what they should be doing, errors which may otherwise have been avoided are the inevitable result.

It was as a result of these intense feelings that as captain of Trinidad I resorted to a certain policy when Trinidad met Barbados in 1951 before our team was selected to tour Australia. The matches played in Barbados were part of the trials for selection for the Australian tour.

Trinidad were without three of her star players – Gomez, Ramadhin and Trestrail – and we were meeting our arch-rivals Barbados at Kensington Oval, Bridgetown. The Barbados team at full strength included eight Test players and their batting line-up of Roy Marshall, Hunte, Walcott, Weekes, the Atkinson brothers, Goddard and Norman Marshall was, to say the least, strong – especially so on their home ground.

In the first match we found ourselves in trouble. Batting second, we were 84 runs behind on the first innings. It was imperative that we should not allow Barbados to score rapidly in their second innings or we should find ourselves in a hopeless position, with playing for a draw over a long period on a possibly deteriorating wicket, the inevitable consequence.

Shortly after the commencement of the Barbados second innings, I decided on employing defensive tactics to carefully set fields. Jones who had already proved his ability to bowl for long spells at the batsman's pads and Asgarali, primarily a batsman but who could bowl accurately at medium pace, were employed to keep the fearsome Barbados batsmen at bay. This they did to great effect, and on the crucial penultimate day's play, the might of Barbados batting was confined to 122–3 in 210 minutes on a perfect pitch with a lightning-fast outfield on the small Kensington ground.

At all events there were boos and jeers from the crowd which, no doubt, had come out to see the great players of Barbados plunder the Trinidad bowling under conditions made to order for batting.

Eventually Barbados were all out for 168 the next day and Trinidad thus had a chance of winning. The game was subsequently drawn when Trinidad lost early wickets by the run-out route in the second innings.

I was not a little upset when the *Barbados Advocate*, a well-respected daily newspaper, ran consecutive editorials that were highly critical of my tactics which, incidentally, had been used on more than one occasion by West Indies teams in the immediate past.

Some excerpts from these editorials which reflected little credit on my sportsmanship are:

It was indeed unfortunate that many schoolboys were at Kensington on Saturday to see how the game of cricket should not be played, and how one of the greatest outdoor sports, devised to test the skill, determination and sportsmanlike qualities of the players, can be made to look ridiculous by grown men.

No one who saw the game on Saturday will continue to wonder why, in certain countries, cricket no longer has the support it formerly did.

Mr Stollmeyer let down Trinidad badly.

His team may not be world beaters but they certainly are not such a third-rate combination that a spirit of defeatism should have been their sole contribution to a game which still had almost two full days of play remaining . . .

It is to be hoped that the defeatist tactics will not be copied by local club captains in the belief that because an international player adopted them they are stamped with the hallmark of great captaincy.

The game of cricket will only continue to be popular as long as it is played in the spirit in which it is intended and true sportsmen are ready and willing to pit their skill one against the other and to try for victory at all times but to accept defeat gracefully should they fail to win.

The laws of cricket have evolved over the long years of the game's existence. New tactics will continue to be discovered and if, as in this instance and in the case of 'body line' in 1932–33, legislation is required to meet a particular circumstance then so be it.

It is completely wrong to ask and expect any captain in first-class competitive cricket not to do his utmost within the laws of the game to win. The reason he has been given the job in the first place is to ensure that his team has the best possible chance of winning.

When this form of attack was outlawed some time later, and the rule whereby only two fielders are allowed behind square leg was introduced, I was among the first to approve. The Indians of 1953 in the West Indies used this tactic to great effect against us, and when at the receiving end I could easily see how the game could be spoiled and brought into disrepute by its indiscriminate use. It was eventually going to become commonplace and was used in 1953 by England against Australia at Leeds and I again employed it in 1954 in the Test match against England in Jamaica after similar tactics had been used against us by England in the previous innings.

My contention is that strategy and tactics in cricket are forever evolving and long may it be so, for it adds the variety and spice so necessary to the enjoyment of the discerning spectator. Undoubtedly there is, however, a line to be clearly drawn between good tactics and sharp practice.

A. G. 'Johnnie' Moyes, in one of his letters to me after our return from Australia, had this to say: 'I agree that West Indies could beat anyone other than the Australians and you have enough natural ability to beat our chaps, however, lack of knowledge of the finer points of the game – so many of your chaps were guilty in this regard – prevented it.'

It was not entirely surprising, therefore, that the West Indies Board decided on a change of policy and appointed a new captain for the home series against India.

Having been appointed to the job, I set about trying to find out as much as possible about the Indians who had been selected to tour. They had recently been badly beaten by England in England, and Fred Trueman, then an unknown tearaway fast bowler, had bowled with devastating effect against them. Our problem was that we had no comparable bowler. Frank King was the only possibility and he had little experience or control at that stage of his career. We would have to depend on the trusted spin combination of Ram and Val and it was spin on which the Indian batsmen were brought up.

The best cricket seen on this tour was when that wonderful leg-spin-googly bowler, Subhash Gupte, now married and living in Trinidad, bowled so well and accurately to the three Ws, with the likes of Gadkari, Umrigar and Gaekwad patrolling the covers like hawks, swooping down and knocking the stumps out of the ground with their returns to the wicket.

There was little doubt that we were the better team all round. So much so that, as soon as we found ourselves in the ascendance with the need to press on for quick runs, the Indians resorted to 'leg theory' effectively exploited by Ramchand, and runs became very difficult to get. I was now at the receiving end of my own medicine!

This was the case in the first Test in Trinidad. Normally we might have chased the 274 needed in 160 minutes but against such an attack it would have been an impossible task.

It was, however, a happy tour and there was much goodwill between the two teams. It was indeed a pleasure to meet most of our visitors some twenty-seven years later in Bombay during the Golden Jubilee celebrations of Indian cricket which I attended as President of the West Indies Board.

West Indians are normally very fond of their Carnival which took place shortly before the Trinidad Test. Several of our players

participated in the 'jump-up' on J'ouvert* morning, with the consequence that there were front-page photographs of the cricketing
revellers in the newspapers. While 'playing mas' we met some of the
Indian players in a car driving through the streets, but our efforts
to get them to join in the revelry regrettably failed.

Carnival goes on for two days, ending at midnight on Shrove
Tuesday. The Test match started on the following Thursday and
when, in the first over, I dropped a relatively simple catch at second
slip from Mankad off King, cries of 'too much carnival' not surprisingly reverberated around the ground.

Everton Weekes continued where he had left off against the
Indians a couple of years earlier. He scored a magnificent 207 in
this match and seldom failed to make a big score during the series.

The only Test finished was the second played in Barbados, and
this was because the wicket was of uncertain bounce and it was a
relatively low-scoring game. It turned out to be an interesting match
in which, batting first, we always held a slight advantage, and it was
Ramadhin who clinched victory for the West Indies, India only
managing 129 in the final innings.

The wicket had deteriorated gradually during the game, keeping
lower and lower as it progressed. In our second innings I advised
our batsmen to make up their minds to play forward even to balls
short of a length as long as they were pitched on the wicket. My
top score of 54 was a result of strictly adhering to this principle.

When India started their last innings, Ramadhin, quickly on, was
asked to concentrate on bowling his off-spinner and quicker ball on
the line of the off-stump. 'Forget the leg-spinner,' I said. 'We can't
give anything away.' These instructions he carried out to the letter,
and from his low delivery, many balls crept along the ground,
presenting insoluble problems to the batsmen. He ended with 5–26
off 24.5 overs and won us the match.

Clarence Skinner, his mentor, was a spectator and with a broad
smile said to me after the game, 'Jeff, none of them could tell which
way he was turning.' Tongue in cheek, I agreed, and left Clarence
deservedly in a state of heavenly bliss.

The third Test due to be played in Guyana was transferred to

---

*'J'ouvert' is the opening of Carnival when revellers 'jump-up' to the calypso
beat of the steel and brass bands on the streets. In those days, it commenced at 5
a.m. on the Monday before Ash Wednesday.

Trinidad after prolonged rain in that country indicated that there would be no chance of starting it.

At the end of the match which was always likely to be drawn on the true jute matting wicket, it became clear to me that if Trinidad, the island which had the most extensive accommodation, the largest crowds, and made the most money, was to be the venue for two Test matches in a home series, then it was time to lay down a grass wicket at the Queen's Park Oval.

The reason for the long delay in the laying down of a grass wicket was principally the ravages of the mole-cricket, an insect with 'claws' (mandibles) which cut through the grass roots. Insecticides had long since been discovered to keep these predators away, however, so this was no longer a problem. A turf wicket had successfully been laid a year or two earlier at Pointe-à-Pierre, so there seemed to be no valid reason for any further postponement of the exercise. I made this the subject of my speech at the official dinner for the Indian team. The authorities took heed and I was among those commissioned to seek out the correct soil for the purpose. This exercise was done the following year.

Guyana was the venue for the fourth Test, but before that there came the selection of the team for the match. I have never, in all my time as captain or selector, known such chaos.

For the Guyana Test, I was surprised when confronted with the suggestion that the resourceful Gomez, who admittedly had been having difficulties with Gupte, should be replaced. I fought against this but to no avail and his replacement, Miller, who had been accompanying the team around the Caribbean as a reserve player, was selected. Miller was hardly Test standard and it proved to be the only Test in which he ever played. There was another selection which mystified me even more, an insistence that G. L. Wight, an opening batsman of a purely defensive nature, should be included. This, to me, was complete madness, for not only were B. H. Pairaudeau and I the recognized opening pair, but we needed to do everything in our power to introduce further aggression into the team in order to press on to try and beat our opponents, whose first instincts had been to play for a draw unless a collapse and the opportunity for a win presented itself.

It was as a result of representations made after the tour that the system of selection was changed, and for the following tour by England, the Selection Committee consisted of the captain, vice-captain and the 'resident' selector. This at least provided continuity but the change was short-lived to the detriment of our cricket over the next two decades. The move was considered to be the first evidence of 'player power'.

The Guyana Test, also spoiled by rain, was drawn but it was not without its moments of drama.

Winning the toss, India were 182 for 6 at the close of play on the first day. It had rained heavily overnight but I was happy in the knowledge that the wicket was covered.

Surprise of surprises, I met bleak faces on entering the ground the next morning. Berkeley Gaskin, that knowledgeable cricketer-administrator, was first with the news. Someone had thrown a lighted cigarette on the tarpaulins. Water had come through the covers and there was a wet spot at one end.

It was more than a spot, it was a wet patch. A quick mental calculation followed, for there was Hazare, my opposite number, coming off the ground as I was going to inspect the damage. 'We can't possibly start,' said Vijay. Quick as a flash, 'I agree with you,' I rejoined.

A 'sticky', if only at one end, and a slow outfield meant that, with accurate bowlers such as Ramchand, Phadkar and Mankad, we could be bundled out for next to nothing and we were already one up in the series. And so, despite the fact that the sun was out and there was a full house, neither of us was in favour of continuing the match. The decision then went to the umpires who agreed with the captains.

Personally, much as I favoured the umpires' decision, I thought they were wrong according to the laws. While they may have delayed for an hour or so in order to let the outfield and bowlers' run-up dry out some more, there was no water either on the ground or on the wicket and there is nothing in the laws to prevent the re-start of the game because of a damp wicket.

Be that as it may, the umpires announced no play before lunch. A further inspection during lunch indicated a start at 2.10 p.m., but as fate would have it, torrential rains came at two o'clock and it was obvious, the ground now being under water, that there could be no play for the day and this was the decision of the umpires.

Further misfortune befell the ground authorities. There was no public address system and the large crowd, justifiably angry, had become openly hostile. A number of administrators, among others, left the ground for their homes, advising me that there would be a riot if, indeed, there was no play for the day.

It was under these circumstances that the captains were instructed by the ground authority that play there must be and we were forced to go on to the field for an hour. Cricket-wise, it was ludicrous because batsmen could hardly run between the wickets, bowlers sauntered on their runs up to the wicket and fielders stood on 'islands' with water all around them.

I remember that fine man and ex-Indian international, Cota Ramaswami, India's manager, saying to me, 'Jeff, don't let anything happen during the hour.' As it turned out, India lost 3 wickets in adding 55 to their score.

The sequel to this was a 'rocket' to the West Indies Board, received from Lord's: 'The game must not be subjected to mob rule.' Wishful thinking, perhaps?

Kingston was the venue for the fifth and final encounter, but this, too, was a drawn game. The three Ws each made hundreds with Worrell scoring 237 so the crowd had their money's worth. Gomez made a welcome return to the West Indies team and, next to Valentine, was our best bowler.

And so came to an end a tour that had been spoiled somewhat by the exploitation of leg-side defensive bowling. But who was I to complain? I wished, however, that the press could have been more understanding of the complexity of the matter.

One lesson had been taught me. Captaining a West Indies team *at home* was no bed of roses.

11
Hutton's England Team
of 1954

As already mentioned, England had wiped the floor with India in 1952 and even more recently, in 1953, had defeated Hassett's powerful Australians, winning one and drawing four, but the fact that England had saved the fourth Test at Leeds by Trevor Bailey slowing up the game and using defensive leg-theory, had not escaped those who followed the series closely. This tactic was once again going to play a significant part in the forthcoming series in the West Indies.

England were at full strength, Bedser being the only notable absentee. Alec Bedser never toured the West Indies. Was it that Alec heard from his fellow-players what the wickets were like and preferred the comfort of his own back garden? Quite rightly, the West Indies were now being treated as equals. Did not England have the 1950 score to settle with us? The visiting team consisting of Hutton (capt.), Watson, May, Compton, Graveney, Bailey, Evans, Lock, Laker, Statham and Trueman, with Wardle among the reserves, was among the strongest ever to represent England abroad, and yet I do not remember feeling otherwise than confident that we would more than hold our own.

It was the first time that a professional cricketer had been asked to captain England overseas. That person was Len Hutton. I had known Len over the years, for we had played against each other many times, and I was a great admirer of his batting technique. We were also both involved with the firm of Slazengers Ltd, he as a signatory of their equipment and I as a shareholder in the local company which represented their merchandise. Communication would be no problem or so I thought.

One of my first duties after arriving in Jamaica where the first

Test was to be played was to invite Len and Trevor Bailey, who was vice-captain, to a dinner party which included Gerry Gomez and Frank Worrell. It turned out to be less than a success. Conversation and pleasantries did not flow as easily as I expected and it set me to wondering if anything was amiss.

It was only some time later on the tour that the truth leaked out through other members of the England team that Len had asked his players not to mix with their West Indian counterparts. His reasoning was, apparently, that you could not get tough enough with the opposition if you fraternized. Although this was apparently the policy enunciated to our visitors, I can't say that it worked because, as the tour wore on, there was fraternization and very little ill feeling engendered between the two teams.

Of course all the participants have now mellowed with age, are good friends and have often since enjoyed each other's company. On the Test cricket field, however, no quarter is given, but I must confess I always preferred playing against the Australians of my period. While on the field it was 'blood', but at the close of play we were in each other's dressing rooms swapping yarns and a glass or two of beer.

How could anyone not be friendly towards, for example, Godfrey Evans or Jim Laker? Godfrey was quite a 'talker' behind the stumps and we have enjoyed many a chat on the field of play. Some well-wishers tried to make out that he was deliberately trying to put the batsman off by disturbing his concentration. If this was indeed so, he never succeeded as far as I was concerned, and in my book he was among the fairest of wicket-keepers. One who seldom appealed unless he was sure that the decision should be in his favour.

An incident concerning Godfrey which took place during the England vs Trinidad match is worth recalling. I was getting near to 100 when I attempted to play a short ball from Fred Trueman off my body to long-leg. The ball touched the inner edge of the bat and then my shirt after which it rested safely in Godfrey's gloves. He duly appealed and I was correctly given out. Godfrey thought that the ball had possibly only touched my shirt so he rather apologetically asked me about it as I passed him on my way to the pavilion. In confessing that I had touched it, I inadvertently flicked my shirt as well, whereupon the home crowd became visibly incensed and directed invective both at Evans and the unfortunate umpire. It was my turn to apologize to them both.

The preliminaries to the first Test match were matches against Jamaica. Players in line for West Indies selection assembled in Jamaica a week or so before the match, but two players who were considered to be certainties missed the game: King, our only really fast bowler, because of a muscle injury and B. H. Pairaudeau who looked completely out of form. Esmond Kentish and Mike Fredericks, both of Jamaica, replaced them. Furthermore, Frank Worrell, who had only recently returned from a Commonwealth tour of India, was also unavailable due to an injury suffered out there. There was, therefore, a vacancy for a batsman.

I had seen George Headley, then aged forty-four, defy the full strength of the MCC bowling at the Melbourne ground in Kingston in scoring 53 not out. That was enough for me; as far as I was concerned there was no one more suited to filling the gap than he was. With our only attacking fast bowler, one of our best batsmen unavailable, and no fewer than five new caps, I reckoned a rearguard action may well be necessary, and in my view and indeed, that of the other selectors, Worrell and N. N. Nethersole, Headley was just the man for the job.

Headley's selection, while popular in Jamaica, was greeted with cries of 'cricket politics' from the other territories – especially after he failed with the bat and did not take any wickets in the match. In fairness to George he was dismissed in the second innings by Tony Lock's faster ball. He claimed he never saw it. Lock was subsequently no-balled by more than one West Indian umpire for throwing. Later events proved there was little wrong with these decisions and Tony was forced to alter his bowling action which, to his credit, he was able to do with equally good results.

The question of Headley's selection was the first of many disagreements which I was to have with the then President of the West Indies Board, Sir Errol dos Santos, disagreements which were to cost me dearly in the future.

One would have had to be a super-optimist before this game started to expect the West Indies to defeat England in this Test match. Our team was at less than threequarter strength, and a sight of the wicket on the first morning before the toss did nothing to encourage any further optimism on our part. It was shining like glass. So much so that England elected to play four fast bowlers and leave out Laker.

When I won the toss and elected to bat, I feared the worst. Pace and more pace on a wicket suited to just that! But how often has the appearance of a wicket fooled everyone? On the first day it proved to be true and quite docile and, at the end of the day's play, we had progressed, if that be the right word, to 191–2.

When Hutton realized that the wicket was not really suited to his fast bowlers and J. K. Holt and I had become entrenched, he slowed the game down. It was the first time that I had experienced an over rate of less than 13 per hour. I shall discuss the question of slow over rates in a later chapter.

We went on to score 417, nearly all the batsmen pitching in with useful scores and J. K. Holt getting 94 in his first Test innings. In reply, England could only make 170 with Ramadhin and Valentine at their destructive best.

At the fall of the ninth English wicket, I realized that I had a problem on my hands as to whether to enforce the follow-on or not. I formed my own views and then went over to Headley and consulted with him. He was in complete agreement that we should not enforce it and so the die was cast.

My decision was greeted with howls of derision by the crowd and I was roundly booed especially when we were restricted by Trevor Bailey bowling wide of the leg-stump at the start of our second innings, and could not push the score along as quickly as we would have liked. The decision was prompted by the fact that our two spin-bowlers had bowled long spells of over 30 overs each and were in need of some rest, apart from which Ramadhin's spinning finger was sore. In addition, we did not relish the possibility of having to bat against Lock in the last innings on a wicket which had begun to show ominous cracks, and which, in the final analysis, looked worse than it behaved.

Let it not be said that we were not in for some anxious moments. Having declared our second innings at 209–6 and setting England 456 to win with unlimited time in which to make them, they were at one stage halfway there before the second wicket fell. In retrospect, there were three turning points from a West Indies point of view in this last innings. The first was when Gomez, bowling off-spin, had the important wicket of Hutton LBW playing forward, the first wicket falling at 130. Len was obviously displeased at the decision but he was not long forward and on hard West Indian wickets the ball turns but little. Then with the score at 220 I bowled a wrong 'un to Watson which he did not read and he lobbed it gently back to me. He was out for 116. May and Graveney took the score safely to 277 until, on the final day, I asked Kentish to bowl at the batsman's leg-stump, and when a superb catch by Weekes at backward short-leg sent back Graveney, the writing was on the wall for England.

It was leg-theory again but with a difference. So accurately did Kentish bowl that he accounted for three of the English batsmen by clean bowling them. In addition, the ball was keeping low on the final day. It was the only day on which Hutton omitted to use the heavy roller. In fact, he used no roller at all. Personally I have never seen a heavy roller break up a wicket nor have I met the man who has!

Kentish had his moment of triumph, 5–49 off 29 overs. It has always been a source of regret to me that he never played again for the West Indies. In the remaining matches of the series, speed was preferred to accuracy and I am not so sure that as selectors we were correct in that decision.

So ended a turbulent Test match. I was afterwards told that I had been placed under police protection for the latter period of the match, and had the result been otherwise, I wonder whether I would have been here to tell the tale!

Bridgetown was the venue of the second Test and this match too produced some incredible cricket. Worrell and Pairaudeau were back in our team, King was fit and Denis Atkinson was brought in for Headley. We felt we were near full strength once again.

Having won the toss and elected to bat, Clyde Walcott's double century helped us to 383 after a disastrous start. Then on the third day we had the unusual spectacle of England scoring only 128 runs from 114 overs in their first innings. Five wickets were also lost in the process. Watching the proceedings from mid-off, as Ramadhin and Valentine bowled over after over accurately to the defensive prodding of some fine English stroke players, I just could not believe my eyes. Apparently, 'stay there and the runs will come' were the orders. Whatever the instructions they proved disastrous. Spin-bowlers get on top if advantage is not taken of the loose ball. True, there were few of these about, but equally there was no effort to score by the batsmen.

Principally because of this sad display and a truly glorious century by J. K. Holt, an innings ranking with the classiest I have seen, we were firmly in the driving seat, and although at one time, with

Compton and Graveney together, England looked like playing out time, Denis misread a googly from me and was given out LBW, again on the front foot. Only in 1981, while chatting to him over a drink during the Lord's vs Australia Test, he reminded me of the incident. 'It was a bad decision,' he said. 'Never mind, you were illiterate anyway and deserved to be out,' was my jocular response.

So against all the prophecies we were two up and the cricket caravan rolled on to Georgetown. Our opponents seemed to be in complete disarray, but it was we who played badly and made the mistakes at Bourda.

The first error was in selection. We packed the team with batting, forgetting that a No. 5 will bat like a No. 10 if he is asked to bat in that position. Bourda had the reputation for being a fast bowler's nightmare so we left out King and brought in another batsman, Christiani. It proved to be an error of judgment.

England won the toss on this occasion and made 435. It was mainly due to Hutton who scored 169 – a magnificent innings. At one stage, Valentine was bowling to him with a packed off-side field, a 7–2 distribution. Repeatedly he was able to hit him firmly over the head of mid-wicket from balls pitched well up outside off-stump.

I believe that the innings went astray when I dropped the dangerous Johnnie Wardle, a relatively simple catch at mid-off off Ramadhin. We had the game reasonably under control until this point, but Johnnie cut loose thereafter and we lost whatever grip we may have had at that stage. I had a most healthy respect for this cricketer on hard wickets. Not only could he bowl his back-of-the-hand stuff accurately and with 'bounce', but he was a sensible and aggressive striker of the ball as well. To me it was no mere coincidence that England won two of the Tests in which he took part and lost the only two in which he did not play.

The first and most formidable nails in our Bourda coffin were hammered in by Statham at the commencement of our first innings. He accounted for Worrell in the first over being caught at the wicket, and bowled me with a beauty which moved from leg off the seam in his second. Clyde Walcott played on to the same bowler shortly afterwards and our innings was veritably in shambles.

Much blame was placed on my decision to allow Worrell to take first ball (the regular opener Holt was injured and needed rest and a runner). In fact, the decision was made on the spur of the moment on our way out to the middle. Frank asked to take first ball. Whether he thought he was doing me a favour or not, I'll never know!

A shameful and inexcusable bottle-throwing incident took place after tea on the Saturday. There was a large crowd tightly packed in the ground and a rearguard action was taking place. Holt, with Atkinson as runner, and McWatt had added 99 for the eighth wicket – a West Indies record against England which still stands today – when McWatt, who hails from the host territory, was run-out by a couple of yards. There may have been bets on the hundred partnership, but whatever the case there was no excuse for the bottle throwing by spectators from certain sections of the ground.

Play was held up for some time while the ground was cleared. Hutton and his men bravely and wisely stayed on the field and eventually play continued without further interruption.

Following our dismissal for 251 in the first innings, England never relinquished her hold on the match and won it comfortably by 9 wickets.

The Trinidad Test, the last to be played on the matting wicket, was, as expected, a draw and run glut. No fewer than 1528 runs were scored for the loss of 25 wickets. There were centuries galore. The three Ws all obliged, Weekes scoring a double, and May and Graveney did the trick for England. As a game of cricket, the less said about it the better. Nor could much be said in favour of the standard of umpiring in the match.

It was as a result of some controversial umpiring decisions during the series (the visitors preferred to have ex-players as umpires when few if any of these take up umpiring in later life in the West Indies), that Gerry Gomez and I enlisted the aid of Norman Ross, a practising umpire, and one or two other interested parties to start a local Umpires Council. With the help of the UK Umpires Association, we set up two subsidiary associations, one in the north and the other in the south of the island. These still exist today and have grown from strength to strength. Through the enthusiasm and dedication of several other individuals too numerous to mention connected with these organizations, a viable West Indies Cricket Umpires Association was formed, and I say without fear of contradiction that our umpires of today are as good as any. This is all the more laudable in view of their comparatively limited first-class experience. The names of Sang Hue, Gosein and, more latterly, Cumberbatch and Archer are highly respected by Test cricketers who have played in matches under their supervision.

When I first started playing for my school in 'first-class' club cricket, players were often subjected to the whims of the umpires, many of whom had peculiar idiosyncracies. There was, for instance, one umpire by the name of Cummins who invariably wore dark shades which extended to the sides of his eyes. These were put on, in all probability, to hide the red of his eyes after his Saturday lunchtime drinks of rum. One of my schoolboy chums, P. B. 'Chappie' Burke, who eventually played for Trinidad, told me a story involving this gentleman.

While playing for the college against a popular club, Burke touched a ball to the 'keeper early on in his innings only to find that Cummins had ruled against the bowler. It wasn't long before he was hit plumb in front to the same bowler, but Cummins's loud 'not out' was evidence that he had got another reprieve. He could not believe his good fortune, however, when shortly afterwards he was run-out at the end where Cummins was presiding. Again he was given 'not out' by the umpire. As he passed his new-found friend on his way to take up his position as non-striker, Cummins removed his dark glasses, winked broadly at him, and said, 'Mr Chappie, look at how they wants to get you out, you are batting like a cat, nine lives.' Humorous though this may be, such incidents would not be considered amusing in a Test match.

But I digress. Kingston was the scene of the fifth and final Test. The score was 2–1 in our favour with one to go. This Test match was memorable from the West Indies point of view if only for the fact that one G. St A. Sobers made his debut at the age of seventeen. He had played very well for his native Barbados against England, showing ability and cricket maturity far beyond his years. In the Test match itself he acquitted himself with far more credit than most if not all of his seniors.

The Sabina Test of 1954 has often been referred to as Bailey's match. Trevor's 7–34 in the first innings was the result of some splendid seam bowling, but he was aided and abetted in two important areas, firstly by the equally admirable bowling of Fred Trueman at the other end, and secondly by some rather irresolute batting. West Indies were all out 139 on a good wicket. No score to bowl at. Valentine was absent with a split finger so there was no spin twin to share the attack with Ramadhin. In fact, Sobers was more than an able substitute for Valentine, bowling orthodox slow left-arm and taking 4 wickets in the first innings, but the other bowlers, King apart, were ineffective and so England progressed steadily and purposefully to 414, of which Len Hutton scored an immaculate 205.

We were all out in our first innings after tea on the first day, and Hutton took Bailey in with him rather than Watson, the other regular opener. I mention this because Hutton refused more than one single to third man so that, as it appeared to us, Bailey, in effect, would have to face up to the hostility of King. Our other opening bowler, Gomez, was only of medium pace and D. Atkinson only a bit quicker. While I don't think that T. E. Bailey particularly enjoyed this tactic, it paid dividends because it was Hutton's innings, following on England's fine bowling, that put the match beyond our reach, and though we performed better in our second innings, England came out easy victors by 9 wickets.

Len Hutton can seldom have played a better innings than this one. He never put a foot wrong. As a result of it, and having retrieved for England what might perhaps have appeared to be a lost cause, Hutton established himself as captain of England, a post which he held until his retirement at the end of the 1954–55 tour of Australia.

For us it was a disappointing end to an absorbing series, but worse was to follow when Australia visited us in the succeeding year.

12
Australia Visits Us for the First Time

'What am I going to say to Frank Worrell?' I kept repeating these words to my friend Cecil de Caires as we sat at the bar of the Hotel Normandie in Trinidad after a West Indies Board meeting in which he had been involved as a member.

The Board, in its wisdom, had replaced Worrell as vice-captain and put in his place the very much younger and inexperienced Denis Atkinson. It was a preposterous decision in any circumstances and was the cause of much of the dissension and bad cricket played by our team in the series.

As a consequence of this decision, I wrote to both men: to Worrell, sympathizing with him, telling him that I had no part in the decision and asking him if he would mind if I consulted him from time to time as may be necessary; to Atkinson, congratulating him on his appointment, and stating that I hoped he would not be offended if, from time to time, I consulted with Worrell.

It was in these inauspicious circumstances that we welcomed a very powerful Australian team captained by Ian Johnson to the West Indies.

Most of the old brigade of 1951–52 were there and, in addition, Richie Benaud, Ron Archer and Peter Burge had joined the ranks. Alan Davidson was also in the touring party but injury kept him out of the Test matches.

A further mistake compounded the errors made by our Board. This was the decision to revert to a selection committee of four persons (one from each territory) and the captain. Gone was the continuity which had been developed in the previous series. This system merely encouraged infighting and parochialism and it was not changed until much later when, as a Board member, I was able to get sufficient support for a selection committee of three (drawn from any of the then five participating territories) together with the captain.

As fate would have it, as I was walking off the field at the Wembley Ground in Jamaica after a stint of fielding practice on the day preceding the first Test, a call went up for a ball hit high in the air. Looking up I saw it coming down towards some unsuspecting spectators. Putting my right hand up to try and catch it, I succeeded only in severely spraining the forefinger of my right hand and as a result I was out of the game. This meant that Denis Atkinson was pitchforked into a crucially important Test as a first-time captain, with several players, professional and otherwise, his seniors in the team.

To say that he was in any way responsible for us losing the test match would be grossly unfair to him. Yet it would be equally true to say that it was well-nigh impossible for him to command the respect of the players and get their full support.

In the Jamaica match before the Test, there were two sterling performances, one by Binns, the Jamaican wicket-keeper, and the other by O. G. 'Collie' Smith. They made over 150 each and did all that was required of them as wicket-keeper in the first instance and as an off-spinner in the second. They were both selected for the Test match.

Australia won the toss, and, batting first, totalled over 500 to which we replied with 259, Clyde Walcott getting the first of his five 100s in the series. Asked to follow on, we did not do any better but Smith fully justified his selection by scoring 104 in his first Test match. On the other hand, poor Alfie Binns had a bad match behind the stumps and made a 'pair' as well. Australia came out easy winners by 10 wickets. It was a bad start to the series and an omen of worse to come.

A short time before the Test in Trinidad was due to start, I became apprehensive about the new grass wicket which had been laid at the Queen's Park Oval. The fact was that it had no grass; the grass had not come through. It was decided, very rightly, to import help in its preparation. Fortunately the services of 'Son' Waldron, the Spartan Club groundsman from Barbados, were available and, in a matter of three weeks, by sheer hard work (but still no live grass) he was able to produce a wicket on which no fewer than 1225 runs were scored for the loss of 23 wickets.

On the first day of the match, there was, perhaps, the largest crowd ever to watch a Test match in the West Indies. The Australians were a tremendous drawing card; they were both powerful and popular. It was to be a frustrating day for the crowd, however, because due to rain, only eighty-five minutes' play in the closing session was possible. But did they get their money's worth! We had won the toss and the decision to bat first, though obvious at the time, was made before the rains came. What transpired in that eighty-five minutes' play was some of the most torrid fast bowling by Lindwall and Miller ever seen in the West Indies, which have themselves produced some of the greatest fast bowlers. It had been rumoured subsequently that Keith Miller was supplied with liberal quantities of gin by his numerous friends in the pavilion. Whatever the truth of the matter he certainly bowled magnificently.

The wicket was so well prepared that not even that prodigious spinner of the ball, Alf Valentine, could get any turn on it. Therefore, when Australia batted after our total of 382, it soon became obvious that we were in for a leather-hunt. The first Australian wicket did not fall until 191 but the batsmen had made slow progress, and when Neil Harvey at No. 3 got settled in, I decided to give him the single and attack G. D. Watson who was in difficulty with Ramadhin. This tactic, although eventually successful, was met with loud jeers from the large crowd which little understood what was going on.

Although Australia made a score of 600–9 declared, this method contributed to their taking more than two-and-a-half days to do so and, in the final analysis, put paid to whatever chances they may have had of winning the match.

Even at this stage of the tour, the major difficulties confronting our team were twofold: that of giving the side a good start against Lindwall and Miller and, secondly, finding the bowlers to get the opposition out. In the event we succeeded in solving neither problem.

The omission of Collie Smith from the team for the Guyana Test caused a furore, especially in his homeland Jamaica. He had made a 'pair' in the Trinidad Test, but what was more important from my point of view was that he never looked like getting any of the opposition out, nor was he accurate enough to keep the runs down. For the Guyana Test match, Norman Marshall, a 'tight' and intelligent off-spinner, got Smith's place. It certainly was not any fault of

Norman's that we lost this match. The truth is that we batted deplorably in both innings and suffered our second defeat by 8 wickets in a comparatively low-scoring match.

After a deficit of 75 in the first innings I was determined to get 'stuck in' in the second and, having got into double figures, thought I might get a good score. It was not to be for, horror of horrors, I mistimed a full toss from Ian Johnson and was caught and bowled. I felt terribly disconsolate at the time. It was to be my last Test innings and a rather ignominious finale to say the least.

Worse was to follow for me for, in chasing a ball to the boundary in Australia's second innings, I trod on it, falling heavily on my right shoulder. Excruciating pain followed and I was lifted from the field. I spent the next few days in hospital with badly torn shoulder ligaments. It meant that I was out for the remainder of the series.

During the time I was in hospital, a concerted effort was being made by the Secretary, Ken Wishart, and certain other Board members, to get the Board to appoint Frank Worrell captain in an effort to salvage something of the series for the West Indies. When the attempt was unsuccessful, it led to one of the most amusing cables in the history of the Board being sent by him to the President. It read, in part, 'suggest the next meeting of the Board be held in Carriacou.'*

Denis Atkinson was to be vindicated, at least to some extent, by his wonderful personal performance in the next Test in Barbados. Facing a first innings score of 668 and with 6 wickets down for 146, Atkinson was joined by de Peiza, the wicket-keeper. They batted together for more than a day, added 348 for the seventh wicket – a world record. Their partnership saved the day for the West Indies and the game was successfully drawn.

The final Test at Kingston proved to be something of a shambles from the West Indies' point of view. Sabina Park is a small ground for the straight hit, and after a prolonged drought it can be a pretty fast-scoring one, especially as the ball normally comes on to the bat and at a height suited to the stroke maker.

Australia went on a run riot, scoring a record 758–8 with no fewer than five centuries in the innings, Neil Harvey getting 200 for good measure. Richie Benaud's 100 took only seventy-eight minutes to compile. The result was that we lost by no less than an innings

*Carriacou is a small island in the Grenadines.

and 82 runs, and this despite a century in each innings by Clyde Walcott.

Only two West Indies players had done anything to enhance their reputations in this series. They were Walcott and Atkinson. The former is the only batsman ever to have scored 100 in each innings of a Test twice in the same rubber and the only batsman to score five centuries in the same Test series. A tremendous performance against such a powerful attack.

But what of Atkinson? Here was a player who was a very good utility cricketer. A batsman who, in the lower middle order, was capable of scoring over 200 against a high-class attack, in addition to which Denis had graduated from bowling rather innocuous seamers to being a much respected and accurate off-spinner. He was a great trier, in his own words, 'a hard red man'. I once saw him, when his bowling was in great need in a Test match, cut off the top of his cricket boot to relieve the pain of an infected big toe so that he could continue a long spell of bowling. But to ask him to captain the West Indies at that stage of his career was to ask too much of him.

There were, however, two shining lights on the horizon among the young players: Garfield Sobers and Collie Smith, both with immense and obvious potential as time was to prove. Generally speaking, however, it was a time for us to lick our wounds, but it was to be some time before they would heal.

13
Time to Retire

Cricket had been my main occupation during the decade following the Second World War. In between times I had occasionally helped my father manage his agricultural estates when he elected to take one of his infrequent holidays, and, by mutual agreement, had built up the agency side of his business, adding to it a complete branded range of sporting goods which my travels had helped to establish.

Due to my many absences abroad, prudence suggested that it would be necessary to get help to run these agencies and it was fortuitous that I was able to form a partnership with old family friends who had an existing and complementary business. The firm of Goellnicht & Stollmeyer Ltd thus came into being with Ken Goellnicht in day-to-day charge. This company has expanded and today it is a small but thriving business in Port of Spain.

A tour by the West Indies to New Zealand was in the offing but I had decided some time before to be a non-starter. It was more than time that I stayed at home with my family for a period.

Denis Atkinson took the team to New Zealand with John Goddard as player-manager, and although it was not a full-strength West Indies side, it was good enough to win the series by three Tests to one.

Playing in the domestic cricket competition at club level, I was finding it more and more difficult to run between the wickets without experiencing considerable pain. A bone-spur at the back of my heel was diagnosed and I was duly operated upon. The wound took a long time to heal, partly because I kept climbing the many stairs at the Queen's Park Oval to watch E. W. Swanton's team which was visiting the West Indies on a goodwill mission.

Jim Swanton is a lover of cricket, most of all English cricket, but he has a soft spot and a corner in his heart for West Indies cricket as well. He thought that the 1954 tour by England had left a nasty taste in the mouths of West Indian crowds and administrators, and he felt that by bringing out a team of attractive cricketers he could do much to heal any breach that may have existed.

He intended that two South Africans, R. A. McLean and J. H. B. Waite, should be members of the party, but even at that time anti-apartheid feelings in the West Indies were such that he was advised against including them; and an opportunity to see and play against those two fine cricketers was missed.

Frank Tyson was among the players selected and I saw him bowl, thankfully from the ring, on a number of occasions. Surely there has never been a faster bowler! We in the West Indies have had a battery of fast bowlers in recent times and Wes Hall, E. A. Martindale and Mike Holding are as fast as they come, but never have I seen one faster than Tyson.

As I have said elsewhere, captaining the West Indies at home is a lot more difficult than doing so abroad, and my final ambition as a player was to captain the West Indies on an overseas tour. The West Indies were due to tour England in 1957.

An opportunity to re-establish my claim came later in the year when an intercolonial tournament was to be played in British Guiana. I captained Trinidad in the series but, short of form and practice, my personal performance and that of the team was pretty dismal. In the second innings of our match with Barbados, the winners of which would qualify to meet British Guiana, an unusual incident occurred which may have contributed to my dismissal. A ball hit to long-leg was fielded in front of the Bourda pavilion by Eric Atkinson. His fast low throw to the wicket-keeper struck the square-leg umpire a terrible blow on the nape of his neck. The umpire was stunned but, after a short period, continued to stand. Was it perhaps because of this that he erred in giving me out caught at the wicket a couple of overs later when I had not touched the ball on the forward stroke?

Umpiring mistakes occur in practically every cricket match. Some-times the luck goes with you, sometimes against, but when all is said and done, it about evens itself out. Be that as it may, this was to be my very last innings in first-class cricket.

A few days later, during the Barbados vs British Guiana match, I was strolling across the ground at Bourda with Cecil de Caires when he turned to me and said, 'Jeff, I have something to tell you.' 'What's that?' said I. 'The President has gone across to Barbados to ask John Goddard to captain the team to England.' For a moment I was literally stunned, then I turned to him and said, 'Cecil, I have played my last first-class match.'

Although it was the straw which broke the camel's back, the fact was that I had been through a series of mishaps during the previous two years which indicated that I had fast become a poor risk physically.

And so it was that, when I returned to Trinidad that evening and a young reporter at the airport asked me what my future plans were, I told him that I was retiring from first-class cricket as I considered myself to be too prone to injury and it was time to call it a day. At the time it caused something of a mild sensation for, despite my poor form, I was still the incumbent and there had been no cry from the public for my dismissal. As things turned out, it was a wise decision because the 1957 tour of England was a complete disaster from the West Indies point of view.

There were a number of reasons why a team which was outstanding on paper and which included such as Weekes, Worrell, Walcott, Atkinson, Ramadhin and Valentine of the old brigade together with young players of the calibre of Sobers, Smith, Kanhai, Gilchrist, Hall* and Alexander, should have performed so badly.

First, the Board was guilty of the unpardonable error of appointing two managers to the team, both with equal status, with the inevitable result that players played one off against the other, and the control which either of them would have enjoyed singly just wasn't there.

Second, the combining of so many old stars with so many potentially great emerging ones into one unit would never be easy unless there was a strong, well-knit and effective management team at the helm.

Before the 1957 team had been selected, there had been trial matches held in Trinidad and I found myself in the position of a critic writing a cricket column in the *Sunday Guardian*. In an article

---

*Hall had difficulty with his run-up on the tour which was not corrected at the time and he did not play in a Test match.

in the *Guardian* four months prior to the commencement of the tour, I had written in part:

The West Indies Board has in its wisdom recently selected Messrs T. N. Peirce and C. de Caires to be joint managers of our team in 1957. I claim both of these individuals as personal friends and I do sincerely wish them well in what may possibly, through no fault of their own, be some very trying moments. It is the first time, so far as I know, that a touring team has had dual (I nearly said duel) managership. Having used the words in brackets I shall follow the Speaker's advice and withdraw them, because I know (a) that the two individuals are both balanced and diplomatic and will do all possible to avoid conflict and (b) that the members of the Board who appointed them would not be so silly as to appoint joint managers without clearly defining the duties of each.

Be that as it may, one wonders whether due regard was paid to our hosts, the MCC, the numerous county secretaries and other officials in the United Kingdom whose duty it will be to deal with the management of our team. Will they know whose duty is Mr X's and whose Mr Y's? Yes, despite the best of intentions, I shall be surprised if there are not embarrassing moments, and these will tend to be more frequent and more publicized in the unhappy event that team performances fall below expectation. Any cricketer of reasonable touring experience cannot help but be surprised at such a decision. A manager and an assistant manager, yes; but joint managers, unequivocally no. In selecting joint managers the Board has created a precedent. My fervent hope is that it will not become an established one.

Then later, when the thirty or forty names for the trials were announced I was flabbergasted at some of the omissions and was strongly critical of the selectors. Whether they paid any attention to this particular article I know not, but the fact remains that three of the names I put forward, not included among those initially invited, were later brought in, and eventually selected in the touring party. These were G. Alexander, N. Asgarali and A. Ganteaume.

Whatever the reasons, things never seemed to go right for the team. At Birmingham in the first Test, we had a commanding lead of 288 in the first innings thanks to Ramadhin, but it was the West Indies who were fighting off defeat in the end after the epic record partnership of May and Cowdrey of 411 for the fourth wicket. In this innings Ramadhin, a bowler who in my opinion usually needed some nursing and was best when used in comparatively short spells unless on top, bowled no fewer than 588 balls (98 overs), and he bowled 774 balls (129 overs) in the match. Both are records which still stand today.

At Lord's in the second Test, close on a dozen catches were dropped during England's innings, and as if to add insult to injury, a dreadful wicket was prepared at the Oval on which Lock and Laker thrived and we were beaten in three days for the third time in the series.

As well as writing for the *Sunday Guardian*, I was also afforded the opportunity of learning something about broadcasting cricket on radio. I continued doing radio commentary for some years until games were televised and I was asked to work in that field. Pleasant as this was to become, these jobs are for the professionals, and one cannot but admire the expertise of Tony Cozier, who is by far the most experienced and able commentator and critic that the West Indies has produced. His work compares favourably with that of all the great commentators of the day.

It was now time for me to turn my thoughts to making a living. My father had turned seventy-five and, Trojan that he was, was still active and able to supervise the running of the estates, but it was long past time for me to help him so that he might enjoy a well-earned rest and retirement. I can pay him no greater tribute than to say that when he handed his affairs over to me, estates of cocoa, coffee and citrus which he developed and cultivated with such pride, energy and love, he never once questioned my decisions or interfered with my actions.

As far as cricket was concerned there was a contribution to be made in coaching the young. And what better place to start than my Alma Mater, Queen's Royal College?

QRC's cricket was in the doldrums. They were by no means a good team, but I could help by organizing their practice and encouraging them to learn the art of fielding and the principles of good out-cricket. My first duty was to dress the boys: good clean whites and caps, and badges for those who deserved them. At least they could now look like cricketers! Among them was a youngster of fourteen, a natural ball player. His name? D. L. Murray. The college had no wicket-keeper so Deryck was commissioned to do the job. So started his long and eventful career as a wicket-keeper.

14
Back to the Land

The responsibility of maintaining and developing our two estates provided me with much personal satisfaction. El Carmen in the Talparo district of Trinidad was a model of its kind. It was not a large estate, 208 acres in all with about seventy cultivated in clonal cocoa, forty in grapefruit and oranges of several different varieties, and the remainder in coffee and guavas.

It was laid out rather like a city, in blocks and around each of the blocks were estate roads. My father used to boast, 'You may drive to any part of the estate.' He was right.

As a corollary to all this I began to take an interest in the Agricultural Society of Trinidad and Tobago which was the organization representing, in the main, the estate owners. At the same time I endeavoured to fill my father's shoes as a member of the Cocoa Planters' Association and the Cooperative Citrus Growers' Association. It was all good experience and, before long, I was to find myself on the management committees of these venerable institutions. I was now totally involved in the three Cs – Cocoa, Coffee and Citrus – and for a time the fourth C, Cricket, took a back seat.

In 1961 I was elected vice-president of the Agricultural Society and was to serve as such for seven years under the stewardship of Sir Harold Robinson. Sir Harold was also Chairman of the Citrus Growers' Association and of the British Caribbean Citrus Association. It was a stroke of good fortune that I should have had the opportunity to watch this outstanding man at work, and to learn from him something of the art of tactics and strategy in business. Sir Harold would set his goal and nothing would deter him from achieving it. He never allowed a minor issue to complicate or intervene in his quest for the major objective. He was a man with an immense capacity for work, highly respected internationally, whose presence at sugar and citrus conferences, where he was inevitably a representative of either the West Indies or Trinidad and Tobago, meant that our islands were being represented by a man of extraordinary ability.

Years later, some time after Trinidad and Tobago became an independent nation in 1961, it occurred to me that only someone of the calibre and drive of Sir Harold Robinson could halt the moral decline of our small twin islands which were drifting like a ship without a rudder. Someone was needed to arrest the *laissez-faire*, the gradual erosion of law and order and of standards generally. Of course the politics of the day would not allow for such a thing. To a white Trinidadian of the so-called 'plantation class', it was just not on.

I still found time from my busy schedule to play club cricket on weekends and continued to keep in touch with events in the cricket world as a selector for Trinidad, broadcasting and writing in the press when tours were coming around and helping in the administration of the newly formed Trinidad and Tobago Cricket Council to which had been recently entrusted the running of domestic cricket competitions.

The Chairman of the Northern Division of the Council was Sir Lindsay Grant, a gentleman of rare quality and high principle. Sir Lindsay, one of the elder members of that distinguished family of cricket personalities, was another from whom there was much to be learned. He was meticulous to a degree, always courteous and unassuming, a pleasure to work with and for. As senior representative on the West Indies Cricket Board of Control, he, with Gerry Gomez as his lieutenant, did much to assist the new president, John Dare, to help West Indies cricket along the narrow and tortuous path through which it was travelling at the time.

Some years later, as Chairman of the Northern Division, I realized that the post was no sinecure, for along with a few hard-working assistant secretaries, the responsibility for organizing and controlling the various domestic competitions devolved almost entirely on the chairmen of the two major divisions, North and South, in a country where communication by telephone or otherwise is, to say the least, wretched.

West Indies cricket was going through an interesting phase at this time. Frank Worrell was pursuing his studies at Manchester University and Gerry Alexander was elected captain. He had conducted two successful campaigns, one at home against A. H. Kardar's Pakistanis, and another abroad in India. The former saw the world batting record broken by Gary Sobers's 365 at Kingston and the emergence of new stars such as R. B. Kanhai, B. Butcher, J. Solomon and C. C. Hunte along with fast bowlers R. Gilchrist and W. Hall.

However, after the tour of India in 1958–59, the West Indies proceeded to Pakistan where the series was lost by 2–1, although reports of bad umpiring were too numerous not to have some basis in fact. This was followed by England's visit to the West Indies under Peter May and a further setback, defeat by 1–0 in the Tests with the other matches drawn.

The West Indies were going through a period of intense political activity at the time with several of the major territories, Jamaica and Trinidad and Tobago included, seeking their independence.

Frank Worrell, his studies now completed, had returned to the team and there was a terrific public outcry for him to be made captain in Alexander's place. I thought this completely unjustified at the time, having regard to the course that events had taken when Worrell had elected to study and became ineligible to undertake the tour to India and Pakistan.

Frank, in his later playing days, was not particularly popular in his native Barbados for he lived both in Jamaica and Trinidad and many Barbadians seemed to feel that he had deserted his homeland. Whatever the reason, he was no fewer than 682 minutes in scoring 197 in the Bridgetown Test. In the latter part of his innings the West Indies were well placed to capitalize on their advantage but Frank was unmoved. Did he have a score to settle with the Barbados public? Or was he just finding his form and re-establishing himself as a member of the Test team? The answer is obscure, but there was the spectacle of messages being sent out to him in the middle and the captain standing on the pavilion steps exhorting him to 'hit out or get out'.

The Trinidad Test which followed was won convincingly by England. It was the first time that bottles were thrown on to the ground in a Test in Trinidad. To me, this was unbelievable.

England had scored 382 in their first innings, and on the Saturday a large crowd had turned up to see the powerful West Indies batsmen go on a rampage on a well-nigh perfect pitch. It was not to be. The batting failed dismally to some fine bowling by Statham and Trueman. To anyone watching the proceedings from the commentary box, there was no excuse for the failure of the batsmen. There were several umpiring decisions given against the batsmen, all, as it happened, from one end, but to most observers they were all correct ones. The running out of C. K. Singh, a local boy playing in his first test, was the breaking point for all hell to let loose.

Picture the scene: a stifling hot Saturday afternoon, the circulation of a considerable amount of rum among the spectators and the local hero, albeit a bowler, run-out when the score was 98–8. Add to this the concerted campaign, particularly in sections of the political press, on placards, etc., that 'Alexander must go' and you have the setting in which the bottle throwing took place.

Perched high up in the glass-enclosed broadcasting booth, I was on the air at the time with Michael Laing, the head of Rediffusion in Trinidad. Michael made the remark to me that it was 'sheer unwarranted hooliganism' and I agreed with him. This was the signal for bottles to be thrown at *us* by the irate crowd and our booth was completely demolished. We spent the next fifteen minutes under the table while glass shattered all around us. Dick Murray, a fellow commentator whose temper was notorious, did not help matters by hurling a cider bottle, which had been thrown at the booth, back into the crowd below. No one was seriously hurt so I would like to believe that it landed safely on the ground.

About the only amusing story about this incident concerns a Canadian lady who was seeing a cricket match for the first time and who had just taken her seat in the stand when the bottles came on to the field. Accustomed to the hurly-burly of ice hockey at home, she thought it was a regular occurrence and all part of the day's work!

Shortly after this, I found myself attending my first West Indies Board meeting at the Board's then headquarters in British Guiana, under the chairmanship of John St F. Dare. It was an important Board meeting and memorable in particular for the appointment of the management team for Australia in 1960–61.

The key positions of manager, assistant manager and captain went to Gerry Gomez, Max Marshall and Frank Worrell respectively, and perhaps the most successful tour of all time had its inception at this meeting.

One rather amusing interlude took place at the meeting which lasted two full days. Communication between the islands was never easy and often hazardous in the matter of getting to one's destination on time. As the meeting was being closed and the chairman was being congratulated for his dexterity in handling it, there was a knock on the door and Dr Cordice, the Windward Islands representative, appeared for the first time. There was the inevitable chorus of 'Dr Cordice I presume!' Poor chap, he had become the victim of airline strikes and missed connections, and thus missed the meeting.

The selection of captain presented no problem, for Gerry Alexander, who had confessed to me that he was suffering from 'Worrellitis', declined to make himself eligible for the post. While in my view this was a wise decision, it could not have been an easy one for him. The fact that on the tour of Australia he was outstanding both as wicket-keeper and batsman, playing several crisis innings in the Tests, earns him the title of 'Alexander the Great'. No praise can be too high for him and my hope is that, as and when his veterinary commitments permit, he will continue to play an important role in the administration of West Indies cricket. He has already proved himself to be a successful team manager.

There followed the golden years of West Indies cricket. The Worrell dynasty had begun and was to continue past his retirement after the tour of England in 1963 until the end of 1966 when, once again, the old brigade needed to be replaced by the new.

It has always been an interesting exercise to compare the great West Indies Test teams over the years. The ones which readily come to mind are those of 1948–50, 1961–63, 1966, 1975–76, and 1980–81.

Taking the 1950 team first, I would rule this out as the best on the grounds of inadequate fast bowling. The batting strength was both long and strong, with all-rounders of the calibre of Worrell, Gomez and the ubiquitous Clyde Walcott. In spin it was blessed with the peerless Ramadhin and Valentine, but there was no shock attack and this was exposed in Australia the following year.

Worrell's team of 1963 gets my vote in a close finish with his team of 1961 in Australia. The latter had no opening bowler to complement Hall, for Sobers bowled chinamen in those days, apart from which it was a bit 'iffish' at the top of the batting order.

By 1963, however, there was Griffith to partner Hall, and Sobers was the world's greatest all-rounder, bowling in three styles as the occasion demanded. Lance Gibbs had reached the apex of his career and the middle order of Kanhai, Sobers, Butcher, Solomon and Worrell had aggression as well as stability. Deryck Murray was having his first tour and showing infinite promise as a wicket-keeper–batsman. Finally, in Worrell it had a mature leader, much beloved by his players, to supply the magic touch. If there was a fault, it was that there was no settled opening pair. M. C. Carew, who was propelled by Worrell into the position of opening bat, would only mature later and much depended on the solidity of Conrad Hunte.

Of the 1966 team, captained by Sobers and which I managed, I shall speak in greater detail later in this story. Suffice to say that it was a well-balanced combination which played with a great deal of determination, but it was never given an adequate start by the openers, and at the end of the day perhaps too much depended on the all-round skill of Gary Sobers.

The 1976 West Indians, captained by Clive Lloyd, were deficient in spin. There was batting to spare and, in Fredericks and Greenidge, a settled opening pair. Richards was now at his magnificent best and he had Kallicharan, Lloyd and the ever-promising Julien to follow him. Roberts and Holding were there with Daniel and Holder lurking in the wings, but where was the spin? Neither Padmore nor Jumadeen were quite Test class and by now there was no Sobers on whom to call.

Perhaps if Packer had not intervened in 1978 the team of that year would have staked claims to be the best ever, but they played only briefly and then only against a third-rate Australian team.

By 1979 and 1980–81, we were back to full strength and Lloyd's great teams of this period could bear comparison with the best of all time. The captain had by now gained both in experience and maturity. There was a slightly brittle middle order, perhaps, and a possible weakness at the level of inconsistent wicket-keeping, but it was, in all fairness, the greatest combination of fast-bowling strength of all time: Roberts, Holding, Croft, Garner. Sustained pace, the last named was two bowlers in one, for which bowler of your knowledge usually averages less than 2 runs per over hit off him and has a more than acceptable striking rate as well? Fast bowlers of the calibre of Malcolm Marshall, Sylvester Clarke and Wayne Daniel would have played consistently for any Test team of the period other than the West Indies. Often they were called upon merely to sit on the sidelines.

You may well ask where were the spinners to come from when they were required? '*When* were they required?' would be Lloyd's answer. Are there any Test pitches today, in this age of covering of wickets, where top-class spinners will be more effective than top-class fast bowlers?

In this day and age, great fast bowlers win Test matches. Perhaps it was always so, but it has never been exemplified before to the extent that the West Indies illustrated it in the period 1979 to 1981.

15

Ten Years in the Senate

Office of the Prime Minister
18th November, 1966

I am directed to forward to you the enclosed Instrument under the hand of the Governor-General appointing you a Senator.
I have the honour to be, Sir
Your obedient servant.
Signed   Permanent Secretary

The die was cast. I was not a little surprised when the first local Governor-General, His Excellency Sir Solomon Hochoy, invited me to be a member of the first Senate of Trinidad and Tobago.

Dr Eric Williams, the Prime Minister who, with his People's National Movement Party, had come into power on a wave of nationalism in 1956, had opted for the Westminster system of Parliament and, thus, a bicameral legislature. The Senate consisted of twenty-four members, thirteen appointed by the party in power, four by the opposition and seven by the Governor-General acting in accordance with the advice of the Prime Minister after he had consulted with religious, economic and social organizations. My appointment embraced the latter category, generally known as the 'independent' senators. The appointment was for five years, the term of the government in power.

Apart from being surprised I was much involved at the time with my work on the estates, at the agency, at the Agricultural Society and with domestic cricket administration. After consulting with my resident brothers Victor and André, it was unanimous that I should serve. There followed a period of ten years as a member of the Senate, years which I never regretted for, apart from the experience of being closely connected with the fortunes of an emerging nation, the Senate appointment was largely responsible for a complete turn-about in my *modus operandi*.

Never one to keep my mouth shut, I joined in many of the debates as the representative of agriculture in the Senate. While these were enjoyable, they involved much hard work and research, especially when early in 1963 I felt disposed to move the first ever motion by a private member in the Senate:

That whereas it was stated in the speech from the throne that agriculture would be the first priority in Government's economic programme for more jobs, higher standards of living and reduction of the cost of living:

Be it resolved that Government declare, without further delay, its agricultural policy for Trinidad and Tobago.

Of course the motion was defeated by the built-in government majority, but it served to highlight the fact that Government was unlikely to put into practice what it was preaching about agriculture, either due to a lack of desire to promote a section of the economy which was mainly the province of persons of Indian ethnic origin who were basically in opposition to them, or because of their preoccupation with destroying the plantation system, which to some extent still existed, and transforming it into a peasant, family-type farming system which concentrated on growing food for domestic consumption rather than export crops, e.g., sugar, cocoa and coffee, the markets for which were controlled by manufacturers abroad.

In many of his public pronouncements, the Prime Minister made it clear that he wished to get rid of the so-called 'plantocracy', and as the years went by it became obvious to many of us who were engaged in growing export crops that it was only a matter of time before we could not hope to compete for labour with the industrial development which was taking place and was to be the main thrust of Government economic policy.

In the meantime, the Senate was called upon to play an even more important role in the affairs of our now independent country. This was when, after the elections in 1966 in which voting machines were used, the opposition Democratic Labour Party, sadly split down the middle, decided to boycott Parliament, and the Senate became the sole source of whatever opposition there was to the Government in the house.

These were exciting years indeed and my nose was kept to the grindstone, wrapped up as I was in affairs of state.

My neighbour seated on my right in the Senate at this time was Sir Patrick Hobson, a man of considerable stature who was the representative of the oil industry, the main pillar on which the industrial strength of the country was built. Sir Patrick had asked me to join the board of the television company which had recently been started and I had accepted.

It was at this period in the country's history that the transformation of business from foreign to local ownership and control had begun to be actively pursued. Pressure was being brought by Government on foreign personnel through the work permit system and other monetary devices to replace them with citizens of Trinidad and Tobago wherever there were people who were capable of doing the job. This policy proved to be of benefit to me personally because, as a result, I started receiving a number of requests to become a director of companies both within and without the agricultural sector.

When Sir Patrick Hobson said to me one day, 'Young man, you will have to make up your mind what you are going to do in the future,' I recognized that I had reached the crossroads and would have to make a decision on whether agriculture or business would be my major future occupation.

Our estates were vested by my father in shares divided between the seven members of the family and there had to be a consensus on what was to be done about them. Four members of the family were living abroad without any likelihood of returning home, and the situation on the estates, what with low prices, wholesale larceny of crops, no subsidies of consequence, difficulties with labour unions and costs of production, collectively led up to the unanimous decision that we should sell out our holdings as soon as the time was appropriate. It was a commonsense decision but, for me, it meant a transfer from the land to the office. I remembered my father's words when he retired from business just before the Second World War: 'People are too devious, I am returning to my trees.' I had elected to do the opposite.

During my term in the Senate, I had the dubious distinction of seeing three of the worthy senators who had occupied the seat directly on my right die so that, when my friend Conrad O'Brien became a senator in 1966, I had the temerity to tip him off and not surprisingly he sought refuge a safe distance away!

The sole excursion abroad which I was invited to join on behalf of the Government was the Commonwealth Parliamentary Association Conference held in Kampala, Uganda in 1967. This conference brought together about 200 serving politicians from all over the Commonwealth and debates on various matters of moment affecting Commonwealth nations were held. However, by far the most memorable part of the conference were the outings organized by the host country to the upper reaches of the Nile and elsewhere.

The Government of Uganda was then headed, as it is now, by Milton Obote, in the period before the Idi Amin coup. Two celebrated Ugandan families of Indian descent, the Mehtas and the Madhvanis, both of whom by their industry had developed industrial and agricultural 'empires' within the country, were delegated to perform the duties of chief hosts, and their kindness and hospitality knew no bounds. Some years later I found myself on West Indies selection duty at Montego Bay, Jamaica when the Indian cricket team was touring the West Indies. Our host at a reception there was Mr Dadlani, a relative of our Ugandan benefactor, Mr Madhvani who, I gathered, had been thrown into gaol by Amin and his holdings confiscated. I wondered whether a similar fate had befallen Mr Mehta and his family. Uganda is a beautiful and fertile country, but it is shameful that its politics since independence have been so disastrous.

In the meantime, Trinidad and Tobago was having its share of political unrest. To many, independence seemed to be interpreted to mean that one could do as one pleased. There was much unemployment, the unions were being militant and the expectations of the man in the street which had been built up by the government of the day were not materializing. The 'black power' movement in the United States, along with student uprisings there, did not escape the notice of their Trinidadian counterparts, and early in 1970 'black power' meetings and protest marches began to take place in Port of Spain and elsewhere in the island.

It was difficult to identify exactly what the protesters wanted because they had a black government. Apparently the more fanatical of the demonstrators wanted a change of the system and the imposition of a revolutionary government. Plantation owners were among the targets selected for attention and abuse, and on one Saturday afternoon a meeting was held by the movement outside our compound in Santa Cruz. Much invective was hurled at me and my family and what we stood for, while cordons of policemen kept the mob away from our premises.

Some time after this event, a 'Molotov cocktail' was thrown on the roof of the great house at Mon Valmont. My mother, then ninety years old and an invalid, lived there alone with a nurse. By the grace of God and good fortune, the hastily constructed kerosene bomb fell and settled against some new galvanized iron which had been inserted along the side of the wooden wall above the roof on the ground floor, and when an alarm was raised and my sons ran over from our home next door, they were able to stop the fire from gaining a foothold. Had the house caught fire – our old wooden home built in 1880 was a tinder-box – the consequences would have been too terrible to contemplate.

The meeting outside our home had its amusing moments. It was observed that, some time before it was due to start, a truck had parked outside our gap and a snow-cone* vendor set up shop on top of it. One person, at least, benefited from the event. At about three o'clock in the afternoon, after several inflammatory speeches had been made, it was suddenly announced by the chief speaker that 'they would have to leave to see Sister Mahalia† perform at the Queen's Park Savannah', whereupon all the leaders jumped into their cars and departed, while their less fortunate brethren hiked the seven miles, waving their green flags in the steamy afternoon heat, back to Port of Spain.

All this saddened me greatly as I recalled our happy youth, mixing and playing cricket and football with our employees and the villagers around. My father put practically all the money he made back into the estates, developing them, often on lands too steep to be properly cultivated, and in the process gave employment to so many. He was much loved and respected by those who worked with him, and in my early youth an air of happiness pervaded the district. Now all this was gone; a new era had dawned. The word 'exploitation' had

---

*A snow cone consists of shaved ice dipped in coloured syrup.
†The Government had hurriedly invited Mahalia Jackson, the celebrated black American singer, to come to Trinidad and give a public concert to try and cool the situation.

been repeated so often by so many that the younger generation had little alternative other than to believe that it was literally the truth.

The situation in the country was extensively debated in the lower house, and when the day arrived for the Senate debate on the subject, I had prepared a somewhat aggressive speech which was highly critical of the Government for not taking firmer action to impose law and order or prevent the marches, wanton destruction and seditious statements from being repeated *ad nauseam*. As it happened, the speech was never delivered because, before I had an opportunity to do so, the Senate meeting was abandoned as a result of a bomb scare in the Parliament building. This may have been a blessing in disguise, for our Prime Minister was not known for taking kindly towards persons who spoke forthrightly in public against Government policy, and after surviving the events of 1970, his power knew no bounds.

My second term in the Senate ended in 1971, when the People's National Movement Party was again elected to power and I was relieved of my responsibility.

I was much less involved in agriculture now that my business commitments were growing, and in any case I believe that ten years is as long as any Senator should be asked to serve under our system of Government.

I had become a member of the West Indies Cricket Board of Control and was attending a meeting of the Board in Barbados on the day of the abortive uprising in Trinidad in 1970. We were in session when the news came through and, together with my colleague Lance Murray (father of Deryck), we caught the first plane home. We arrived at Piarco airport at dusk to find that there was a curfew in operation. I hastened through customs wondering how I would get home to Santa Cruz, but the fates were on my side. The last car to leave the airport happened to be going to my destination and the driver willingly gave me a lift. I was happy to be reunited with my family in such disturbing circumstances.

How the day was saved by the Coast Guard commander shelling the bank of the only road and preventing the rebel Defence Force from driving their transport through to Port of Spain; and the subsequent successful efforts by the ex-commander of the Defence Force to get the ringleaders to surrender is a matter of history.

Trinidad and Tobago struggled on with a diminishing budget until 1973 when two important events took place simultaneously. New discoveries of oil and natural gas off the east and north coasts of the island were made, and a substantial increase in the price of oil was imposed by the newly formed Organization of Petroleum Exporting Countries (OPEC). The twin islands suddenly found themselves caught up in an economic landslide, the likes of which they had never experienced in their previous history.

16
1966 and All That

Following on the retirement of Sir Frank Worrell after the successful 1963 tour of England, there was much speculation as to who would be the next West Indies captain. There were two possible contenders: Conrad Hunte, the vice-captain, and the great all-rounder Gary Sobers, who had shown such individual flair on the field. It is no secret that Frank advised the Board that, if he had to make the choice, it would go to Sobers and so the decision was made.

Conrad Hunte successfully disguised his disappointment and continued to play and support Sobers to the full. He was fully committed to the development and preservation of the highest standards in West Indies cricket, and as an opening batsman he was a tower of strength. Conrad is a serious-minded and highly religious person who has made a name for himself as a leader in Moral Rearmament as well as on the cricket field. He was a very sound and correct player, outstanding against fast bowling.

I have no doubt myself that the decision to appoint Sobers was the correct one at the time. West Indies players on the whole do not take kindly to rigid discipline off the field and are more likely to respond to persuasion on matters not directly related to the field of play. Conrad may have been rather too paternalistic and sanctimonious for their liking, and as regards his efforts thus far as captain, the word had spread that in difficult situations he would ask questions in the expectation of answers from above and those that came down were not always the right ones!

It was soon after this, in 1966, that I was asked to manage a very strong West Indies combination for the tour of England, with Gary Sobers as captain and Conrad Hunte as vice-captain. The Test team of Hunte, Carew or McMorris, Kanhai, Butcher, Nurse, Sobers, Holford, Hendriks, Hall, Griffith and Gibbs proved to be a powerful and highly effective combination, and the series was comfortably won by 3–1.

I found managing a cricket team to be an easy job when compared with the multiplicity of different duties that I was called upon to perform at home. It was almost a piece of cake. I say this while fully admitting that, if a team does badly, there will be problems – many more than I had in England in 1966. The first week of the tour was hectic with numerous engagements and matters to be organized, but after this was over, things ran quite smoothly.

I approached the job knowing as I did that the first essential was for the captain and manager to work together in harmony. My experiences on two previous overseas tours as a player had taught me this lesson, and on the flight to London, I impressed upon Gary that full cooperation between us was essential and that no one should be allowed to come between us during the tour. If either of us had problems, we should raise them with each other and see that any potential 'wounds' were attended to before they 'festered'. The other rule on which we agreed was that, in broad terms, he would be in complete charge on the field of play and I would be likewise off it. We stuck to these conditions implicitly and succeeded in going through the tour without any major internal problems.

Gary was then at the height of his great powers. He never seemed remotely capable of putting a foot wrong in anything he did on the field of play. His performances were superb in every department of the game, and I could only marvel at the quality and quantity of the superlative performances that he produced.

At Trent Bridge in the third Test, after Kanhai and Butcher, by some superb back-to-the-wall batting, had extracted us from a difficult position – performances which, incidentally, were not appreciated either by the crowd or sections of the press – Sobers arrived and, after settling in, regaled the crowd with a series of magnificent strokes, compiling 94 in quick time before he apparently gave his wicket away, caught at long-off about an hour before the close of play. As he was taking his pads off, I remonstrated with him for throwing his wicket away when so near his century and going so well. 'Never you mind, Mr Manager,' said Gary, 'I want to pick up two or three this afternoon.' In the event, he did not succeed in achieving his objective as he had done in England's first innings when he had Boycott LBW with a beauty for no score, and having taken a superb catch to dismiss Milburn off Hall, we had England reeling at 13 for 3. Still, it was an illustration of his positive approach and the supreme confidence which he had in his own abilities.

We did agree to disagree on one subject. Gary was determined to bat at No, 6 and the rest of us on the tour selection committee, which included Kanhai, Hunte, Hall and Gibbs, thought his proper place was at No. 3 or 4. He was so capable of dominating the game that sound cricket sense indicated that his great talents would better serve the team up front. But he preferred his chosen position from which he claimed he could save the situation or push on, whichever was necessary. And who was to say he was wrong? He certainly wasn't proven wrong on this tour.

What about the second Test at Lord's when he found himself fighting a lost cause with his cousin David Holford? The score in our second innings was 95 for 5 and we faced a deficit of 86 on the first innings. It was before lunch on the third day of the match when Gary, with only a few to his name batting at No. 6, was joined by David. We were inwardly blaming Gary for not batting higher in the order for he, above all, would have been able to stem the tide. Now, here we were 'in the cart' with little hope of survival. Billy Griffith, Secretary of the MCC at the time, came into our dressing room after lunch and informed me that Her Majesty the Queen was due to meet the teams the following day at the tea interval. 'Should we ask her to bring it forward and come today?' Quite naïvely, I asked Billy to wait another hour, if possible, before deciding. Sobers and Holford were still together undefeated the *next* day at tea time, and the Queen arrived at the originally appointed hour and the teams were duly introduced to her.

It was one of the most amazing partnerships of all time. Gary made no attempt whatsoever to dominate the strike. He allowed his less illustrious partner to face the bowling from the outset and he, himself, displayed not one iota of anxiety. It was incredible. Often, too often, in the early stages Holford played and missed and he had his share of the luck, but gradually he found touch and towards the end of his innings he was in no way overshadowed by Sobers. They added 274 in an unbroken partnership which is still the highest for the West Indies sixth wicket in all Tests.

The day after the match was saved, the team was invited to

Wimbledon. We entered the centre court, appropriately dressed, during a break in the play. The entire crowd stood up for the team and cheered. It was a moment to be cherished for all time.

Another highlight was the visit of Muhammad Ali to the team's dressing room during our match with Middlesex. It was all a part of the publicity for his bout with Henry Cooper which was due to come off shortly in London. Ali's knowledge of cricket was no greater than mine of boxing, but the boys were elated over his visit and he clowned and shadow-boxed with them for the cameramen during the tea interval. I couldn't get over the fact that his face did not bear a single mark or scar as a result of the many battles he had fought in the ring.

One of the problems which I inherited on the tour was a press campaign which was designed to get Charlie Griffith branded a 'chucker' and thus out of the series. The campaign was a concerted one and a hang-over from the previous series in the West Indies when Australia, under Bobby Simpson, had been beaten by us for the first time. All through that tour the controversy raged, with Richie Benaud and Bobby Simpson at the head of the protesters. On the other side of the fence were Keith Miller and Alan McGilvray, and so the Australian camp itself was divided in its views.

Certainly if one viewed Griffith's action on delivery in *slow motion*, it did not look fair. His elbow appeared bent and he was inclined to splay his left foot wide at the moment of delivery. But umpires don't see things in slow motion when in the middle and therefore are in no position to pass judgment on this basis. An umpire can only act on what he sees. During the fifth Test in Trinidad, I was doing radio commentary along with Alan McGilvray during a certain period of play after lunch when Graeme Thomas was batting and playing well. Alan turned to me and said, 'Jeff, Charlie hasn't put a foot wrong today.' I agreed with him, but at that very instant Charlie slipped in an extra fast short ball which lifted, touched the top of Thomas's bat and he was caught at the wicket. In a flash Alan and I turned to each other and we both raised our eyebrows. We silently but mutually felt that that particular ball was unfair. After so many fair deliveries it was unlikely that any umpire could be expected to call the exception to the rule. There and then I got the impression that Charlie could bowl but he could throw as well if he so desired.

The press campaign was unrelenting and offensive and Charlie, not unexpectedly, reacted adversely to the criticism. My public pronouncement was that 'the umpires were in charge and we would abide by their ruling'. It was not long before Charlie and I found ourselves seeking legal advice as he wished to sue one newspaper for libel. He was a professional cricketer and his livelihood was at stake. I sympathized with him fully in his predicament.

In the meantime we had been playing all over the country without comment on Griffith's action, and the matter of his 'chucking' seemed to be a thing of the past when, late one afternoon in the gloom at Old Trafford in our match against Lancashire with nothing at stake, Arthur Fagg, umpiring at square leg, suddenly called Charlie once for throwing. None of us could believe it! He had been bowling during the day without any adverse comment and he was bowling no differently at the time. There was hardly anyone on the ground and the incident appeared to have passed unnoticed except by a few officials who read nothing into it, but Arthur Fagg, for reasons best known to himself, contacted the press and once again the telephones were clanging.

I spent much time answering calls by the press with 'it is an isolated case and he was not called by an umpire chosen for the Tests so we are not paying any attention to it.' Charlie was not called again on the tour nor did he deserve to be, except perhaps once. The incident of which I write took place in the Test match at Leeds, and it brought forth one of the finest pieces of umpiring I have seen.

Tom Graveney was batting and Griffith was bowling from the Kirkstall Lane end with that big stand in the background. All of a sudden he let one go and the ball whizzed past Tom Graveney's nose into Hendriks's safe gloves. Umpires. Buller and Elliot immediately consulted each other. I heard later that they said words to Griffith to the effect that 'Charlie, you can bowl and you can throw. Stick to your bowling' and that was the end of any further transgression by the bowler.

I will not deny that Charlie became somewhat anti-social during the tour, but if he did he was certainly provoked into that frame of mind. There were incidents, for example, during the Test match at Trent Bridge when Derek Underwood suffered a terrible blow on the head from a ball from Griffith and the latter showed little sign of remorse at the time. He was later persuaded to write Underwood an apology for this incident and his reaction afterwards indicated that he had indeed regretted it. Brave little Ken Suttle received some stitches from a nasty ball from him on a dreadful wicket at Hove when there was nothing in the match, but such incidents are commonplace these days except that helmets now prevent serious injury. For my part, Griffith played his heart out on the tour and he never stopped trying. The withholding of his bonus at the end of the tour by the West Indies Board was not, in my opinion, justified under the circumstances.

Undoubtedly our selectors had been guilty of errors in selecting the seventeen for the tour. When our test team was in the field, we were well-nigh invincible, but if the reserves were playing we weren't worth going around the corner to watch. Clive Lloyd and Charlie Davis were two notable absentees. They would have lent admirable support to the front-line players as, indeed, time was to prove conclusively.

There was an obvious anomaly in the quantum of fees and allowances paid to our players at this time, and in my report to the Board at the end of the tour, I thought it was best illustrated by pointing out that Gary Sobers was receiving the same amount of basic pay as, for example, Rudy Cohen, our reserve fast bowler who had played least on the tour and had failed to gain selection in a Test match. This was palpably absurd and I am glad to say that, as a result of my recommendation, players were categorized in the future on the number of Test matches previously played.

No mention has been made of the part played by Lance Gibbs in the success of the tour. Lance was a great off-spinner, especially so on hard wickets. He wouldn't have held the record for the greatest number of Test wickets if he wasn't! He used the air and bowled flighted off-spin, depending on subtle changes of flight and spin to obtain his wickets. Among many sterling performances, he disposed of the England batting in both innings of the first Test at Old Trafford, and he could always be counted on to bowl 'tight'. If he could be faulted it would be on the grounds of inflexibility. He positively hated to bowl around the wicket, and when he was asked to do so, his control suffered. His obvious enthusiasm knew no bounds and he took a very tough line with the younger players where discipline on the field was concerned, yet he was never seriously considered for the post of captain. His efforts in that direction on behalf of his native Guyana were not crowned with any degree of success. Unfortunately, on his retirement Gibbs appeared to sour and had little good to say about the administrators and the game which had done so much for him.

Having taken a short break away from the team to watch Charlottown's Derby, I rejoined the lads at Bradford and was asked to join a group of players who wished to lodge a complaint. The objection was to what could be termed 'Barbadian chauvinism'. There were no fewer than ten Barbadians in the tour party of nineteen and the view was expressed that the tour was being dominated by them. The tour committee of five had three Barbadians on it: Sobers, Hunte and Hall. Frankly, I had neither noticed nor conceived of any inclination to favouritism of the Barbadians and said so, but immediately called a meeting of the team so that any such fears might be dispelled.

I mention this because it is one of the disturbing features surrounding the future of West Indies cricket. The territories which form the core of West Indies cricket are now nearly all independent. A revival of the short-lived federation of the islands is now further away from becoming a reality than ever. More and more nationalism on the part of the individual territories that form the whole is the order of the day. The matter of raising funds for West Indies cricket is a case in point. Repeatedly, the view is being expressed that each should look after its own. I can foresee that pressures will build, as the years go by, to separate country from country. Due warning should be taken of this trend for, without unity, we shall count for nothing in the world of cricket.

17

Selection Duties

The quirks of fate are seldom predictable. Late in March 1969 I found myself in Georgetown, Guyana as a member of the West Indies Selection Committee to select the team for Australia the following winter. Gerry Gomez, the selector from Trinidad, could not make the trip, and as his alternate I was asked to fill the breach. Little did I know that I was about to be involved in the most unusual team selection of my experience.

Colin Cowdrey's England team was touring the West Indies at the time and the meeting was held on the rest day (Sunday) of the fifth and final Test match. It rained throughout the day, and the weather was as dismal as the proceedings.

Perhaps a short résumé of what had taken place during the MCC tour is in order, for it had considerable bearing on the team finally selected.

Three of the four Test matches played had involved extreme tension and excitement. The first in Trinidad had only been saved by the West Indies due to an incredible eighth wicket partnership between Sobers, who had elected to bat at No. 7 in the second innings, and Hall, after we had been asked to follow-on.

In Kingston a game of high drama saw crowd disturbance intervening at a crucial stage, and some misguided police action involving the use of tear gas that halted play for the day, with England poised for the *coup de grâce*. Although the lost time was made up, the match, when resumed, took a different course with Sobers once more in the role of match saver. Aided and abetted by a few of his team-mates, in particular Nurse, he scored 113 not out on a treacherous wicket on which large cracks had appeared as though after an earthquake. Technically I am sure this must have been the best of the many superlative performances by this great player. Not only had he restored his team's fortunes but, in the end, his opponents were in disarray, and when time was called, they were eight wickets down and facing imminent defeat.

The Barbados Test was also drawn, the excellence of the wicket and inclement weather contributing in equal measure.

This was the prelude to the fourth Test played in Port of Spain which, until the last day, was also headed for another stalemate, until Sobers made his remarkable declaration. I say remarkable because in my view the result, unless the greatest miracle of all time occurred (we had already had two minor ones in the series), would either be a draw or a win for England. This I said at the time to television viewers.

The *Wisden Book of Test Cricket* merely states that England, set to score 215 in 165 minutes, won by 7 wickets with three minutes to spare. These are indeed bare facts. What is not mentioned is that the wicket was still an absolute beauty and that, in the five days' play up to that time, only 18 wickets had fallen to the bowlers. In addition, Griffith, the only fast bowler playing and the only bowler capable of slowing down the over rate, and thus the scoring rate, had been injured and could not take the field. In the event, we were treated to the spectacle of Lance Gibbs opening the bowling at a brisk medium pace, and leg-spin bowlers of the calibre of Rodriguez and Butcher, neither notable for their containment capabilities, having to bowl a number of overs.

After the match, in his defence Sobers claimed that it was time the stalemate was broken and he was fed up with the negative tactics of England. Be that as it may, cricketers do not like losing Test matches and West Indians are no exception. West Indian crowds react even more unfavourably and, overnight, the hero became an object of ridicule.

It was indeed ironic that such a miscalculation should follow two match-saving innings for his team, one of which defied description in terms of its skill and tenacity.

The series was eventually lost by 1–0, although the final Test at Bourda did not lack for excitement, England staving off defeat on the final day, aided and abetted by the forward pads and bats of Cowdrey, Knott and Snow.

This, then, was the background to the scene of the team selection for Australia. Incredible as it may seem, at the end of a full day's session a team was agreed upon by the six selectors (one from each of the five territories together with the captain), but the following day the chairman requested and we were advised to sit again and re-think our decisions. This was done and a new team with a number of different names was finally chosen. This volte-face was nothing to be proud about and, in the light of what happened on the tour, it would probably have been better to have sent the team which was originally selected.

It is not my intention to divulge any details of the selection, but the omission of Deryck Murray, who had kept wicket (albeit poorly) throughout the series with England, was to have severe repercussions in Trinidad. It was not anticipated that Hendriks would be available due to a chronic back injury, but his doctors had given him the all clear and as such he was indisputably the best in the region, and the second wicket-keeper's place went to the promising Mike Findlay by a substantial majority.

Later in the year at the Annual General Meeting of the Queen's Park Cricket Club which was responsible for appointing the two representatives to the West Indies Board, much was made of the non-selection of Murray and considerable criticism was directed at the two representatives on the Board, Sir Lindsay Grant and Gerry Gomez, both of whom were abroad at the time and unable to attend the meeting. In the matter of selection, I rose to the defence of Gomez, being at pains to point out that I and not Gomez was on the selection committee for the tour. Sir Lindsay at this time had come to the conclusion that, due to failing health and his desire to give up some of his commitments, he should retire from the Board. He had, indeed, done more than his share. The management committee of the club took the view that the meeting had expressed a vote of no confidence in Gomez, and it was in these unusual and somewhat inauspicious circumstances that Lance Murray and I were appointed to the West Indies Cricket Board of Control late in 1968.

The tour to Australia was a disaster – the series was lost by 3–1. The great Wes Hall was but a shadow of himself and had reached the end of a great career. Of all West Indian fast bowlers of my experience, only E. A. Martindale and M. Holding could compare with Wes both for speed and fluency of motion in action and delivery. But Australia 1968–69 proved to be one tour too many for Hall and Griffith, and a team with nine players over thirty and an average

age of twenty-nine proved to be no match for a young Australian side on the make.

Considerable criticism was directed at Sobers who, it was reported, spent too much time on the golf course and too little with his team. There was apparently little tactical planning and, in any case, any plan may have been thwarted by faulty catching and ponderous outfielding.

A three-Test series against New Zealand followed which ended one match all, and on a short tour of England later in the year, the West Indies lost by the only Test which was completed. The golden era of the early sixties was at an end.

India were our visitors in 1971, and I became a regular member of the selection committee. It was another disappointing tour from our point of view. Our team, although superior to the Indians on paper, succeeded in losing the series by 1–0. Young Gavaskar, playing in his first series, put his stamp on each of the four Tests in which he played, causing the Trinidad calypso singer, Lord Relator, to produce a classic song, the chorus of which ran:

> Gavaskar the real master,
> Just like a wall.
> We couldn't out Gavaskar at all.

Our team's performance could best be described as a leaking ship out in mid-ocean without a rudder. The fielding was shoddy, the catching poor and guidance at the top was a commodity in short supply.

There was no improvement when New Zealand visited us the following year. The first Test was frittered away despite the brilliance of Lawrence Rowe who contributed a double of 214 and 100 not out in his first Test match: a new star had apparently arisen in the West. By dint of resolution and determination, a New Zealand team of limited talent succeeded in drawing all five Tests, and in one of them they had the upper hand at the end of the game. The West Indies used no fewer than eighteen different players in each of these series, an indication of signs of panic and the result of having a selection committee with frequent changes in its composition along the way. So often it happened that, for the final couple of places, too many different ideas and viewpoints were forthcoming, ending in compromise with the selection of a player who had not originally merited consideration. It was time for this outmoded form of selection committee to change.

It is common knowledge that there was more than a measure of dissatisfaction with the performance of Sobers as captain. Ever since the poor performance of the team in Australia in 1968–69, there had been mounting disquiet in this area. On more than one occasion during this period, there were moves behind the scenes to replace him. The majority of the Board, however, remained loyal in their support of Sobers and the matter was never raised at a Board meeting.

The fact was that Gary Sobers was a tired man who was playing cricket summer and winter, year in year out, without a break. He was stale and appeared to be worn out both mentally and physically. He was still a great player although unable to dominate a game as he had done so often in the past.

The possible replacement was Kanhai or Carew. The former's form against India had not been of the best and he had not elected to make himself available for the New Zealand visit. Carew, on the other hand, had been scoring many runs in the Shell series and had been one of the few successes in Australia. As a captain he had led Trinidad to victory in the Shell series in 1970 and 1971, and his astuteness on the field was obvious to the discerning onlooker, but his form in the more recent Tests had not been as convincing and, apart from being the victim of minor leg injuries, he gradually appeared to lose interest. It was unlikely also that a predominantly professional team, which was in a large measure loyal to Sobers, would cooperate fully with a non-professional captain. So the status quo remained until 1973, when Sobers asked to be relieved of the captaincy and Australia toured the West Indies for the third time under Ian Chappell.

In the summer of 1972, Sobers had undergone a cartilage operation in England and he was still recovering from this when the West Indian season started. The West Indies had won only two of its last twenty-six Tests, and the time for change appeared somewhat overdue.

The appointment of Rohan Kanhai to captain the team was generally well received, but the dapper little Guyanese had a tall order ahead to weld a team with several changes in its make-up into a Test combination.

Under the positive and aggressive captaincy of Ian Chappell, the

Australians proved too good for us, but the series was not without its merit from the West Indies' point of view. The 2–0 win for Australia could well have been 1-all, for the third Test in Trinidad was only lost by 44 runs and the ball had not rolled with us on this occasion. Most of all, the team appeared to be rejuvenated and the batting collapse which took place in Guyana could in no way be attributed to the fault of the captain.

Before the second Test match, an unfortunate and distressing controversy arose over the non-selection of Sobers. In February, Sobers had captained Barbados in a Shell Shield match in Trinidad at which the selectors, including myself as chairman, were present. It was obvious that Gary was not fit. He limped badly, walked from slip to slip and, when he bowled, he did so in his easy action, slow left-arm fashion. At the end of a game during which his knee swelled up, I suggested to him that he should play in the Shell game for Barbados at home in order to satisfy the selectors that he was fit. Gary decided against playing and, prior to the team's selection for the Test, we asked, as is normal in such circumstances, for him to produce a medical certificate certifying his fitness or otherwise. Despite repeated attempts and arrangements made for him to visit a doctor, he refrained from doing so, and it was the unanimous decision of the selectors to leave him out of the team.

The fact that the Test was being played in his native Barbados, where he was (no doubt with justification) an object of hero worship, did not help matters, and a bitter controversy developed with the selectors being flayed openly in the press. Unfortunately, Gary made a public statement in which he was reported to have said: 'I have been playing for the West Indies long enough for them to take my word' (i.e., about his fitness).

Regrettably, the Prime Minister of Trinidad and Tobago, Dr Williams, saw fit to enter the controversy and invited Sobers over to Trinidad for a private conference after which, at a public meeting, he implied that the selectors had not consulted Sobers and that he was being discarded 'on the wayside like an old car'. This was, of course, far from the truth and I felt constrained to rise to the defence of my fellow selectors whom I described as 'men of integrity, most of whom were former test players with the best interests of West Indies cricket at heart'. It is perhaps significant that Dr Williams never asked any member of the selection committee, including the chairman who lived in the same island as he did, whether there was another side to the story. This incident merely serves to illustrate how close politics is to cricket in the West Indies.

The only occasion on which I saw the error of Sobers batting at No. 6 or lower in the order exposed for the mistake we thought it to be was in the Trinidad vs Barbados Shell Shield match referred to earlier, which was comfortably won by Trinidad although the Barbados team looked to be the stronger. They had not been doing too well when Sobers arrived at the wicket, and as soon as he had settled in, Carew, the Trinidad captain, gave him the single which he invariably took, and saw to it that most of each over was bowled at Sobers' less illustrious partners. This paid dividends because Sobers was left 'high and dry', with just a few to his name at the end of the innings. It struck me as strange that so few captains ever followed this strategy when faced with a similar situation.

A basic difference of opinion between myself and my fellow selectors arose when we met before the tour started to select the President's XI to meet the Australians at Montego Bay in one of the early matches of the tour. It was on a matter of policy. In the past, this game had been used in part to determine the final place or two in the team, but on this occasion I was in a minority of one, the other four selectors feeling that no one should be put 'on trial' in this match and that a young team with a more experienced player as captain should oppose the Aussies. We were all good friends around the table and had known and respected each other's views over the years. When about half an hour had gone by, the chairman of the meeting turned to me and said, 'Jeff, you are very quiet, what's the matter?' I replied that I was not 'with them' as regards their policy of selection and that there were established players whose form was at the time suspect but who should be present in Jamaica and playing in the match. Unfortunately, my views did not carry and a young inexperienced team under the captaincy of Clive Lloyd, with whom I sympathized, was literally thrown to the wolves.

I felt sure that this decision contributed to the premature retirement of Charlie Davis who had been, apart from Sobers, the outstanding batsman against India and New Zealand during the two previous home tours. His local form had been poor at the beginning of the season and he needed match practice; however, he was not asked to join those invited to be available for the first Test in Jamaica. It was, in my view, a lamentable error, and after playing in the fourth and fifth Tests in which he did little of note, he retired at the early age of twenty-nine. Maybe my assessment of this is wrong, for the time of the amateur West Indian cricketer was now at an end. To keep up with the greatly expanded cricket programme, one had to turn professional or retire. Trinidadians could generally obtain alternative employment at home, and the future of the individual and his family came first.

It was on Good Friday 1973 that my attention was forcibly diverted from cricket. It was midday and we had just finished selecting the team for the fifth and final Test. I was on the way home to Santa Cruz when, from an open spot on the highway, I saw huge columns of smoke billowing into the air over the hills to the east. The end of the dry season was at hand and it was a bush fire, the scourge of my agricultural life, and one look told me that it was in the area of our cocoa lands. Being a public holiday, there were only three others besides myself to go to the scene of the fire, and by the time we got there, our efforts to stem the tide could be compared to trying to put out the Fire of London with a bucket of water. My family lost seventy-two acres of cocoa and limes that day, and our overseer and friend Knolly George stood with tears running down his face. He had laboured with us for over forty years, going into those hills daily to keep the steep lands cultivated as if they were his own. In three hours all was burned and lost for all time.

18
From Agriculture to Business

The period of transferring from agriculture to business had now arrived in earnest, and in no time I found myself involved as a director on a number of boards as well as being chairman of some.

Agricultural and sporting connections did much to enhance these opportunities. Caroni Ltd, then owned by Tate and Lyle, and the West Indian Tobacco Company, a subsidiary of British American Tobacco, were among the first to ask me to join their boards. Then there was the television company, Metal Box Trinidad Ltd, the Trinidad Publishing Company – producers of the *Trinidad Guardian* and *Evening News* – and finally Barclays Bank DCO which was in the process of being converted into Barclays Bank of Trinidad and Tobago Ltd.

In addition, I was persuaded by some young entrepreneurs to accept the chairmanship of the first fully locally owned insurance brokerage company, Consolidated Insurance Consultants Ltd. This company was destined, in ten short years, to become a multi-million dollar concern, with a substantial building of its own in Port of Spain, and brokers to the Government of Trinidad and Tobago.

Business experience was being gained through practice in the field, and it was to prove of great value when, in the course of time, I took over the reins of the West Indies Cricket Board of Control. I have never underestimated the part that cricket has played in my acquisition of some of these business positions.

An example of this was when, in 1966, while managing the West Indies in England, I suddenly received an invitation to lunch with Lord Thomson of Fleet. I recall that Sir Learie Constantine was present, among others, and that we swapped yarns long into the afternoon. Although I never suspected it at the time, 'Lord Thom' must have been giving me the once-over, for not long afterwards there arrived the invitation to join the board of his newspaper in Trinidad and, later on, to become its chairman. I am happy to state that I still hold this post, in spite of the fact that the paper has changed ownership and is now owned by a local conglomerate.

As I have already related, my father had suffered great financial loss during the period of the market crash in 1929. He had entered the merchandizing of cocoa along with the growing of it, and had had a large tonnage of this commodity, for which he had already paid, stored in New York waiting to be sold, when the crash had come. Overnight, he had been virtually bankrupt. One of the main sources of finance which had enabled him to effect his recovery had come from Barclays Bank, the manager of which had sympathized with his plight and, being aware of his industry and integrity, had supported him in his hour of need.

It was, therefore, a source of great satisfaction to me to be asked not only to join the board of the Trinidad and Tobago network of this great banking institution, but to be its chairman. The bank is now majority-owned by citizens of Trinidad and Tobago, and its recent name change to Republic Bank Ltd has not made one iota of difference to its clientele. The new bank is, of course, an associate of the Barclays group of banks, and that institution's vast resources of training and experience are still available to it. It was a stroke of good fortune that my schoolmate and 'Triumph' wicket-keeper of old, Ken Ball, then happened to be the London parent's director in charge of the Caribbean area, apart from having been for some years manager of the main branch of the bank in Trinidad. His knowledge of the local scene and our close past connection made my job considerably easier than it may otherwise have been.

Trinidad and Tobago has been fortunate in the extreme. Having a surplus of oil for export and considerable reserves of natural gas has made the economy buoyant, but riches, especially if accumulated as they were almost overnight, bring problems with them: problems of congestion on the roads and corruption to name but two.

As in all communities, there are fringe elements of the extreme right and the extreme left, but the saving grace of this small country has been the building up of a substantial middle class. This has meant that the majority of the people now own something tangible, be it a house or a car and, as such, they have a stake in the country and good reason to ensure that stable government continues.

It is impossible, when involved day to day in business, not to feel the frustrations due to the absence of some of the normal amenities of civilized living such as reliable telephones, a regular supply of water, electricity, and roads which, despite the availability of both oil and asphalt, are distinctly substandard. The fact is, however, that the twin islands have been growing at too fast a pace for the infrastructure to keep up, although it is difficult not to admit that we could have done better.

New riches have encouraged free spending, and a certain brashness, discourtesy and lack of discipline on the part of the population which did not exist in earlier times, for we are generally a happy-go-lucky people. Perhaps the worst feature of the current scene is the system whereby peace is being kept in part by the dubious expedient of paying some of the unemployed (and some unemployables as well) for not working. This, in the view of many, including myself, is likely to create a Frankenstein which a future generation may not be able to control.

Withal, in these troubled times world-wide, we have much for which to be thankful, and if, as we are prone to do, we complain about the various ills around us, then we may truly count our blessings as well. Democracy survives, schools have been built apace, there has been a significant redistribution of wealth and small businesses have sprung up everywhere.

The uncertainty lies in the long-term future. What will happen when the oil runs out or the wealth dries up? Will there be a repetition of 1970? This is in the hands of the new generation. If the slogan adopted by our late Prime Minister Dr Williams, 'Discipline, production, tolerance' counts for anything and is put into practice, then we are worrying unnecessarily.

19
President of the West Indies Cricket Board of Control

The West Indies Cricket Board of Control has been blessed with a number of dedicated and able presidents. During the period of my involvement with West Indies cricket, Karl Nunes, Sir Errol Dos Santos, John Dare, Noel 'Tom' Peirce and Cecil Marley had all discharged this responsibility with a signal devotion to the cause of West Indies cricket.

It came as something of a shock and a surprise when, after the meeting of the Board held in Jamaica in 1974, Cecil Marley said that, for personal reasons, he wished to retire from the Presidency in November of that year and would I be prepared to accept the position of President if asked? Cecil was not due to retire, if at all, until May the following year when the Annual General Meeting of the Board came around. He had served as President since May 1970 and, although our team had met with little success during the early part of his stewardship, it had concluded with a crushing victory against England in 1973 and an indication that its fortunes had turned.

Marley had been an admirable President and was respected by all who knew him both at home and abroad. His trained legal mind enabled him to conduct meetings with admirable facility. He would sift the wheat from the chaff and, after a long discussion, would summarize and convey the Board's decision precisely and concisely to the notetakers. In his onerous task, he was admirably assisted by the jovial and enthusiastic Secretary, Johnnie Groves.

There were, of course, many memorable incidents and occurrences during his term of office. On one occasion at a Board meeting in Jamaica it was noticed that the member for the Leeward Islands was absent and no word had been received from him. Later the same day a cable was sent to the Board regretting the absence of the member, the reason being that he had been incarcerated the day before for leading an illegal political protest march!

Perhaps the most difficult moments experienced by Cecil Marley were in the period following Gary Sobers's visit to Rhodesia.

We were aware that Gary had gone to Rhodesia to have a bit of a holiday and play with and coach players of all races for reasonable remuneration. The visit would probably have passed unnoticed but it so happened that Prime Minister Burnham of Guyana was touring African frontline states at the time and was voicing public support for the isolation of South Africa and Rhodesia, both economically and as regards sporting contacts. While on the platform in one of these countries, the news of Sobers's visit to Rhodesia was thrust under his nose. He had no political alternative other than to condemn it in the strongest possible terms. Not only did he do this but he stated that the West Indies captain would not be welcome in Guyana. A crisis had developed out of the blue and Gary in all innocence had found himself in an invidious position.

Hurried meetings followed. Prime Minister Barrow of Barbados, whose relations with Guyana were not of the best at the time, intervened on the side of Sobers but, the issue being highly political, the solution had to encompass an apology in a form that was acceptable to Barrow, Sobers and Burnham, no easy task. Prime Minister Williams of Trinidad decided to act as an intermediary and summoned Wes Hall to Trinidad. An emergency meeting of the Board was held in Barbados at which a statement was drafted which apparently met the wishes of all parties.

After its publication, the matter died a slow and painful death, but the inference was plain for all to see. Cricketers from the West Indies who elected to play or coach in South Africa and/or Rhodesia would find themselves *persona non grata* at home. It was not easy for those players who spent most of their time playing in the atmosphere of county cricket in England, with and against players from these two countries, to understand the strong anti-apartheid feelings that enveloped the West Indies, and if some of them appeared to be insensitive to these feelings, my sympathy went out to them.

When Cecil Marley first spoke to me on the subject of the Presidency he named my problems as mainly two-fold – politics and finance. To this, I added a third: the Queen's Park Cricket Club.

'Why?' he asked. Although a member of the management committee, I was neither President nor Vice-President of the club and felt that there would be opposition within the club to such an appointment. Secondly, I knew that the time would shortly arrive when the club would be forced to relinquish its authority as the Board's representatives in Trinidad and Tobago and I would be caught in the middle of this controversy as and when it arose.

I afterwards learned that support for my appointment came from what may have been considered an unexpected source, none other than Sir Errol dos Santos.

Sir Errol had been Vice-President of the club since 1943, and when the rule whereby the Governor was ex-officio President was changed in 1962, Sir Errol became the club's President and has held that post to this day at the ripe age of ninety-two!

Since his retirement from Government service in which he held the high post of Treasurer, following which he became the territory's first locally born Colonial Secretary, Sir Errol had entered business and had become chairman of one of the largest local business firms. He was something of a financial expert, and his business acumen was used for the benefit both of the club and the West Indies Board of which he had been President from 1953 to 1959.

In retirement, Sir Errol's major public interest has been the Queen's Park Cricket Club. It has been described as his second home, and the vast stadium which can hold nearly 30,000 spectators is a tribute to his foresight and ability to get things done. The club owes him a debt of gratitude which cannot be repaid even with the passing of years.

Sir Errol has always held very strong views on matters affecting the club and the island's cricket, and he was one of the founders of the Trinidad and Tobago Cricket Council, the forerunner of the Trinidad and Tobago Cricket Board of Control, the controlling authority for cricket in the islands.

The first duty of a Board President is to choose his 'team' and in this I was lucky. Harold Burnett, my choice as Secretary, had been an ex-intercolonial cricketer and assistant to the manager of the successful 1963 West Indies team in England. he had often managed West Indies teams on home tours in his native Trinidad, and we had worked together often as manager and captain of Trinidad teams. Harold was dedicated to West Indies cricket and we would have a happy working relationship. In the words of another former Board

Secretary, 'he pays meticulous attention to minute detail' – a virtue I would need because I knew my propensity for being precipitate and this would provide the essential brake. His recent premature death shortly after vacating office was suitably acknowledged and mourned by the cricket fraternity.

No less important was the post of Treasurer, and when the name of Richard 'Dick' Hobday was suggested to me, I responded with alacrity. Dick was a chartered accountant and the senior partner of the firm of Pannell Fitzpatrick, and it would be a major triumph if he would accept. In the event, he agreed to do the job, not knowing, I am sure, what it would entail. But my troubles in this area were not over. Dick, born in Ceylon, of English parents and married to a Trinidadian, was considered to be an Englishman, and there was pressure to appoint a 'local' as Treasurer. I took my problem to Sir Errol and have been ever grateful to him for his advice to stand firm on my selection. It was the wisest decision possible, for Dick has been a tower of strength over the past six years and has earned the respect of all with whom he has dealt, including our players. Whether one likes it or not, more than half of our Board meetings are taken up with financial matters, and our financial survival to this day depends on the successful negotiation of overseas tours to England and Australia. In these and other matters, Dick Hobday has played a significant role. If we had been required to pay him or his company for the time he has devoted to this job, the fee would have run into hundreds of thousands of dollars.

A few months after the Board headquarters had been transferred to Trinidad, we ran into our first controversy. It was really a storm in a teacup, but in view of the intense rivalry between the territories and the legitimate desire of the Combined Islands (Windwards and Leewards) to make their mark in the Shell Shield, the incident, fanned by extensive media coverage, was magnified into a major issue and was the cause of a certain amount of acrimony.

An important match – Combined Islands vs Trinidad and Tobago – ended in a draw with the scores tied at the end of the match, with Trinidad and Tobago, 3 wickets in hand, batting in the final innings. I was present at the match and there was a sizeable crowd in the ground, all clamouring for the result to be announced. Was it a draw or a tie? And if the former or the latter, how many points would each team receive? A check with the laws of cricket confirmed that the match was a draw and I announced this, but there was nothing in our points system to cater for such a circumstance.

Public controversy raged during the weeks that followed, and when our Board met shortly afterwards, it decided that, in accordance with the existing rules, Trinidad and Tobago should be awarded 6 points for a win on the first innings and the Combined Islands 2 points for losing on the first innings in a drawn match. The latter suggested that 6 points each should be awarded. This decision meant, in effect, that the Combined Islands fell 2 points short of the eventual winners, Guyana. The decision of the board received the confirmation of the ICC when the matter was referred to them, although we were careful to state in our press release that it was our Board's decision and no one else's.

In the meantime we had sent a team to India which won an exciting Test series by three Tests to two, and Andy Roberts, hailing from the small island of Antigua, had put his name indelibly in the scorebook. He was at his fastest and learning all the time. After the India tour, two Tests played in Pakistan were drawn. Viv Richards, also from Antigua, was beginning to show the spark that was to kindle the fire later on.

Later in the same year, we became world champions at the one-day game when we were successful in winning the first Prudential World Cup. Two of the most exciting games of this type ever to be witnessed at the top level were the one we played against Pakistan at Edgbaston, a game which we won against all odds, Roberts and Deryck Murray pulling our chestnuts out of the fire at the eleventh hour; and the final at Lord's, a spectacle never to be forgotten where, due in the main to a superb innings by our captain, Lloyd, we beat Australia in a photofinish.

I was sitting next to G. O. Allen when Lloyd came in, and after he had played the first two or three balls, 'Gubby' said to me, 'Mr Lloyd looks in good nick today. Watch out Australia.' And how right he was. His innings of 102 rightly earned him 'Man of the Match'.

There was another memorable innings played earlier in the series by Kallicharran against Australia at the Oval. Kalli hooked, cut and drove the irrepressible Denis Lillee to all parts of the field. In Lillee's position, I would not have known where next to bowl to the little man. To his eternal credit, Lillee just kept on trying and his wave to the cheering crowd as he took his place at third man following

the over, when he was hit out of sight, was a suitable acknowledge-
ment of the batsman's prowess.

Full of confidence and enthusiasm, our attractive team then toured
Australia for a six-Test series, but after making the score 1-all at
Perth, our team effort degenerated and we were conclusively beaten
5–1 in the series. The team was nicknamed 'the happy hookers' by
the Australian press and this aptly described a feature of the batting.
Bouncers from Lillee and Thomson were hooked with abandon, but
what would have been 6s on the smaller West Indian and English
grounds proved instead to be catches at long-leg. On occasion, most
of the batsmen produced big scores but they seldom clicked together.
An innings of 169 by Roy Fredericks at Perth was said to be one of
the all-time classics by those who saw it.

Our team was kept busy for, on their return to the West Indies,
we were at home to India. However, the inconsistencies continued,
for, whereas we looked much the better team on the faster wickets
of Barbados and Jamaica, we were vulnerable and beaten in one of
the two Tests played on the slow turner which was the Trinidad
wicket.

The first signs of real success came when our team toured England
in 1976. The series was convincingly won by a 3–0 margin and the
all-round supremacy was there for all to see. Roberts, Holding and
Daniel, all fast and with contrasting styles, were too much for the
England batsmen and the name of I. V. A. Richards was repeatedly
making the headlines.

As I write, Richards is acknowledged as the world's finest
batsman, the only other real contender for this honour being Greg
Chappell. Doubtlessly Richards is in the class of the greats of West
Indies cricket and must be ranked along with such as Sobers and
Weekes of the recent past. He has a wonderful eye and sense of
timing and is ruthless in dealing with the short ball. He is a magnificent player of the hook stroke and is especially strong in the mid-
wicket area. Those bowlers who feel that he plays too often across
the line of the ball are seldom rewarded and few will dare to bowl
at him without at least two fielders patrolling the mid-wicket region.
In the 1976 series he scored a magnificent 291 in the final Test at the
Oval, but this is only one of the many great innings he has played.

However, while the tour of England progressed, the storm clouds
were gathering. Earlier in the year, during the course of the Shell
series, Barbados had included one of their regular players, Geoffrey

Greenidge, in their team to play against Guyana at Georgetown. To the surprise of many, including myself, Greenidge on arrival in Guyana was deemed *persona non grata* on the grounds of having played and/or coached in South Africa, and was not given permission to stay in the country. The Barbados team returned home forthwith and the fixture was abandoned. This incident was very nearly the cause of an international confrontation between Barbados and Guyana whose governments took differing views on the issue. For West Indies cricket, signs of trouble ahead were unmistakably clear.

Parallel to this event, Richie Benaud had taken a team, which included several Australian Test players, numbered among whom were the Chappell brothers, Ian and Greg, to South Africa to play against teams ostensibly composed of all races. I say 'ostensibly' because at this point few if any blacks played cricket in South Africa. It is not their game. Asians yes, but Africans no.

The anti-apartheid movement was quick to seize on the issue and it was not long before West Indian politicians were drawn in, and there were strong indications that if the Australian team, due to visit us in 1978, contained players who had recently toured South Africa, they would not be welcome in certain West Indian countries, notably Guyana and Jamaica.

Our Board had met in May of 1976 and released the following statement on South Africa:

The West Indies Cricket Board of Control wishes to reiterate its total opposition to the systems of apartheid as obtain in South Africa and Rhodesia and advises that all players from Caribbean territories under its jurisdiction who play cricket or coach in South Africa or Rhodesia will not be permitted to participate in matches organized under the auspices of the Board either at home or abroad.

In addition, the Board re-affirms that no official team from any country which tours South Africa or Rhodesia will be welcome in the West Indies unless and until there is complete multi-racial cricket and teams are selected solely on merit in those countries.

The pot was kept boiling by both the Guyanese and the Jamaican governments indicating that neither Les Lenham (assistant manager) nor Christopher Cowdrey (captain) would be welcome in either Guyana or Jamaica when Young England toured the West Indies in the summer holidays, the reason being that they had both either played or coached recently in South Africa. In the event, the tour came off after the matches due to be played in these two countries were rescheduled. A 'Test' match was played in Trinidad, and players from both Jamaica and Guyana took part without comment from their governments. At least in this respect the third-party principle did not apply.

As the end of the year approached, the matter of the Australian visit was far from resolved and a further media release was issued by the Board:

On the question of South Africa and Rhodesia the West Indies Cricket Board of Control has gone as far as it can. It has made its position over the years as a member of the International Cricket Conference as clear as possible and again this year endorsed the official position of the Conference, i.e., 'That no official team from any country, which is a member of the ICC will exchange visits with South Africa unless and until it is fully satisfied that cricket is played and teams are selected in that Country on a multi-racial basis.'

The Board went further in May this year to declare publicly its total opposition to apartheid and racism in sport in general and cricket in particular as practised by the regimes in South Africa and Rhodesia and advised that players from Caribbean territories under its jurisdiction who play cricket and/or coach in any of these territories will not be permitted to participate in matches organized under the auspices of the Board either at home or abroad until there is complete multi-racial cricket and teams are selected solely on merit in those countries.

The Board has noted that recently efforts have been made to bring about a new policy for genuine integration in sport in South Africa. This is a positive step in eliminating apartheid and racism in sport.

The Board will continue to use its influence amongst other cricketing nations to encourage the complete elimination of apartheid and racism and welcomes similar efforts by other countries and by the nationals of other countries.

Cricket is an integral part of life in all West Indian territories and it has proved to be the most unifying force in the Caribbean. Negotiations for the tour of Australia to the West Indies in 1978 have already begun and the possibility that some Australians may not be permitted to enter some West Indian countries will have the effect of bringing about the rescheduling of the proposed itinerary. This in itself will cause stresses and strains within the framework of West Indies cricket administration. It is the duty of the Board to ensure that West Indies as a cricket entity does not disintegrate.

The Board, therefore, earnestly hopes that before the negotiations for and the planning of the Australian tour are concluded at its next meeting in May 1977, the policies of all governments of the West Indian territories will enable the Board to schedule matches in all territories.

As a Caricom Heads of Government Conference was due to be held early the following year in Trinidad, much thought was put into the preparation of a position paper which was sent to each of the delegates at the conference in the hope that the matter would be discussed and a solution found which would enable the various governments to formulate a policy within which West Indies cricket would be able to operate successfully. Unfortunately the matter was not placed on the conference agenda and no decisions could be taken. An important opportunity at which the problem could have been debated and thrashed out was therefore missed.

In the meantime there was no rest for our players. Pakistan were engaged with us in what turned out to be an exhilarating series. They played attractive cricket and their team was deservedly popular. By this time, 'Big Bird' Garner and Colin Croft had joined the fray. Well as Majid, Raja, Mushtaq and Co. played, the four-pronged pace attack proved a bit too much for the visitors and an exciting series saw West Indies winning out by two Tests to one with two drawn.

The Heads of Government meeting took place during the first Test match with Pakistan and several of the islands' prime ministers attended the match from time to time. In talking to them, the desire to find a solution came through to me strongly, but the question was how could it be achieved without sacrificing a principle to which the governments were committed?

Time was getting short and both the Australians and ourselves were more than anxious to know where we stood. Accordingly after the meeting of our Board in May, a letter was written to the prime ministers of both Jamaica and Guyana, seeking a meeting with them in order to discuss the proposed visit of the Australians so that the itinerary could include all the traditional cricket territories. It was also thought appropriate to indicate to them the serious repercussions for the future of West Indies cricket and international cricket in general before their departure for the Commonwealth Heads of Government Conference which was due to be held shortly in London.

Both Michael Manley and Forbes Burnham were keen followers of the game, and together with Allan Rae, who was a long-time

personal friend of the former and more than an acquaintance of the
latter, I set forth on this rather unusual mission. We were most
cordially received and left with the impression that they would leave
no stone unturned to try and find a solution to the problem.

However, in the event that none could be found, our Board was
determined that the tour should take place and I continued my
travels to include Bermuda to survey the chances of holding a Test
match there. In the company of Alma 'Champ' Hunt, I met with all
the appropriate government officers whose help would be necessary
if the ground was to be converted into a Test arena. Financially I
was left in no doubt that a Test match played in Bermuda would
be successful.

It is now a matter of history that the Gleneagles Accord, negotiated
at the Commonwealth Heads of Government Conference, was the
means by which the question of sporting links with South Africa
was, for the time being, deferred. But as time was to prove, the
agreement was not sufficiently clear cut and was open to differences
of interpretation. This was to become only too obvious in the days
that lay ahead.

During the course of one Board meeting and while we were pre-
occupied with the problems of South Africa, a cable was received
from Jack Bailey, Secretary of the International Cricket Conference,
saying that a special meeting was being called the following month
to discuss 'a proposed cricket circus in Australia'. Simultaneously
we received a cable from a Mr Kerry Packer asking for a meeting
with his representatives, to which we replied that we were unable
to confer other than through recognized cricket authorities.

We were not unduly perturbed by these communications and I
remember saying, 'One bridge at a time. We'll cross this one when
we come to it.'

No one, least of all myself, conceived at that time the holocaust
that was to be unleashed on the complacent cricket world. The next
three years were to prove the most testing ever experienced by
international cricket and its administrators.

20

The Packer Intrusion: The West Indian Viewpoint

Allan Rae and I had, for the previous couple of years, represented the Board at the annual meetings of ICC, but in view of the fact that we had made arrangements to attend the regular meeting in July, previous commitments made it impossible for us to be present at the hastily summoned meeting in June, when discussions would be held by the representatives of Test-cricket-playing countries with Mr Kerry Packer.

I have always regretted not being present at this meeting as it was undoubtedly the most important of all.

As a result of what transpired, there was a parting of the ways for all time. Mr Packer is reported to have made a statement to the effect that television rights in Australia were not an area for negotiation as far as he was concerned. This was unacceptable to the Australian Cricket Board, who had a long-standing arrangement with the Australian Broadcasting Commission, and they insisted on competitive bidding. And so it was that the West Indies (and other cricketing countries) were drawn into a dispute that was basically an Australian quarrel.

One has heard reports from all sides of the aggressiveness and discourtesy with which Mr Packer treated the cricket authorities; nevertheless, I was of the view then, and still am now, several years later, that the door should not have been closed, and that not keeping a line of communication open with Packer was a serious mistake. After this meeting there was no real dialogue between Mr Packer and the cricket authorities until irreparable damage had been done.

At the opening of the ICC meeting in July, I made a formal request of the chair: 'Mr Chairman, in my not inconsiderable experience I have learned not to have confrontations with three "Ps", the Politicians, the Press and the Police. Is it that we are about to wage war against a fourth P? Has a line of communication been left open with Mr Packer so that further dialogue may take place?' The answer was in the negative. Perhaps the mention of the word 'war' was a mistake for I was made to feel somewhat like Chamberlain after Munich as a result of having made this statement!

The die had been cast and much of the Conference was devoted to the legal implications of the proposed resolution to debar the Packer players from playing Test cricket. Allan, being a lawyer, was in his element and was obviously unhappy and not as satisfied as his legal colleagues representing ICC that the Conference could successfully defend any action which may be brought by Packer against ICC. We thereupon made our stand clear to the Conference.

The West Indies position was somewhat different to that of any other country. Those of our players who had been contracted by Packer at that stage were not under contract to the Board and would, inasmuch as the itineraries did not clash, be available to play against Australia in the West Indies in 1978. We were opposed to the principle of retroactivity implied in the ICC resolution: 'Any player who after 1 October 1977 is contracted to or played in a match organized by the Packer promotion will not be eligible to play for their country in a Test match unless prior approval is obtained from the Conference.'

Nevertheless, our players knew that we were due to tour India the following year and that this tour would clash directly with their Packer contracts. The crunch had to come sometime along the way.

It is now common knowledge that the West Indies, with only two votes out of 12, were a minority of one when the decision was taken to pass the resolution. It is a fact also that we were persuaded neither to vote against nor to abstain from voting for the sake of unanimity with ICC. In view of the fact that the Conference had decided on this course of action, it would have been foolhardy for us to exhibit, by voting against the resolution, a chink in the armour of ICC. If we were going to fight, then we must fight together whatever the differences of opinion. I shall defend this action to the last, although it was not acceptable to the majority of West Indians at the time.

We were applauded by the other ICC representatives for our change of heart but we insisted that our reservations should be recorded in the Minutes of the Conference. Our reservations embraced the following:

1. That it was morally unfair to penalize retroactively players who were at the time free to enter into contracts.
2. That this circumstance would give Mr Packer a weapon with which to fight against the Conference in court.
3. That the fact that Mr Packer was offering the players more money would carry weight in that he would be shown to have improved the players' circumstances.

In my statement to the Chairman, I made it clear that we were 'taking the easy way out', but warned that the repercussions by press and public in the West Indies would be severe, for paramount in their minds would be the increased wages for the players and this would transcend all other considerations. Prophetic words these proved to be, not only in respect of the reaction in the West Indies to our stand, the details of which we could not fully disclose, but also in the unsuccessful defence of the court action instituted by Packer shortly afterwards!*

At home we were never able to convince either the majority of the press or the cricketing public of the ICC viewpoint to which we were now a party. The issue became highly emotional, and although through media conferences we tried to explain our position and that of ICC and the dangers which lay ahead for the future of international cricket, Kerry Packer became something of a hero and his 'more bread for the players' syndrome carried the day.

Realizing as I did that money would be required to keep West Indies cricket going and to pay our players higher wages (we certainly could not match Packer), I set about trying to raise funds on a grand scale under deeds of covenant. The oil companies, the banks and businessmen all over Trinidad (the only reasonably wealthy country) were approached, and the problems were explained over specially held luncheons. While the response was admirable, I detected a certain reticence which was no doubt due to public reaction that was anti-Board at the time. Would it be good publicity for a company to contribute to a cause which did not have popular support?

---

*The West Indies were made to pay their full share of the cost of the court case. I have always thought that this was morally indefensible.

Further setbacks were forthcoming when the Trinidad and Tobago Inland Revenue Department, no doubt influenced by the Government, refused to allow donations under covenant for tax-relief purposes, and in the midst of it all Packer triumphed in his court case and the ICC was found 'in restraint of trade' in its efforts to disqualify the Packer players from playing in Test matches. Later on, however, many companies and individuals supported us and we would have been hard pressed to survive financially were it not for their generous help.

In the meantime, the Australian Cricket Board had decided not to select any of their Packer players. The number of Australians engaged by Packer was almost enough to form two teams, so what was perhaps a third XI was selected to tour the West Indies in 1978. This team had, however, done well that winter against the visiting Indians and we hoped that all would be well.

The West Indies Board, at its November meeting, had decided to retain its Packer players, holding the view that, until they made themselves unavailable to us, we would continue to select them. At the same time we imposed a deadline by which they would have to commit themselves one way or another for the forthcoming tour of India.

The first two Test matches against the 'new' Australian team were overwhelmingly won by our full-strength West Indies team. Neither game went the distance; in fact, both were over in three days and it was obvious that our aggressive fast-bowling combination of Croft, Roberts and Garner was too much for the untried and inexperienced Australian batsmen.

One of the more base aspects of the Packer intrusion was the fact that his scouts were ever present at Test venues, looking for new talent and 'creaming off' the top-class players on whom a great deal of money had been spent in order to enable them to attain Test-match standard. Three such players were Croft, Haynes and Austin and, on behalf of the Board, I had promised these three players contracts which would be prepared for their consideration before the third Test match, due to be played in Guyana. In spite of this, the Packer scouts had, with their usual propensity for secrecy, signed them up during the Test match in Barbados. However, the news was leaked to us before the Packer camp could make the announcement, and we were able to put out a strongly worded release which enlisted some public sympathy for the Board. But whatever we did, we were in no position to match the money being offered by Packer.

All of this, not surprisingly, pitted player against player and, even more so, player against administration, and it would be no understatement to mention that I, among others, felt like a stranger in the West Indies dressing room. This was ironic in the extreme for we were the only country to have put in a plea (unsuccessful though it had been) for their players.

Between the second and third Test matches the players' deadline had passed, and a communication received at the eleventh hour from Deryck Murray, acting as secretary of the Players' Association which the Board was assisting the players to form, sought to put off the deadline further and encourage a meeting with Packer representatives. This the Board was not prepared to do, for we had given an undertaking at ICC that we would not meet unilaterally with Packer or in any way seek to undermine the authority of ICC.

Our selectors in their wisdom, and with the forthcoming tour of India in view, then decided on three changes in the team for the third Test due to be played in Georgetown. The players omitted were Deryck Murray, Haynes and Austin. The last named would probably have been omitted in any event as he had not had any degree of success in the two previous Tests. Clive Lloyd, as captain, was a party to the selection but was in all probability in the minority. At the end of the selection, he announced to the media his withdrawal from the team, and in this he was supported by the other Packer contracted players, Greenidge, Richards, Roberts, Garner and Croft. In anticipation of some such action the Board had hurriedly made arrangements to fly replacements into Guyana. The fat was now truly in the fire!

Under pressure from the Guyanese cricket administrators, I realized that it was my duty to fly to Georgetown at short notice in order to try and help bring order out of chaos. I was accompanied on the flight by Peter Short, one of the representatives of the Board from Barbados. An experienced and able administrator, Peter was a former secretary of the Board and had, at the request of ICC and with our approval, been summoned to give evidence in the court case. His help in the difficult exercise we were about to undertake was considerable.

The main question to be answered was, could we do in practice what in all conscience we should do in theory? That is, accept the withdrawal of the captain and other Packer players and replace them with the players we had flown in?

Guyana's politics are extremely sensitive and the thousands of cricket followers there are highly emotional and very fond and conscious of their cricketing heroes. What was more, Clive Lloyd was Guyanese. Would there be a riot if we did what we had to do, I wondered.

Arriving late in the evening together with Short, I held a conference with Berkeley Gaskin, President of the Guyana Cricket Board, Joe Solomon and Glendon Gibbs, the Guyana Board representatives, Sir Lionel Luckhoo and others who had the ear of the Government. 'There will be no riot,' I was told and so, mercifully, I received the green light to proceed along the straight and narrow but difficult path that my conscience dictated.

Of the meeting held the next day with Lloyd and some of the other Packer players present in Guyana, little needs to be said. I do believe that they expected to be asked to return to the fold and that the Board would capitulate and not dare to accept their withdrawal.

At a press conference afterwards on the same day, my pent-up emotions were released, for the pressure had been terrific over the past months. I have a tape recording of what I said on that occasion which, in retrospect, could be a collector's item and form a part of the archives of West Indies cricket which one hopes will some day be developed. It was as though a heavy weight had been lifted from my shoulders. At least we knew the road along which we had to travel until further developments in this high drama unfolded.

Mr Packer arrived in Guyana in his private plane the same afternoon. Perhaps, in anticipation of a different decision by our Board, he had come to do a deal with us. If so, he must have been disappointed for he flew out early the next day.

In quick order, a new team was selected. Kallicharran, who had elected not to join Packer, was made captain and an exciting and closely fought Test match was lost by 3 wickets. The pressure quickly built up again, and although the 'new' West Indies team won the fourth Test in Trinidad by a wide margin, it was poorly attended. The crowd, egged on by sections of the media and an ill-informed public, decided to boycott the match, the original omission of Deryck Murray being the main plank on which the boycott was built.

The final Test match in Jamaica also had its traumatic moments. When I left Kingston on the day before it was due to finish, it seemed headed for a quiet draw, but the Australians gained the ascendancy on the last day, and would most probably have won had the thirty-eight balls of the final 20 overs been bowled on the day following the scheduled end of the match. However, in spite of representations made by the cricket authorities, the umpires ruled that the regulations under which the game was being played would not permit this and this provided an unfortunate finish to an equally unfortunate tour.

The West Indies Board, because it is unable to make a profit on home tours due to limitations of population and ground accommodation, is seldom far removed from financial embarrassment. Following on the disastrous tour by Australia, the Board once again went into the red, and when the position was explained to members at the end of 1978, it was clear that we were fighting for financial survival. It was purely on these grounds that we saw fit to allow the Packer organization to stage matches in the West Indies early in 1979. The games came and went. There was some good cricket and some bad, but I have no doubt these games, like so many of the other Packer contests, will be quickly forgotten for they form no part of cricket records. I would accept Mr Packer's money for our Board's survival, but I could not bring myself to attend any of his matches.

Events continued to unfold by the hour. More and more players joined World Series Cricket, as the Packer contests were now named, and it was generally recognized that the real crunch would come when England toured Australia in the winter of 1978. The Australian representatives at ICC were overwhelmingly confident that this tour would sound the death knell of Packer who, by this time, may have been himself worried over the lack of public support. But his organization and promotional operatives had improved beyond measure, learning by their past mistakes, and the contrary proved to be the case. The England tour was a financial flop and the Packer games drew more crowds and, even more important, their television ratings increased significantly.

At the same time we had sent a team of 'seconds' to India under Kallicharran and they were holding their own. New names were coming to the fore. Sylvester Clarke, Malcolm Marshall, Larry Gomes, Faoud Bacchus and David Murray were all making their mark. There would be keen competition for Test places when normal cricket resumed.

While the Board had authorized certain of its members to have informal discussions with World Series Cricket representatives during their tour to the West Indies, they were held with a view to ensuring that our WSC players would be available for all Test matches and as much domestic cricket as their contracts would allow. The 1979 Prudential Cup was due to take place in July and we wished to have our full team for this series. It was more than time to heal the breach. We constantly pressed ICC to hold talks with WSC, for we knew that the traditional Test series in Australia was not going well.

It would be churlish of me not to record the immense amount of good work put in by such devoted servants of the game as David Clark and Charles Palmer who, as Chairmen of ICC in 1978 and 1979, bore the brunt of organized cricket's responsibility during the Packer years. They travelled far and wide in their attempt to achieve a consensus among the cricketing nations and it is to their everlasting credit that their efforts were eventually crowned with success.

In the end, with financial ruin staring them in the face (and this went for the West Indies as well), the Australian Board opened negotiations with the Packer organization and, bargaining from a position of weakness, were forced into making several decisions which would seriously affect the future of the game as a whole and especially so in Australia.

The position taken by the Australian representatives at the 1979 ICC meeting was a complete volte-face from that taken the year before – incredible but true! The fact was that they had been able to remove (a not unwilling) Mr Packer from the cricket scene, but in doing so they had to pay a steep price.

At this meeting we found ourselves as mediators between Australia and the UK. Our overriding consideration was the financial salvation of West Indies cricket and, concurrently, the return of our players, therefore we left no stone unturned to effect a compromise between the two foundation members, so that a proposed joint tour by England and the West Indies to Australia could take place in the winter of 1979–80. This tour, when it did come off, certainly saved us financially and safeguarded our foreseeable future; and I have no doubt that the Australian Cricket Board breathed more freely as well. What is more, with a second World Cup championship under our belt as well as a convincing victory in the three-way series including the one-day internationals in Australia, we were undisputed champions of the world.

Our euphoria, however, was short-lived. A short tour of New Zealand followed and with it more difficulties. This time the problems were of a different but equally serious nature.

21
The Aftermath

Early in 1980 the Board of Control for Cricket in India invited administrators from all of the Test-playing countries to celebrate their golden anniversary with them. It was a gala occasion and it took Sara and me to Bombay for India's Golden Jubilee Test match with England.

The match itself was memorable for the exhibition of all-round prowess by Ian Botham, who won the match for England almost single-handedly, and a generous display of sportsmanship by the Indian captain, Viswanath, who asked the umpire to recall Bob Taylor when he had been wrongly given out caught at the wicket. As is oft-times the case, this proved to be the turning point of the match.

After the celebrations we wended our way back to the West Indies via London where, although we were understandably tired on our arrival, I found a message awaiting me that I should call our team manager, Willie Rodriguez, in New Zealand. There had been articles in the international press indicating that the tour had not been going smoothly, and various incidents which had apparently taken place on the field did not reflect at all well on the West Indies team.

At around midnight I got through to the manager, only to be told that the team had decided unanimously to return home by the first available opportunity. Momentarily I was lost for words. 'Are you out of your minds?' I asked. 'Do you realize the implications of such action?' In a flash I visualized writs against our Board, isolation in international cricket and goodness knows what other damage to the future of West Indies cricket.

After a conversation lasting several minutes, during which I listened to numerous complaints about bad umpiring and substandard conditions to which the team was being subjected, I succeeded in obtaining from the manager a promise to call another team meeting at which he should leave no stone unturned to persuade the team to complete the tour.

There was also, of course, the necessity to offer suitable apologies to the New Zealand Cricket Council over alleged unsportsmanlike incidents on the field in which Holding and Croft had been involved, and for an equally serious charge that the team had failed to take the field at the appointed hour after the tea interval during the second test at Christchurch.

There followed further talks on the telephone with Bob Vance, President of the New Zealand Cricket Council, and also with the captain and manager of our team. For the time being, a crisis was averted and the tour was completed with New Zealand winning the series by 1–0. There was no doubt, however, that feelings had run high and many were the intemperate statements made to the press by our manager and some of the players.

While there was, on the one hand, a loud outcry in certain areas, notably New Zealand, for immediate action to be taken by our Board against the players involved, the West Indian press, fed with reports by our manager and some of the players, found every justification for the players' actions. It was decided in the circumstances to wait until a full enquiry into the events could be held. This was done at our Board meeting which followed shortly after the end of the ill-fated tour, at which members were able to view on videotape the incidents on the field as well as some of the controversial umpiring decisions which we had been told precipitated them.

After viewing the films, there was no doubt in the minds of members that the conduct of Holding, who had kicked down the wickets at the batsman's end after a decision for 'caught behind' went against him, and of Croft, who had, apparently with some deliberation, barged into the back of the presiding umpire after being no-balled repeatedly, were nothing short of a demonstration of extremely bad sportsmanship.

On the other hand, Willie Rodriguez, Clive Lloyd (captain) and Deryck Murray (vice-captain) were all unanimous on the subject of several acts of provocation both on and off the field in New Zealand.

It has been said of our Board that we were too lenient in our dealings with the captain and players over the issues involved. In essence the Board decided:

1. That the Captain should write a suitably worded public letter of apology to both the New Zealand Council and the West Indies Board.
2. That both Holding and Croft should apologize publicly to both Boards, failing which they would not be selected for the then imminent tour of England.
3. That our contracts with the players should be tightened up to include disciplinary clauses calculated to prevent any such recurrence.
4. That the authority of the umpire must remain supreme at all times.

These decisions were duly conveyed to the New Zealand Cricket Council.

This was not to be the end of the story, for it appeared that our players were now unhappy with the Board's decisions, and after the completion of financial negotiations for the England tour and further protracted bargaining on the question of fees and allowances for the tour, we were faced, literally on the eve of their departure, with a proposed 'strike' by the players.

I am fortunate to possess a 'retreat' on the small island of Monos off the coast of Trinidad, and I had retired to it after considering that all matters pertaining to the tour had been settled. Shortly after sun-up on the day prior to the team's departure, I was awakened by our worthy secretary, Harold Burnett, who had hired a boat and presented himself at my bedroom door with the words, 'Mr President, the Secretary of the Players' Association has informed me that the team will not fly out tomorrow unless certain adjustments are made to the fees and allowances.' Would the problems never end, I wondered.

Experience, by this time, had taught me not to panic, so we lingered awhile over a cup of coffee before setting out for Port of Spain to start the round of telephone calls that this new crisis had precipitated, calls to Donald Carr in London, Board members around the Caribbean, etc. Fortunately, Clive Lloyd coincidentally called us from his home in Manchester, and after a discussion with him, the matter was presumed to be settled by the addition of a minimal increase all round, but we were aware that he would have the difficult job of conveying this to the players. Not to be caught napping again, we arranged for the fees and allowances to be published on the day after the team was due to fly out, for by this time the fees were considerable.

All this contributed to further and renewed estrangement between the players and the Board. The team, however, was playing magnificent cricket and their performances on the field were exemplary. The series and one-day internationals were convincingly won and, without doubt, we were the best and most attractive team on the circuit. The bowling of Holding, Croft, Roberts and Garner and the batting of Greenidge, Haynes, Richards and Lloyd were too consistently powerful for the opposition.

While in London to attend ICC, Allan Rae and I held a satisfactory meeting with the players at their hotel and this did much to clear the air. With our players scattered as they are all over the globe, it is seldom possible to hold such meetings, but they are absolutely necessary if that bugbear 'suspicion' is going to be eliminated.

Much emphasis these days is being placed on slow over rates and their effect on the course of a match. The West Indies, with four fast bowlers usually employed, has been a prime target for these complaints. Over rates are now talking points for radio and press commentators, particularly in England where they seem to compete equally for broadcast time with the score itself.

Obviously the over rates depend on a number of factors: whereas Ramadhin and Valentine averaged around 21 overs per hour, Holding and Croft would average about 14. However, the imposition of fines and other penalties for slow over rates is not the answer. These touch only the tip of the iceberg. For my part, the answer lies in two main areas. First and foremost, the umpires must step in and take action under Law 46 – unfair play – if there is any indication of anyone, bowler or batsman, deliberately wasting time. Umpires have been encouraged, nay instructed, by cricket authorities all over the world to take such action but, so far, I have rarely if ever seen or heard of them doing so. Second, the LBW law should be altered to encourage spin-bowlers, particularly those who turn the ball from leg, back into the game.

It is generally accepted by all thinking administrators and spectators as well as by most players that the absence of wrist-spinners from the modern game robs it of considerable interest. We seem in this day and age to be presiding over the demise of the leg-spinner. Under the present laws, he has been 'sorted out' by the batsman and there is no room for him in first-class cricket; he is no longer 'value for money'.

I have been advocating for some time the application of the current LBW law to balls pitched outside of the *leg-stump* as well; with the one proviso that the ball must be delivered from the opposite side of the wicket. The reason for the proviso is obvious, for without it the fast left-arm-over- and right-arm-around-the-wicket bowlers would be unnecessarily helped by the law.

After all, it is conceded that outswerve and leg-spin are the two most difficult balls to bowl, and under the present LBW law they are the least subsidized. It is only logical that what now applies to the off-side should apply equally to the leg-side. The fact that only two fielders are allowed to be placed behind square leg will eliminate the possibility of too many balls being bowled too wide of the leg-stump.

Some support for this proposal has been obtained at ICC, notably from Australia, and the change is being experimented with at the present time in several of the Test-playing countries. Such knowledgeable ex-Test players as Sir Donald Bradman, with whom the theory originated as far back as 1938, and Bill Bowes among others have declared themselves in favour of such an experiment, for it is only by experimenting that we may tell whether such a change is worthwhile or not.

The International Cricket Conference itself will have to move with the times. A valid criticism of its deliberations is that it has no 'teeth'. Its recommendations are invariably subject to confirmation by individual member boards of control. It has no funds of its own which severely limits its functions, and the time is fast approaching when its constitution, with the power of veto residing with the two foundation members, England and Australia, will have to be changed. This is something of an anachronism in this day and age.

Recently there has been an attempt by Pakistan to introduce the idea of neutral observers to be present at Test matches whose terms of reference are to report on every facet of the staging of the match, both on and off the field. While the idea has much merit, the absence of funds to put it into practice is a stumbling block to its development.

This idea was also put into effect experimentally during the West

Indies tour of Pakistan in 1980 and its usefulness became apparent when another unhappy incident involving one of our players, Sylvester Clarke, took place during the Test match at Multan. Jack Bailey, Secretary of ICC, was the independent observer at the match and our Board was in receipt of his report as well as those of the captain and manager of our team.

There was little doubt that Clarke – who was fielding in the outfield after bowling and under some provocation from the crowd, which were throwing a variety of missiles – lost his cool and retaliated by throwing a brick which formed a part of the boundary's edge back into the crowd. A young student was seriously injured as a result, and a dangerous situation was only averted by the prompt action of our manager, Jackie Hendriks, Captain Lloyd and other members of the team, along with the Pakistani authorities who could not have been more helpful and understanding.

Here we were, then, once again having to hold an enquiry into an ugly incident in which one of our players was the central figure; and here again we were not going to be rushed into precipitant action as was being called for by elements of the cricketing press.

At the enquiry held sometime later, Clarke was most contrite and did not attempt to deny the essential facts. He impressed us all with the straightforward manner in which he gave his account of what happened. He was duly suspended for a number of matches which effectively kept him from being a contender for a place in our Test team which was meeting England at home at the time, but it in no way prejudiced his professional contract in the UK or his future in the game.

These incidents, which are becoming more and more frequent and have in no way been confined to the West Indies, call for more effective control of cricket worldwide by ICC, and the time is long overdue for the world's controlling body to examine what may prove to be the more suitable constitutions of FIFA and ILTA in an effort to increase its role in international cricket.

When the England team of 1981 arrived in the West Indies for a five-match Test series, all was set fair except the weather which was deplorable from the outset. Our problems were not over, however, and when our selectors in their wisdom decided to substitute the young wicket-keeper David Murray for Deryck Murray, now approaching the age of retirement, we were once again facing another boycott. This, together with the inclement weather, the one-sided nature of the game which was won by the West Indies in three days and the fact that we had decided to allow the match to be fully televised, all made it a financial disaster. Worse was to follow.

When Bob Willis, the England fast bowler, became unfit and had to return home, his replacement was Robin Jackman of Surrey who, it turned out, was married to a South African and had been a regular visitor to that country, both to play and coach in the off-season. These events did not escape the notice of a Jamaican journalist and a press report by him on the subject received wide publicity throughout the Caribbean and was the cause of an immediate reaction in Guyana to which country the England team had travelled for the second Test.

Overnight, despite diplomatic and other protests, the future of the tour was placed in jeopardy when it was officially announced by the Guyana Government that Robin Jackman would not be welcome to stay in Guyana. As a result, the England team packed up, lock, stock and barrel, and left for Barbados where, on the initiative of the Barbados Government, a conference attended by representatives of Barbados, Jamaica, Antigua and Montserrat was hurriedly called and the Gleneagles agreement rescued from the files.

The England team manager, Allan Smith, acted with great restraint and, after consultations with his headquarters in the UK, stated that, in addition to their belief that Jackman's selection had not violated Gleneagles, England would not be dictated to as to whom they should select. Unfortunately, however, also included in the statement was the request for an assurance with which we could not conceivably comply, namely that there would be no more interference by any West Indian Government for the remainder of the tour. Once again, therefore, there was confrontation on the South African issue, only this time it was taking place in the middle of a tour, and apart from the financial implications, the whole future of international cricket where the West Indies were concerned was in jeopardy.

Under no illusion that in any country it is the politicians who are in charge, and realizing that the remainder of the tour was due to take place in two independent countries, Barbados and Jamaica, whose policies on the subject in all probability differed, I decided to seek the advice of the Trinidad Minister of Foreign Affairs. Also to be considered were the views of a third state, Antigua, shortly to become independent and about to stage a Test match for the first time with all the prior arrangements that this entailed.

As far as our Board was concerned, I wanted to ensure that I had the best political information available before making any statement on such a controversial affair. Finally it was decided to state publicly that 'The West Indies Cricket Board of Control would not act in contravention of the principles governing sporting links with South Africa to which the governments of the various West Indies territories have subscribed.'

Only those who have lived in the West Indies will be able to understand the extent to which emotions are aroused in this part of the world by the system of apartheid which operates in South Africa. It is most unfortunate that sport happens to be the major vehicle by which anti-apartheid campaigners hope to accelerate the demise of that system, and it is a shattering thought that, unless governments are prepared to compromise on the issue, international sport, and cricket above all, may well be sacrificed at the altar of politics. The danger is very real, I assure you. There are so many other important sectors where anomalies exist, trade for instance.

First and foremost, the area for compromise must be on the so-called 'third-party principle'. Taking cricket as an example, if a professional cricketer wishes to visit South Africa as an individual to play or coach in order to earn his keep and that of his family, then that must be his right, for it is more than likely that under the laws of most countries, positive action by any organization to prevent him doing so would find that organization in the position of being in 'restraint of trade'. It seems to be an untenable position for even governments to hold.

Boards of Control may use various methods of persuasion which will vary in degree. The West Indies Cricket Board has instructed its selectors not to select any player for the West Indies who has played or coached in South Africa since Gleneagles. England, on the other hand, has merely advised their players of the possible consequences if they do so, but has not gone further than moral persuasion. The sanctioning of official tours to and from South Africa is another matter, and I do not see this taking place in cricket in my lifetime. If such an event does happen, then the Test-playing members of the International Cricket Conference are likely to become polarized on racial lines, a circumstance that would be disastrous for the game.

In the particular case of the Jackman affair, the future of the tour hung in the balance until the announcement came from the Barbados conference that it would be allowed to continue. In essence, the release from the meeting indicated that interpretation of the Gleneagles agreement was open to ambiguity and that the governments of the Caribbean and the wider Commonwealth should consult with a view to *strengthening* the Gleneagles agreement at the Commonwealth Heads of Government Conference due to be held in Australia later in the year. So far as I am aware no such consultations have taken place. In short, we obtained a reprieve but no framework of policy within which our Cricket Board could operate in future. This unfortunate and unhappy situation still exists as I write.

So the tour continued and three enthusiastically attended Test matches, in which the best of spirits and camaraderie existed between the teams, saw it to a successful conclusion. The West Indies were a superior team, but two of the last three Tests were drawn by an increasingly tenacious England team. Our margin of victory was 2–0. The finances, however, were in ruins and our board lost heavily on the tour.

Our outstanding player in the series was the captain, Clive Lloyd, who at age thirty-seven batted magnificently in the middle order, caught superbly in the slips and led his side most capably. It is true that he had an excellent team under him, but Clive has become more than just a captain to his team. He is now something of a father figure who is much respected by those who play under him. West Indies cricket has much for which to thank this outstanding player who has been the most successful of all West Indies captains in terms of Test matches won. He has grown considerably in stature as the years have gone by, has survived operations to both knees and conquered a number of other, perhaps lesser, injuries, but his purpose to blend into one combination the best cricket team in the world has never varied. Our relationship, fraught as it has been with difficulties of one sort or another, has mellowed to what I hope may be considered more than just mutual respect, and he will be sorely missed whenever he elects to leave the scene.

Although reluctant to accept a fourth term as President of the Board, I felt that my job was not yet done because the Board's finances were in the red, and the vexed question of the smooth transfer of authority by the Queen's Park Cricket Club to the Trinidad and Tobago Cricket Board of Control had not yet been achieved.

The control of the twin islands' cricket by a single club was undoubtedly an anachronism in this day and age, but long and tedious were the negotiations that eventually brought the transfer to a satisfactory conclusion. The Queen's Park Cricket Club is the equivalent of the MCC to cricket in Trinidad and Tobago and it played a significant part in the establishment and promotion of the game in the West Indies, but the time had arrived for a more democratic organization to take over and this has now taken place.

The financial setback resulting from the ill-fated tour by England has been abolished by receipts expected from our winter tour of Australia, and by the direct financial help of the Government of Trinidad and Tobago so, once again, we shall be in the black and hopefully in a position of relative solvency.

At the Board's meeting held in tranquil Tobago in November of 1981, I felt that I could safely lay down the burden of West Indies cricket, and no one was happier than me when my opening partner and life-long friend, Allan Rae, was elected my successor.

22
Reflections and the Future

This is one man's story. It is one man's experiences. It tells one side of the picture. Far be it from me to admit that in matters of controversy there is not 'another side', but many of the incidents and events were recorded at the time they took place and of these there can be no dispute.

What about cricket's future and, in particular, the part to be played by the West Indies? Taking the former first, there is little doubt that more and more one-day, limited overs cricket will be played – at least in the near future – for in many parts of the world this is what the spectator wants, and at the top level of commercial cricket the customer has to be right. To the professional player and to those interested in tactics, the limited overs game has its limitations. There are too few variations on the same theme. The clamour of the majority of spectators today appears to be for action and a finish to a match in one day. If this is indeed what the spectators want, then they will get it, but the sameness of the one-day game from match to match may prove its undoing in the longer term.

What of the future of Test cricket? With the object of bringing the crowds in, Test cricket must undoubtedly put much more of an emphasis on winning. In factual terms, those Test teams which have played the more positive cricket have been the successful ones. Isn't there a moral in this? England's apparent approach to Test matches in recent times is a case in point. Her team selection has tended towards safety-first tactics, and the potential stroke player has not been sufficiently encouraged. So many of the imported players in county cricket show the way to success by playing their strokes. The example is there to be followed. At the other end of the scale, the

West Indian batsmen can and do play shots and the accent is generally on attack rather than defence. The same applies to our bowlers and here lies the secret of our numerous successes.

Turning to the future of West Indies cricket, it may not be an over-simplification to state that it is all related to the South African issue. While there will be continuing problems over matters of finance and keeping our diverse small countries and territories integrated into one unit, both of these problems are essentially related to South Africa.

The West Indies in the foreseeable future will continue to earn its money through overseas tours, to England and Australia in particular. In India and to a lesser extent Pakistan, where large crowds watch the game, there are apparently stringent exchange control regulations to be surmounted and this restricts the profits to be made on these tours. New Zealand has similar financial problems to ours with a limited population to support home tours as well as limited accommodation. So what is to happen if the world of cricket, through external forces beyond its control, becomes divided, due to differences of political opinion on the South African issue, into the so-called 'white' and 'black' countries? Do we disappear from the scene because of lack of finance?

In another but equally important sphere, there are considerable differences of opinion between the governments of the West Indies over the extent to which they should take steps in practical terms to show their distaste and disapproval of apartheid in South Africa, for make no mistake: unless my reading of the situation is wrong, West Indian governments will not permit their Board of Control to accept the return of South Africa to the International Cricket Conference unless and until the *system* of apartheid is abolished. Internally, a constant struggle will have to be waged to keep our cricket integrated because of this divergence of views and we shall continue to find it necessary to walk the existing tightrope.

This is not a particularly happy note on which to end this book which essentially tells a happy story. The story of one who has had many wonderful years playing and talking cricket and helping in the administration of the great game. The travel, the experiences, the friends made have all added up to the making of a life well worth living.

Index

Adelaide Oval, 68, 123,
125, 126–7
Adhikari, H., 64
administrator, cricket, 162,
164–5, 168, 173,
193–221
Agard, Joey, 47
Agricultural Society of
Trinidad and Tobago,
161, 168
Alexander, Gerry, 158,
159, 163, 164, 165
Ali, S. M., 46
Allen, G. O., 9, 52, 53, 55,
60, 77, 79, 197
Altham, H. S., 87
Amarnath, L., 61, 62
Ames, Les, 83
Amin, Idi, 171
Andrews, Bill, 38
Archer, Ron, 116, 151
Arlott, John, 78, 92–3
Asgarali, N., 49, 135, 159
Ashdown, W. H., 100
Atkinson, Denis, 69, 117,
126, 127, 146, 148,
150, 151, 152, 154,
155, 156, 158
Atkinson, Eric, 157
Auckland, 132–3
Austin, 206, 207
Australia, tours to:
1951–52, 117–33;
1960–61, 113, 164–5;
1968–69, 184–5;
1979–80, 210

Australian tours to West
Indies: 1954–55,
151–5; 1973, 186–9;
1978, 206–9

Bacchus, Faoud, 209
Bailey, Jack, 202, 217
Bailey, Trevor, 85, 86, 89,
94, 105, 142, 143,
145, 150
Ball, Ken, 27, 191
Barbados Advocate, 135–6
Barclays Bank of Trinidad
and Tobago Ltd
(renamed Republic
Bank), 21, 26–7, 50,
190, 191
Barnes, S. F., 77, 78
Barnett, Charles, 35, 36
Barrow, Errol Walton, 194
Barrow, Ivan, 20, 34
batting records by the
author, 49, 88
Baxter, Alex, 17
Bayley, Peter, 32, 34, 38
Bedser, Alec, 52, 85, 88,
89, 95, 96, 105, 142
Benaud, Richie, 132, 151,
154, 178, 199
Berry, R., 85, 86, 87, 91
Beyond the Boundary, 19
Binns, Alfie, 152
Birkett, Lionel, 31, 33, 39
Bombay, 58, 61, 67, 69,
70, 71, 101, 137, 212
Borwick, 80
Botham, Ian, 212

Bourne, C. L. C., 46
Bowes, Bill, 30, 35, 38,
216
Boycott, Geoff, 177
Bradman, Sir Donald, 23,
35, 36, 67, 80, 117,
125–6, 216
Bramall Lane, Sheffield,
96–102
Branch, Mr, 53
Bray, Charles, 52, 84
Brennan, Don, 97, 100
Brisbane, 80, 113, 119–21,
124, 125–6
British Guiana Chronicle,
33
Brookes, Dennis, 52, 55
Brown, F. R., 77, 94, 105,
106
Brown, W. A. (Bill), 125
Buller, J. S., 179
Burge, Peter, 151
Burke, Boysie, 23
Burke, Jim, 126
Burke, Oliver, 43
Burke, P. B. (Chappie), 23,
24, 149
Burnett, Harold J., 24,
195–6, 214
Burnham, L. F. S., 194
Burtt, Tom, 88
business activities, 190–91
Butcher, B., 163, 166, 176,
183
Butler, Harold, 52
Butler, L., 118

Caires, Cecil de, 151, 158, 159
Calcutta, 68–9
Cameron, J. H., 34, 49, 59, 92
captain of: West Indies vs India (1952–53), 137–41; vs England (1954), 142–50; vs Australia (1954–55), 153–4
Cardus, Neville, 35, 36, 78–9, 96–7
Carew, George, 55, 59, 69, 176, 186, 188
Carew, M. C., 166
Caroni Ltd, 190
Carr, Donald, 214
Casuals Club, 42–3
Ceylon, tour of (1948), 73–4
Challenor, George, 53
Chapman, A. P. F., 77
Chappell, Greg, 198, 199
Chappell, Ian, 186, 199
Cheeseman, E. E., 32
Christchurch, 132, 213
Christiani, R. J. (Bob), 64, 75, 82, 85, 102, 117, 122, 127, 128, 147
Clairmonte, Fred, 45
Clark, David, 210
Clarke, C. B., 34, 92
Clarke, Sylvester, 166, 209, 217
Cocoa Planters' Association, 161
Cohen, Rudy, 180
Collymore, Allan, 45
Colombo, 74
Compton, Denis, 52, 94, 105, 142, 147
Consolidated Insurance Consultants Ltd, 190
Constantine, Sir Learie (later Baron), 34–6, 92, 190
Cooperative Citrus Growers' Association, 21, 161
Copson, Bill, 38
Cordice, Dr, 165
Cowdrey, Christopher, 199
Cowdrey, Colin, 159, 182

Cowie, Jack, 88, 132
Cox, George, 88–9
Coxon, Alec, 97, 98, 99, 101, 102
Cozier, Tony, 9, 160
Cricketer, The, 110
Croft, Colin, 166, 201, 206, 207, 213, 214, 215
Crooks, Joe, 43
Cumberbatch, 148
Cummins, 149

Dadlani, Mr, 171
Daniel, Wayne, 166, 198
Dare, John St F., 162, 164, 193
Daunt, Achilles, 25
Davidson, Alan, 151
Davies, Albert Cory, 21
Davies, Dai, 91
Davis, Charlie, 180, 188–9
Delhi, 58, 63–4, 66, 90
Dewes, J. G., 81, 82, 96, 105
Doggart, G. H. G., 81, 82, 85
Dollery, H. E. (Tom), 85, 89, 103, 104
Donnelly, Martin, 60, 88, 132
Doorly, Rev. C. Stokeley, 25
Drayton, Lionel, 45
Duckworth, George, 77, 78

East Molesey, 30
Eastbourne, 79–80
Edgbaston, Birmingham, 103–4, 159–60, 197
Edrich, Bill, 52, 85, 87, 90, 94
education, 13, 25–30, 32–4
El Carmen estate, Talparo, 161
Elizabeth II, Queen, 177
Elliott, C. S., 179
England, tours of: 1939, 33–40; 1950, 75–106; 1957, 159–60; 1966, 175–81; 1970, 185; 1976, 198

England in the West Indies: 1948, 52–7; 1954, 142–50; 1960–61, 163–4; 1968–69, 182–3; 1981, 217–21
Etzler, J. A., 15–16
European schoolboy tour, 29–30
Evans, Godfrey, 53, 55, 85, 86, 95, 96, 104, 142, 143
Evening News, 87–8

Fagg, Arthur, 179
Farnes, Ken, 27
Ferguson, W. (Fergie), 34, 76, 80, 84, 112, 118
Ferguson, Wilfred, 49, 64, 69, 117
Findlay, Mike, 184
Fingleton, Jack, 118, 119, 125
Fishlock, Laurie, 102
Foster, Mike, 53
Fredericks, Mike, 144
Fredericks, Roy, 166, 198
Fry, C. B., 36
Fuller, Dickie, 49

Gadkari, 137
Gaekwad, A. D., 137
Ganteaume, A. G., 46, 47, 49, 55, 59, 108, 159
Garner, Joel, 166, 201, 206, 207, 215
Gaskin, Berkeley, 49, 140, 208
Gavaskar, Sunil, 185
George, Courtenay, 21
George, Knolly, 189
George VI, King, 89
Georgetown, 182, 207–8
Bourda ground, 31–2, 55, 147–8, 158, 183, 199
Ghulam Ahmed, 73
Ghulam Mahomed, 61
Gibbs, Glendon, 208
Gibbs, Lance, 123, 166, 176, 177, 180–81, 183
Gilchrist, Roy, 158, 163
Gilligan, Arthur, 77
Gimblett, Harold, 84, 94

Gittens, Dr Cyril, 44
Gittens, Stanton, 46
Gleneagles Accord, 202, 218, 219, 220
Goddard, John, 9, 47, 48, 54, 56, 59, 62, 65, 67, 68, 69, 72, 75, 85, 91, 92, 106, 117, 119, 120, 121, 125, 128, 130, 134, 135, 156, 158
Goddard, Tom, 40, 46
Goellnicht, Ken, 156
Goellnicht & Stollmeyer Ltd, 156
Gomes, Albert, 19
Gomes, Larry, 209
Gomez, Gerald Ethridge, 10, 23, 26, 28, 31, 33, 34, 38, 42, 43, 46, 47, 48, 49, 54, 55, 56, 62, 66, 67, 70, 72, 75, 81, 82, 83, 85, 90, 98–9, 105, 111, 117, 119, 120, 121, 122, 127, 128, 130, 134, 139, 141, 143, 145, 148, 150, 162, 164, 165, 182, 184
Gore, Leo, 48
Gosein, 148
Gover, Alf, 77
Grace, Dr W. G., 36
Grant, Sir Lindsay, 162, 184
Grant, Rolph S., 19, 20, 31, 33, 34
Graveney, Tom, 142, 146, 147, 148, 179
Greenidge, Geoffrey, 198–9
Greenidge, Gordon, 166, 207, 215
Griffith, Charlie, 165, 176, 178–80, 183, 184
Griffith, S. C. (Billy), 53, 55, 88, 177
Grove, Charlie, 103
Groves, Johnnie, 193
Guillen, S. G., 49, 117, 126, 128
Gunn, George, 77–8
Gupte, Subhash, 137, 139

Hadlee, Walter, 132

Hall, Wesley, 53, 157, 158, 163, 165, 176, 177, 181, 182, 184, 194
Halliday, Harry, 101, 102
Hammond, Walter, 23, 30, 34
Hannays, Sir Courtenay, 17–18
Harbin, Len, 46
Hardy, F., 32
Harvey, Neil, 117, 122, 128, 131, 153, 154
Hassett, Lindsay, 117, 119, 122, 123, 128–9, 130, 131, 142
Haynes, Desmond, 206, 207, 215
Hazare, V. S., 61, 67, 72, 73, 140
Headingley, Leeds, 179
Headley, George, 10, 33, 34, 36–7, 39, 40, 49, 54, 56, 58, 59, 63, 64, 65, 66, 69, 70, 73, 83, 144, 146
Hendren, Patsy, 77
Hendriks, Jackie, 176, 179, 184, 217
Hill, David, 31
Hilton, Malcolm, 105
Hitler Youth, 29–30
Hobbs, Sir Jack, 60, 77
Hobday, Richard, 196
Hobson, Sir Patrick, 170
Hochoy, Sir Solomon, 168
Holding, Mike, 157, 166, 184, 198, 213, 214, 215
Hole, Graham, 117, 121, 128, 131
Holford, David, 176, 177
Hollies, Eric, 80, 85, 86, 87, 89, 96, 103
Holt, J. K., 49, 145, 146, 147, 148
Hue, Sang, 148
Hunt, Alma, 202
Hunte, Conrad, 135, 163, 166, 175, 176, 177, 181
Hutchinson, Henley, 50
Hutchinson, Ruby, 50
Hutton, Sir Leonard, 39,

52, 56, 81, 85, 86, 87, 90, 91, 93, 94, 98, 99, 100, 105, 106, 109, 142–3, 145, 146, 147, 148, 150
Hylton, L. G., 34, 38–40

Ikin, John, 80
Imitiaz Ahamad, 66
Imperial College of Tropical Agriculture, 32–4, 42
Imran Khan, 66
India, tours of: 1948, 58–73; 1958–59, 163; 1978, 209
India in the West Indies: 1952–53, 137–41; 1971, 185
inter-island tournaments, 31, 33, 45–9, 108–9, 134–6, 157
Shell Shield, 186, 187, 188, 196–7, 198–9
International Cricket Conference (ICC), 197, 202, 203–7, 209, 210, 215, 216, 219

Jackman, Robin, 218
Jackson, Mahalia, 172
James, C. L. R., 19
Jardine, Douglas, 77
Jehangir Khan, 66
Jenkins, R. O., 89, 95
Jinnah, Mohammed Ali, 65
Johnson, Hines, 49, 56, 59, 75, 83, 85, 86, 89, 94, 104, 115
Johnson, Ian, 117, 120, 124, 127, 129, 151, 154
Johnson, Tyrrel, 33, 34, 40
Johnston, Bill, 116, 117, 120, 122, 129, 130, 132
Jones, Prior, 27, 46, 49, 54, 68, 70, 71, 72, 75, 81, 85, 89, 94, 98, 101, 103, 104, 117, 119, 123, 126
Jones, Willie, 102
Julien, B. D., 166

Jumadeen, 166

Kallicharan, Alvin, 166,
　197–8, 208, 209
Kampala Commonwealth
　Parliamentary Associ-
　ation Conference, 171
Kanhai, Rohan, 10, 37,
　158, 163, 166, 176,
　177, 186
Karachi, 64, 65
Kardar, A. H., 163
Kelshall, Joe, 45
Kennington Oval, 40, 80,
　81, 102, 104–6, 117,
　160, 197, 198
Kensington Oval,
　Bridgetown, 46, 48,
　52, 135, 146–7, 163
Kentish, Esmond, 144,
　146
Kidney, J. M., 34, 40, 75,
　89, 103
King, Frank, 118, 137,
　138, 144, 146, 147,
　150
Kingston, 59
　Melbourne ground, 144
　Sabina Park, 56, 141,
　149, 154–5, 163,
　182–3
Kingston Cricket Club, 48
Knott, Alan, 183
Knowles, R. E., 29
Kumar of Vizianagram, 70

Lacy, Donald, 58, 61
Laing, Michael, 164
Laker, Jim, 46, 54, 85, 87,
　89, 142, 143, 144,
　160
Langley, Gil, 117, 120,
　127, 129, 131
Langridge, James, 89
Larwood, Harold, 77
Leadbeater, E., 102
Lenham, Les, 199
Lester, Ted, 101
Leveson-Gower, H. D. G.,
　60
Leyland, Maurice, 37
Lillee, Denis, 197–8
Lindwall, Ray, 10, 116,
　117, 118, 119–20,

121, 122, 123–4, 128,
　130, 131, 132, 153
Lingwood, Daphne (sister),
　19, 20
Lingwood, Don, 20
Littlepage, R., 42
Lloyd, Clive, 166, 167,
　180, 188, 207, 208,
　213, 214–15, 217,
　220
Lock, Tony, 142, 144,
　145, 160
Lord's, 34, 38, 39, 75, 82–3,
　84, 89–92, 97, 116,
　147, 160, 177, 197
Lowson, Frank, 98, 100,
　101
Loxton, Sam, 118–19
Lucas, Johnnie, 76
Luckhoo, Sir Lionel, 208

Macartney, C. G., 88
McDonald, Colin, 131
McGilvray, Alan, 118,
　122, 178
McIntyre, A. J., 105
McLean, R. A., 157
McMorris, 176
McWatt, Cliff, 64, 148
Madhvani, Mr, 171
Madras, 56, 59, 70, 72
maintaining and
　developing the estates,
　161, 168
Majid Khan, 66, 201
managing the 1966 tour to
　England, 175–81
Mankad, M. (Vinoo), 61,
　67, 138, 140
Manley, Michael, 201–2
Manning, Charlie, 27–8
Marley, Cecil, 49, 193,
　194–5
Marsden, E. J., 45
Marsden, Edgar, 23
Marshall, Malcolm, 166,
　209
Marshall, Max, 164
Marshall, N. E., 59, 118,
　135, 153–4
Marshall, Roy, 59, 75, 85,
　93, 98, 99, 102, 104,
　117, 121, 126, 127,
　135

Martindale, E. A., 34, 35,
　36, 53, 157, 184
Matthews, Austin, 55
May, P. B. H., 81, 142,
　146, 148, 159, 163
Mayer, J. H., 81
Mead, Phil, 77
Mehta, Mr, 171
Melbourne, 113, 127–9
Mello, Anthony de, 58, 63,
　69
Menzies, Sir Robert,
　118–19
Mercer, Jack, 111
Merchant, Uday, 67
Merchant, V. M., 67
Merry, C. A., 26, 33, 34
Merry, Clara, 34
Merry, David, 26, 46
Metal Box Trinidad Ltd,
　190
Milburn, Colin, 177
Miller, Keith, 10, 116,
　117, 118, 120, 121,
　122, 123, 128, 130,
　131, 132, 153, 178
Modi, R. S., 67, 72, 73
Moir, Alec, 133
Mon Valmont, Santa Cruz,
　15, 17, 22–3, 172,
　173, 189
Montreal, 17, 18, 40, 42
Morris, Arthur, 117, 124,
　126, 128
Moyes, A. G. (Johnnie),
　122, 136–7
Mudie, George, 70
Muni Lal, 62
Murray, David, 209, 217
Murray, Deryck, 160, 166,
　173, 184, 197, 207,
　208, 213, 217
Murray, H. R. (Dick), 44,
　164
Murray, Lance, 173, 184
Mushtaq Ali, 61, 69, 201

Nayuda, C. K., 61, 68
Nayuda, C. S., 61
Nethersole, N. N., 39,
　144
New York, 18–19, 21,
　42
New Zealand, tours of:

1951–52, 132–3;
1955–56, 156; 1970,
185; 1980 revolt,
212–15
New Zealand in West
Indies, 1972, 185
newspaper critic, 158–9,
160
Nichols, Maurice, 35
Nicole, C. R., 9
Nimbalkar, R. B., 67
Noblet, Geoff, 124, 126
Nunes, Karl, 58, 59,
69–70, 79, 193
Nurse, Seymour, 176, 182

Obote, Milton, 171
O'Brien, Conrad, 171
O'Dowd, Alty, 45
O'Reilly, Bill, 118
Old Trafford, Manchester,
10, 35, 83, 85–8, 115,
179, 180

Packer, Kerry, 10, 166,
202, 203–10
Padilla, 44
Padmore, 166
Pairaudeau, Bruce, 118,
139, 144, 146
Pakistan, tours of: 1948,
65–6; 1959, 163;
1980, 217
Pakistan in the West
Indies, 163, 201
Palmer, Charles, 210
Palmer-Barnes, Rev. R. C.,
75
Parkhouse, Gilbert, 89,
105
Patiala, 61–2
Patiala, Maharajah of,
61–2
Paynter, Eddie, 77
Peirce, Noel (Tom), 47,
159, 193
Peiza, de, 154
Perks, Reg, 35
Phadkar, D. G., 71, 73,
140
Pierre, Lance, 46, 75, 93,
98, 99–100, 102, 104
Pilgrim, Grant Elcock, 13,
25

Place, Winston, 55
political career: Senator of
Trinidad and Tobago,
representing agri-
culture, 11, 168–73
political unrest, 171–3
Poona, 58, 66–7
Port of Spain, 17, 18, 50,
54, 123, 156, 171,
172, 173, 183, 190
Queen's Park Cricket
Club, 32, 42, 48, 49,
184, 194–5, 220–21
Queen's Park Oval, 18,
31, 38, 46, 48, 49, 79,
108, 139, 152–3, 156
Queen's Royal College,
9, 13, 18, 23, 24,
25–30, 32, 160
Port of Spain Gazette, 22
President of the West
Indies Cricket Board
of Control, 10, 48,
193–221
Prudential World Cup,
197, 210

radio commentator, 160,
164, 178
Rae, Allan, 9, 62, 63, 66,
67, 68, 70, 71, 75, 82,
84, 85, 86, 88, 90, 95,
96, 105, 117, 119–20,
122, 126, 129, 130,
132, 133, 201–2, 203,
204, 215, 221
Ramadhin, Sonny, 36, 75,
76, 81, 82, 84, 85, 86,
88, 90, 91, 94, 102,
105, 107–10, 111,
112, 117, 119, 120,
121, 123, 128, 129,
131, 132, 134–5, 137,
138, 145, 146, 147,
149, 153, 158,
159–60, 165, 215
Ramaswami, Cota, 141
Ramchand, G. S., 137, 140
Rangachari, C., 63
Relator, Lord, 185
retirement from first-class
cricket, 158
Rhodes, Wilfred, 77, 95
Richards, Vivian, 10, 37,

48, 166, 197, 198,
207, 215
Richardson, A. J., 28
Richardson, Vic, 122
Rickards, Ken, 49, 68, 69,
117, 127, 128, 129
Ring, Douglas, 117, 120,
123, 127, 129
Roberts, Andy, 166, 197,
198, 206, 207, 215
Robertson, Jack, 55
Robertson Glasgow, R. C.,
80
Robinson, Sir Harold, 21,
161–2
Rodriguez, Willie, 183,
212–13
Ross, Norman, 148
Rowe, Lawrence, 185
Russell, A. C., 77

Santos, Sir Errol dos, 45,
144, 193, 195, 196
Sapsworth, Captain, 93
Saram, Derek de, 74
Sealey, Ben, 33, 46
Sealy, J. E. D., 34, 47, 49
selection duties, 182–9
Sellers, Brian, 83
Sen, P., 72
Shackleton, Derek, 95
Sheppard, C. Y., 32–3
Sheppard, Rev. David, 81,
82, 105
Shinde, S. G., 61
Short, Peter, 207, 208
Silva, H. De, 42
Simpson, Bobby, 178
Simpson, R. T., 85, 89, 96,
105
Sims, Jim, 82, 83
Singh, C. K., 164
Skinner, Clarence, 107,
109, 138
Smart, Cyril, 35
Smith, O. G. (Collie), 152,
153, 155, 158
Snow, John, 183
Sobers, Sir Garfield, 10,
37, 53, 149–50, 155,
158, 163, 165–6, 175,
176–7, 180, 181,
182–3, 185, 186,
187–8, 194, 198

Sohoni, S. W., 61
Solomon, Joe, 163, 166, 208
Sperry, Bob, 38
Statham, Brian, 142, 147, 164
Stollmeyer, Ada Kate (mother), 16–17, 22, 80, 172
Stollmeyer, Albert Victor (father), 15, 18, 20–22, 80, 156, 160, 170, 172, 191
Stollmeyer, Alex (brother), 18
Stollmeyer, Allan (son), 50
Stollmeyer, André (brother), 18, 19, 168
Stollmeyer, Brian (son), 50
Stollmeyer, Conrad Frederick (great-grandfather), 15, 16
Stollmeyer, Donald (son), 50
Stollmeyer, Elizabeth, 18
Stollmeyer, Hugh (brother), 19
Stollmeyer, Kathryn (daughter), 50
Stollmeyer, Marjorie, 18, 42
Stollmeyer, Rex (brother), 17–18, 42
Stollmeyer, Sara (wife), 22, 50–51, 69, 212
Stollmeyer, Sheila, 27
Stollmeyer, Teckla, 19
Stollmeyer, Victor H. (brother), 19–20, 23, 27, 31, 33, 34, 40, 42, 46–7, 48, 92, 168
Strudwick, Herbert, 77
Sunday Guardian, 158–9, 160
Sutcliffe, Bert, 88, 132
Suttle, Ken, 179–80
Swanton, E. W. (Jim), 52, 95, 156–7
Sydney, 10, 84, 118, 121, 122–4, 125, 130–32
Sydney Morning Herald, 124

Tallon, Don, 120

Tang Choon, Rupert, 34, 46
Tate, Maurice, 77
Taylor, Bob, 212
Taylor, Don, 104
Thomas, Graeme, 178
Thomson, Jeff, 198
Thomson, Phil, 23
Thomson of Fleet, Lord, 190–91
Tremlett, Maurice, 52
Trent Bridge, Nottingham, 78, 84, 88, 94–6, 104, 111, 112, 176–7, 179
Trestrail, Arthur, 23
Trestrail, Dick, 23
Trestrail, Ken, 47, 75, 82, 83, 98, 135
Trim, John, 68, 69, 70, 71, 117, 119, 124–5, 127, 128, 129
Trinidad Publishing Company, 190
Trinidad uprising (1970), 173
Triumph Club, 25–7
Trueman, Fred, 137, 142, 143, 149, 164
Turnbull, Maurice, 35
Tyson, Frank, 157

Umrigar, Polly, 61, 137
Underwood, Derek, 179

Valentine, Alf, 36, 75, 76, 84, 85, 86, 88, 90, 91, 93, 96, 98, 99, 103, 104, 105, 106, 107, 110–12, 117, 119, 120, 121, 127, 128, 129, 131, 137, 141, 145, 146, 147, 149, 150, 153, 158, 165, 215
Vance, Bob, 213
Verity, Hedley, 30, 34, 37, 38
Viswanath, G. R., 212
Voce, Bill, 77, 80

Waite, J. H. B., 157
Walcott, Clyde, 9, 10, 36, 37, 47, 48, 52, 53, 56, 61, 63, 67, 69, 75, 82, 85, 90–91, 99, 100, 101, 102, 112, 115–16, 117, 122, 123, 126, 132, 135, 141, 146, 147, 148, 152, 155, 158, 165
Waldron, 'Son', 152
Wallace, Merv, 132
Walling, Sydney, 48
war years, 42–8
Wardle, Johnny, 89, 91, 101–2, 142, 147
Warner, Sir Pelham, 53–4, 60, 79, 82, 89, 92
Washbrook, Cyril, 89, 90, 91, 96, 105
Watson, G. D. (Australia), 153
Watson, Willie (England), 142, 145–6, 150
Weekes, Everton, 9, 36, 37, 47, 52, 53, 56, 57, 62, 63, 64, 67, 69, 71, 75, 82, 85, 88, 90, 92, 93, 95, 98, 99, 100, 112, 113–15, 118, 120, 122, 131, 132, 135, 138, 141, 146, 148, 158
Weekes, K. H., 34, 35, 49, 198
Wellard, Arthur, 38
Wellings, E. M., 87–8
West Indian Tobacco Company, 190
Wharton, Alan, 84
White, Crawford, 52
Whitehead, J. P., 102
Wight, G. L., 139
Wilkin, Calvin, 48
Wilkinson, Arthur, 25
Williams, C. B., 75, 82, 83, 98, 100, 102
Williams, E. A. V., 34
Williams, Dr Eric, 168, 169, 173, 187, 192, 194
Willis, Bob, 218
Wilson, J. V., 101
Wishart, Ken, 49, 154
Wood, Arthur, 40
Wood, Donald, 16
Woolley, Frank, 77
World Series Cricket, 209–10

Worrell, Sir Frank, 9, 10, 36, 37, 47, 48, 52, 53, 56–7, 75, 80, 81, 82, 85, 87, 88, 89, 91, 93, 94, 95, 96, 98, 99, 101, 102, 105, 112–13, 114, 117, 118, 119, 120, 121, 122, 124, 127, 128, 130, 132, 141, 143, 144, 146, 147–8, 151, 154, 158, 163, 164, 165, 166, 175

Wright, Douglas, 38, 105

Wyatt, R. E. S., 36, 60, 77, 81, 83

Yardley, Norman, 77, 80, 85, 86, 87, 89, 91, 92, 94, 97, 98, 99, 100, 101